D0886641

The New Deal and American Indian Tribalism

The
NEW DEAL
and
AMERICAN INDIAN
TRIBALISM

THE ADMINISTRATION OF THE INDIAN
REORGANIZATION ACT, 1934–45

by

Graham D. Taylor

UNIVERSITY OF NEBRASKA PRESS

Lincoln and London

Library of Congress Cataloging in Publication Data

Taylor, Graham D   1944–
  The New Deal and American Indian tribalism.

  Bibliography: p. 187
  Includes index.
  1. Indians of North America—Government relations—1934– 2. Indians of North America—Legal status, laws, etc. 3. Indians of North America—Tribal government. I. Title.
E93.T39   323.1'19'7073   79–9178
ISBN 0–8032–4403–7

To Deb and Charlotte,
my people

CONTENTS

Preface   ix
1. Background to Reorganization   1
2. Designing the Indian Reorganization Act   17
3. The Administrative Approach to Reorganization   30
4. Problems of Tribal Organization: Assimilation and
    Factional Rivalry   39
5. Problems of Tribal Organization: Councils
    versus Communities   63
6. Tribal Government in Theory and Practice   92
7. The Economics of the Indian New Deal   119
8. The Waning of the Indian New Deal   139
    Appendix 1: Data on Assimilation   151
    Appendix 2: Indian Ethnic and Economic
    Characteristics Correlated with Vote on Indian
    Reorganization Act; Indian Economic Status
    Correlated with Vote on Indian Reorganization
    Act; Indian Participation in Indian Reorganization
    Act Referenda, 1934–35   155
    Notes   159
    Bibliographical Essay   187
    Acknowledgments   195
    Index   197

PREFACE

In May 1977, an American Indian Policy Review Commission, established in 1974, submitted to the U.S. Congress a lengthy report on the economic, social, and political conditions of the Indians of the United States. The report concluded that even though Indian lands encompassed fifty million acres and contained rich deposits of oil and gas, coal, uranium, and phosphate, "for the most part . . . Indian people lack credit, remain poor, uneducated, and unhealthy. From the standpoint of personal well-being, the Indian of America ranks at the bottom of virtually every social statistical indicator."

The commission reviewed a number of factors that contributed to this anomalous situation: fractionated landownership on Indian reservations, widespread leasing of Indian resources to non-Indian enterprises, lack of education and technical skills which would enable Indians to develop their resources, and poor coordination of government programs to provide services and opportunities to Indians. But "most serious," according to the report, was "the lack of responsiveness, particularly on the part of the Bureau of Indian Affairs . . . to adhere to the principle of 'self determination' as expressed by Indians and the law." The commission recommended that future government policy should be guided by two concepts: first, that the federal government has a special

responsibility toward Indians, based on the historical relationship
of trust, which had not "been consistently honored in spirit as
well as name"; and second, that "Indian tribes are sovereign political bodies, having the power to determine their membership, and
power to enact laws and enforce them within the boundaries of
their reservations."[1]

Neither the analysis nor the prescription is new. The report
constitutes an astonishing replica of the proposals of a variety of
studies and statements by government officials and advocates of
reform in the 1928–33 period which provided the backdrop for
programs of the Indian New Deal. History may not repeat itself,
but to the reader of this 1977 report it is almost as if the Indian
New Deal had never happened. For the fundamental aims of the
Indian Reorganization Act of 1934, which was the heart of the
Indian New Deal, were the development of Indian economic resources and the restoration of Indian self-determination through
the revival of tribal governments.

Until recently our understanding of the aims and achievements
of that earlier period of Indian reform was filtered through the
accounts of those who participated in it, notably John Collier,
United States commissioner of Indian affairs from 1933 to 1945.
Collier's views, buttressed by those of former colleagues in the
Indian Service such as William Zimmerman and D'Arcy McNickle
and of anthropologists whom Collier brought into the administration of the Indian New Deal, also provided both a coherent
explanation for the origins of the reform movement in the 1920s
and the reasons why the Indian New Deal was ultimately frustrated and supplanted.

For Collier, American Indians were not simply an exploited and
ignored minority group, but a people whose "way of life . . .
realizes . . . man and nature intimately cooperant and mutually
dependent . . . the individual and his society as wholly reciprocal."
That way of life required preservation in its own right "as a gift
for us all." Threatened with total submergence of their traditional
cultures by the dominant white society, as well as the loss of their
remaining resources to western business interests, American Indians and sympathizers such as Collier joined forces to resist
further destruction in the 1920s. They designed a program of
reform that would enable Indian tribes to develop economically
while preserving their cultural institutions and restoring their
traditions of self-de nination. Resisted by representatives of

"many and powerful groups" in Congress, the reformers were nevertheless able to force the passage of the Indian Reorganization Act of 1934. During the following twelve years that legislation, in Collier's words, helped "scores of ancient tribal systems reorient themselves toward modern tasks, while more than a hundred tribal democracies have been newly born and have lived and marched out into life." Despite these successes, the forces of reaction restricted funding for Indian reorganization throughout the New Deal era, while white misconceptions about Indian needs and aspirations contributed to a return to the disastrous policy of rapid assimilation in the years following Collier's departure from the Indian Service.[2]

Although these reasons for the failure of the Indian New Deal, advanced by its proponents, were colored by a certain amount of ex post facto self-justification, there is a good deal of merit in them. But scholars who have examined some of the more controversial aspects of the Indian New Deal have developed a more complex picture of the course of American Indian reform in that period and a more critical judgment of its strengths and weaknesses.

This revised view of the Indian New Deal proceeded from analyses of the Navajo experience during the New Deal, for the Navajos were the largest cohesive tribe in the United States, and it was with them that the reformers met their most serious setback. In 1968, Lawrence C. Kelly, in *The Navajo Indians and Federal Indian Policy, 1900-1940*, argued that the issues which initiated the Indian reform movement in the 1920s were less clear-cut than Collier and his supporters had made them out to be, and that the impetus for reform came from white sympathizers like Collier, not from the Indians themselves, who by no means agreed with Collier or among themselves on those issues. Furthermore, Kelly's review of the New Deal programs among the Navajos revealed that the Bureau of Indian Affairs had not been free of misconceptions and blundering attributed to earlier, less enlightened administrations. More recently, Donald H. Parman, in *The Navajo Indians and the New Deal*, has elaborated on this subject, delving into the intricate internal politics of the Navajos. Parman discusses divisions among the Indians between traditional leaders and those favoring assimilation, as well as rivalry between religious and community factions, revealing the rather simplistic nature of Collier's views about Indian cultural homogeneity. Parman also demonstrates how government efforts to introduce tribal reorganization, herd reduction and range controls, and educational reforms exacerbated these internal conflicts and failed to resolve many basic problems on the reservation.[3]

In 1977, the first full-scale reassessment of Collier and the Indian New Deal, *John Collier's Crusade for Indian Reform, 1920– 1954*, by Kenneth R. Philp, was published. More sympathetic to Collier than Parman or Kelly, Philp supported the view that hostility in Congress and misunderstanding of Indian needs in the white community substantially hampered the reform program. At the same time, he noted flaws in Collier's assumptions about Indians and the inept administration of New Deal programs which weakened them and contributed to the ultimate eclipse of reform in the 1950s.[4]

The present study is somewhat narrower in focus, but examines those elements of the Indian New Deal which Collier, in particular, regarded as fundamental: tribal political reorganization and its integration with the development of Indian economic resources. The critique of the Indian New Deal proceeds from this focus. There can be little doubt that the indifference or hostility of Congress hampered the reform program, but the reformers were in control of the Bureau of Indian Affairs for more than a decade, and Collier demonstrated considerable political ingenuity in acquiring financial and technical assistance from other New Deal agencies in surmounting these difficulties. There was administrative bungling by the bureau, particularly in handling the Navajo problems, and Collier's abrasive personality often alienated potential supporters. Yet at the same time, the Collier administration moved steadily toward a more coordinated approach to economic planning than most other federal agencies of the period had, and pioneered in the systematic use of social scientists in administration.

The basic argument of this study is that the Indian New Deal, however enlightened in contrast to previous or subsequent Indian programs, was fatally weakened by its emphasis on tribal reorganization and the assumptions about contemporary Indian societies which formed the basis for the tribal idea. Furthermore, the failure of the Collier administration to achieve genuine tribal revival, or to recognize the reasons why that effort failed, undermined as well the ambitious and farsighted plans for ensuring Indian economic self-sufficiency. No amount of technical aid, funding, administrative sophistication, or outside support could guarantee the success of the economic programs unless the Indians themselves were prepared to provide support; and this, for a variety of reasons, they did not do. The reforms of the Indian New Deal failed to endure because, in the last analysis, they were imposed upon the Indians, who did not see these elaborate proposals as answers to their own wants and needs. The most durable legacy of the Indian New Deal, the tribal governments established under the Indian Reorganization Act, evolved into a form far removed from that which Collier and his fellow reformers intended or anticipated, and are today focal points for rivalry and contention among Indians rather than spokesmen for their aspirations.

The record of the Indian New Deal is not unrelievedly bleak, and this study also attempts to demonstrate where and under what conditions a genuine sense of Indian self-determination developed. For Collier's argument that some sense of indigenous Indian commitment, some sense of participation in the determination of their future, must undergird any lasting transformation of social and economic conditions is neither misguided nor necessarily hopelessly idealistic. Perhaps the more critical studies of the Indian New Deal that have now appeared will provide a degree of historical depth, a greater sense of the complex nature of Indian problems, which will contribute to a more successful approach to American Indian policy in the future.

The New Deal and American Indian Tribalism

1
BACKGROUND TO
REORGANIZATION

"The Indian's right of self-government," Felix Cohen, the fore-most authority on American Indian law, wrote in 1941, "is a right which has been consistently protected by the courts, frequently recognized and intermittently ignored by treaty-makers and legislators, and very widely disregarded by administrative officials." Because of their peculiar position in the American federal system, Indian tribes, theoretically "distinct, independent political communities," were in practice regulated by federal laws administered by the United States Bureau of Indian Affairs. In this situation tribal self-government became "the Indian's last defense against administrative oppression . . . his only alternative to rule by a government department."[1]

During the nineteenth-century military conquest, fraudulent or unobserved treaties and the increasing pressure of advancing white settlement dispossessed the Indian tribes of virtually the entire continental United States. White encroachments on their lands, military subjugation, and even intermarriage, had not, however, disrupted the political organization of many Indian tribes. In 1832, John Marshall, chief justice of the U.S. Supreme Court, recognized Indian tribes as legally independent communities with limited sovereignty. Although the Cherokee Indians whose rights Marshall sought to protect were forced to leave their lands in

1

Georgia, they were not destroyed as a tribal entity.[2] Up to the 1870s government officials negotiated with Indian tribes as corporate bodies, even though the officials often tried to divide and dominate tribal leaders. Congress recognized existing tribal organizations as agents in such matters as annuity payments for tribal lands. While two centuries of white impact had weakened the internal cohesion of traditional Indian societies, the political framework of Indian life had not been eradicated.

The form and size of organization varied considerably among Indian groups. Some possessed an elaborate and highly sophisticated tribal organization. Among these were the Iroquois Six Nations of New York and the Civilized Tribes, who were removed from the southeastern states to present Oklahoma before the Civil War. The Cherokee, Choctaw, Chickasaw, and Creek confederacies had written constitutions with legislative assemblies and court systems. At the other end of the scale were groups like the Shoshones and Paiutes of the Great Basin region of Nevada, Utah, and Wyoming, who appeared to have no form of organization beyond the extended family. Ranged between these extremes were a wide variety of groups, including agricultural village societies such as the Pueblos of the Southwest, and the nomadic warrior and hunter bands of the Great Plains.[3] Generalizations are consequently hazardous, particularly for the late nineteenth century, when Indian tribes were collapsing before white encroachment, the rapidly changing economic environment, and the transition to reservation life.

Tribe is most appropriately a cultural concept. Except for some eastern woodland confederacies, few Indians had tribal organizations that governed their activities. Some, like the Comanches, Apaches, and Navajos, were nomadic families with little in the way of larger organization. Similarly, the Pueblos of New Mexico lived in settled villages rarely, if ever, in contact with each other. Even among the more organized nomadic groups of the Northern Plains, such as the Cheyennes, Sioux, and Blackfeet, the tribes assembled only occasionally, while daily affairs were left to smaller bands. Participation in tribal religious ceremonies or annual buffalo hunts reinforced a sense of larger community, but did not alter the fact that an individual's life focused mainly on the family and clan.[4]

Colonial governments, and later the federal government, recognized tribal control over land well into the nineteenth century, and the courts continued to honor tribal claims in specific cases. But this was a distorted picture of the actual land distribution characteristic of most tribes. The tribe retained a residual claim to land, but in practice the assignments were made by villages or bands, and land or other property was held by an individual or family so long as it was actually in use. White officials often assigned to the tribe a more formal structure and greater powers than it actually possessed.[5]

Although few whites understood Indian societies and political organization, they recognized tribal governments and, before 1870, did not substantially challenge their control over tribal members and property. After the Civil War, however, while the last independent tribes of the plains were being conquered, demands for a new policy increased, aimed at the assimilation of Indians into white society. This new policy directly assaulted traditional Indian concepts of property and government.

From the Indian point of view, assimilation posed a more insidious threat to tribal institutions than the random violence and racial intolerance of western expansionists. Tribal organization was rooted in religious traditions and communal ownership of land. The proponents of assimilation would strike at these roots through Christian proselytizing, education, and the allotment of lands to individuals. Furthermore, the line between the humanitarian reformer and the land-seeking frontiersman was not necessarily clear. Their goals often seemed to converge. As Bernard Sheehan has noted, "Since the tribal possession of . . . surplus acres constituted one of the major signs of savagery, the abandonment of the land was a positive step toward civilization. Simply stated, the philanthropic program abetted the white man's desire for land."[6]

Proponents of assimilation such as the Indian Rights Association of Philadelphia did offer substantial arguments for their case. Tribal governments were corrupted as the responsibilities of leaders diminished and the amount of money they controlled increased. As the commissioner of Indian affairs complained in 1873, "The traditional chieftain, losing his hold on the tribe, ceases to be distinguished for anything except the lion's share of goods or monies which the government endeavors to send through him to his nominal subjects."[7] Among some of the tribes in which intermarriage was prevalent, such as the Choctaws of Oklahoma, mixed-blood Indians and white adventurers with Indian wives jockeyed for control of tribal councils in order to conspire with neighboring whites and railroad companies to lease tribal lands and resources and siphon off tribal annuities.[8] Tribal governments may have been no more corrupt than other local governments of the time, but they wasted irreplaceable assets.

By 1887 allotment of Indian lands was a virtual necessity. The government could not protect remaining Indian lands from further settlement and the demands of the railroads and other enterprises. As Delos S. Otis, a critical historian of the allotment policy, pointed out, "The friends of the Indian looked to allotment and patents in fee as a means of giving the Indian sufficient, but above all, secure lands." Westerners accepted allotment but "would have preferred to take all of the Indian lands."

In 1887 a General Allotment Act sponsored by Senator Henry L. Dawes, a Massachusetts Republican, passed with little opposition. Under the act tribal lands were divided and plots of 160 acres allotted to each family head, with lesser amounts given to single persons and orphans. Title to these lands would be held in trust by the U.S. government for not less than twenty-five years, and longer if deemed necessary. Surplus tribal lands could be sold to the government, which usually opened them directly to white settlement. Indian allottees who resided off reservations and formally broke all tribal ties were, in theory, entitled to American citizenship.[9]

The Dawes Act signaled a new era in Indian policy. In 1898 a similar law was imposed on the Civilized Tribes of present-day Oklahoma, at the same time summarily uprooting their traditional governments. In 1889 Indian Commissioner Thomas J. Morgan outlined the policy that the Indian Service was to follow until the 1920s. Education was to effect "the disintegration of the tribes." Compulsory schooling emphasizing the English language and Anglo-American culture was recommended, and all tribal history and traditions were to be suppressed. While adult Indians had to adjust to individual ownership of land, the new generation would be educated to desire it. "This civilization may not be the best possible," Morgan declared, "but it is the best the Indians can get."[10]

The basic aim of the Dawes Act was to transform the Indian into a homesteader. But most reservations were in the arid plains region where small farming was virtually hopeless. These lands were better suited to large-scale farming or ranching. Ironically, allotment was carried out most thoroughly on the reservations of the Northern Plains and the Northwest Coast, where tribes had traditionally hunted and fished. In the Southwest, where Indians had long successfully practiced dry farming and ranching, reservation lands were not allotted, primarily because the surplus lands were too desolate to attract neighboring white landowners.

The Dawes Act resulted in opening the remaining Indian lands to white exploitation. Between 1887 and 1932 the Indian land base diminished from 139 million acres to 48 million acres. Of the 91 million acres lost, two-thirds disappeared during the first decade of allotment, although only 5 million acres were actually allotted in this period. The remainder consisted of surplus lands sold to white settlers.[11]

Under the Dawes Act, allotments were to be held in trust by the government for a minimum of twenty-five years. The Burke Act of 1906, however, allowed certain allottees to receive a patent in fee which permitted them to sell or lease the land. This law, intended to encourage Indian ownership, opened the way for questionable arrangements between bureau agents and local whites. An Indian allottee would be persuaded to petition for a fee patent with the promise of ready cash for immediate sale. In some cases fee patents were allegedly issued to Indians without their application and the lands sold for prices far below their market value.[12]

Ultimately more damaging, however, were the efforts of those who sought to force the pace of fee patenting in order to encourage assimilation. Between 1915 and 1920 a federal "competency commission" ordered the issuance of twenty thousand patents to Indians of less than one-half Indian blood, despite the protests of the recipients, who would be unable to pay state and local taxes on their lands. The commission was most active among the tribes of the Great Lakes region and in the Dakotas. The results of this misconceived policy were to plague administrators throughout the New Deal era, setting the scene for conflict between landless mixed-bloods and full-bloods who had retained their allotments.[13]

A study by the National Resources Board in 1935 revealed the extent of land loss through alienation of fee patent allotments. The practice was most prevalent in Oklahoma, Minnesota, Wisconsin, and the Dakotas. In Oklahoma the Five Civilized Tribes had alienated 40 percent of their lands since 1898. Among other tribes the state of depletion was greater. The Osages had sold 70 percent of their allotted lands, mostly during the oil boom of the 1920s.

The Shawnees and Potawatomis had lost all but 5,000 of more than 425,000 acres of allotted land. The Chippewas of Minnesota had alienated 80 percent of their lands, with the Red Lake Reservation, which had successfully resisted termination of trusteeship, as the outstanding exception. The Sioux tribes had lost 30 percent of their total allotted acreage. On some reservations, such as Lower Brulé and Rosebud, almost 40 percent of the land was gone. The Oneidas and Winnebagos of Wisconsin had alienated virtually all their allotments. Although these were the worst cases, the National Resources Board estimated that almost one-half of all Indian allotments had been released in patents in fee between 1900 and 1934, and the majority of these lands had been sold or seized for nonpayment of taxes. Indian owners of these lands had no other resources once the profits from land sales, which were also subject to state taxation, were gone.[14]

During the trust period the allotted land could be leased, and Indians were encouraged to lease their lands for relatively modest fees. In the case of the Civilized Tribes in Oklahoma, local real estate agents selected the sites for allotment, then rented the land from the Indians and sublet it at a profit to white farmers. In other cases the bureau, as trustee, administered the leases but failed to ensure that the Indians received the maximum possible rent from the land.[15] While leasing did put money in Indian hands, it was not a practice that prepared them for farming or managing property. Moreover, income from leases was likely to diminish or disappear in periods of depression.

Another virtually insoluble problem developed as original allottees died and left their paltry estates to numerous heirs. The so-called Meriam Report on Indian administration, prepared by the Brookings Institution in 1928, reviewed the difficulties of this situation:

Heirs had to be determined. The estate had to be partitioned among heirs or sold so that the proceeds might be partitioned. If it was not sold or partitioned, but was leased as an estate, the lease money had to be divided among heirs. In some cases the heirs were numerous and records of their relationship poor, so that the work of determining them is long and difficult. Divisions of lease money among them may require many small entries on the books, some of them so small as to be of little monetary consequence. With inheritance came all the problems of wills and will-making, a difficult and expensive matter.[16]

These were the problems of bureau administrators. The Indians faced graver hardships. Heirship lands might be sold and distributed among the heirs. Alternatively, where the heirs were minors, the land might be assigned to a white guardian who could then use the land as he chose. Even when the land remained in Indian hands, the process of dividing allotments among heirs only aggravated the basic problem, that the lands were too small to be used productively. A National Resources Board survey of sixteen reservations in 1934 and 1935 estimated that 70 percent of the heirship lands were leased and another 23 percent lay idle, leaving only 7 percent actually used by Indians.[17]

Forty years after its inception, allotment had failed to improve the Indians' economic condition. The Brookings study documented the magnitude of this failure in its analysis of the personal wealth of Indians. In 1928, 55 percent of the Indians had a per capita income of less than two hundred dollars per year; only 2 percent had incomes greater than five hundred dollars per year. This income derived primarily from rent rather than labor: 96 percent of all Indians earned wages of less than two hundred dollars per year. A study made in 1933 by the Civil Works Administration found that 49 percent of Indians on allotted reservations were landless, and that the per capita value of those lands remaining in Indian hands was about eight hundred dollars.[18]

Allotment also failed as a means to promote assimilation. Indeed, no policy could better have prevented assimilation than allotment as it was conceived and executed between 1890 and 1930. Lack of credit, remoteness from markets, and insufficient technical assistance from the bureau contributed to this situation. But most crucial was the failure of the government to provide the incentives and institutions that would make it possible for Indians to benefit from or even function effectively in the emerging industrial society.

There was a fundamental contradiction in the policy of assimilation. On the one hand, the Indian was to be forced to accept the responsibilities of individual ownership and American citizenship, while at the same time he was to be deprived of the political system that provided the basis of social stability in his community. In the absence of any indigenous institution for the allocation of resources and settlement of disputes in the community, the federal government assumed guardianship over the Indian. How this paternalistic administration would transform Indians into self-sufficient and independent members of the larger society remained a mystery.

To make matters worse, the Bureau of Indian Affairs was poorly organized and failed to develop uniform and coherent policies. As the agency's tasks became more complex after 1890, new divisions were established in specialized areas such as irrigation, forestry, agricultural extension, schools, and hospitals. Rather than drawing on the technical knowledge available in other government agencies, the Indian Service created duplicate organizations and staffed them with their own appointees.

These specialized services were poorly coordinated. Even worse, in developing special programs in such areas as health, education, or land management, varying conditions among reservations were ignored. In the early part of the twentieth century the local Indian agent retained control over virtually all matters relating to his reservation. After 1920, however, this situation changed. New programs were inaugurated by the Washington offices of the specialized staffs for application in all jurisdictions. The central office had no way of reviewing the results of these programs and the local superintendent had no incentive to assume greater responsibility. The Indian Service was highly centralized but lacked a focal point for administrative control.[19]

In these circumstances there was little reason for anyone of ability or initiative to enter the bureau or remain very long. The Brookings study of 1928 found that the overall quality of employees was lower in the bureau than in other federal agencies. Officials exhibited little interest in the people they were supposedly serving; indeed, the policy of assimilation discouraged any such interest. Local agents were shifted about constantly, further inhibiting the acquisition of knowledge about the specific needs and traditions of different Indian groups. Indians who might have filled the gaps were denied positions of any authority in the bureau, even at the reservation level, ostensibly because of their inability to meet the standards required under civil service regulations.[20]

The continual fluctuations in policy had an equally devastating impact on the Indians. During the congressional hearings on the Indian reorganization bill in 1934, John Collier pointed out this problem: "There is no Indian tribe whose memory is not filled with the recollection of the constantly fluctuating policies of successive Commissioners of Indian Affairs . . . and the situation is one under which Indians cannot be expected to go to work in earnest to build up a stable domestic government. They are dependent on the whims of the Commissioner."[21]

The combination of a misguided policy of rapid, enforced assimilation and an arrogant and undirected administration had a disastrous effect upon a people already demoralized by more than a century of conquest and exploitation. The results could be seen on every reservation: landless Indians living in incredible poverty, an infant mortality rate more than twice that of the white population, widespread alcoholism and crime. Forty years of assimilation had crushed traditional Indian communities but had seen relatively few Indians successfully or willingly adopt white cultural values. During the same period, however, attitudes toward Indians and Indian policy were changing, culminating in the emergence of a new Indian reform movement in the 1920s which challenged the basic premise of assimilation and instead emphasized cultural pluralism and the right of group self-determination.

In 1881, Senator Henry Teller of Colorado, one of the few open opponents of assimilation in Congress, predicted accurately that "when thirty or forty years shall have passed and these Indians shall have parted with their title [to allotments], they will curse the hand that was raised professedly in their defense to secure this kind of legislation."[22] But his was a voice in the wilderness, and once the policy of assimilation was firmly established, open advocacy of tribal self-determination or Indian rights was virtually extinguished for almost a generation.

In 1911 the Society of American Indians was established by graduates of the Indian boarding schools, particularly Carlisle and Hampton. Members were largely of mixed blood and accepted the basic premises of assimilation. Their leaders, especially Arthur C. Parker and Charles A. Eastman, sought to help Indians blend into white society while preserving the best of Indian cultures.[23] Nevertheless, the society rapidly became a forum for demands for changes in Indian administration. Some of the more extreme members hoped to dissolve the Indian Service completely, and proposals for greater Indian autonomy emerged.

In 1912 a bill proposing that "the right of nomination of agents be given to the Indians" was introduced by Representative John Stephens of Texas, chairman of the House Committee on Indian Affairs. This bill was actually wider-ranging than its title suggested, requiring the establishment of elected tribal business committees to manage tribal funds, preferential hiring of Indians for government positions on the reservations, and approval of new superintendents by a two-thirds majority of adult Indian residents on each reservation.[24]

The Society of American Indians endorsed the Stephens bill at its 1912 convention and provided many of the witnesses on behalf of the bill before the House subcommittee. All of these witnesses were educated mixed-bloods who stood to gain from the provision concerning reservation appointments. The bill was reported out of committee favorably but did not pass the House. In 1916 a similar bill was introduced by Senator Edwin Johnson, a Republican from South Dakota, and endorsed by Senator Robert La Follette of Wisconsin. It also failed to get through Congress, but was taken seriously enough by Interior Secretary Franklin K. Lane, who argued: "If enacted these provisions would place in the hands of designing and unscrupulous persons a most dangerous weapon. . . . It is a well known fact among those acquainted with the Indian character that Indians can be easily influenced and that agitation of questions of but slight importance arouses much interest and is prolonged to the neglect of important duties."[25] Lane's statement reveals much about the attitude taken by government officials toward the people they were supposedly grooming for full citizenship. Many of the Indians were at this time being released from trusteeship while the official responsible for them was asserting, in effect, that they were unprepared to manage their own affairs.

The Stephens bill itself indicated the caution with which even sincere white sympathizers approached the subject of Indian self-determination. It would have given the proposed tribal business committees some authority over reservation superintendents, but the superintendents were already losing much of their control over local matters. While the provision giving the committees control over the spending of tribal funds would have been a step toward genuine autonomy, the tribes would still have needed special congressional action to get access to those funds. Furthermore, the major assets of Indian tribes were their lands, forests, minerals, and other resources that would remain under the control of the Interior Department.

The limitations of the Stephens bill reveal the dilemma which supporters of Indian self-rule were to face again in the New Deal. The desire to reduce the often destructive and at best paternalistic control the government exercised over the Indians was tempered by a reluctant conclusion that many Indians, collectively and individually, were ill prepared for complete control over their resources and would be hard pressed to withstand pressures to part with their remaining property. The experience of the fee patent allottees under the Burke Act reinforced this belief. The difference between Secretary Lane and supporters of the Stephens bill was a matter of degree. Neither believed in the last analysis that the government's control over the Indians could soon be abandoned.

Even while the prospect of reform of Indian policy was being inconclusively debated in Congress, however, the bureau embarked on its most ambitious effort to promote allotment and assimilation, the competency commission. Almost another decade was to pass before a more substantial attempt to reorient Indian policy was attempted.

Ironically, the new reformers did not focus on the difficulties of the allotted reservations. The Indians whose problems became the initial center of controversy in the 1920s were the Pueblos of New Mexico, whose culture and social organization had been relatively undisturbed. They were threatened, not by well-meaning advocates of assimilation, but by western politicians, notably Interior Secretary Albert B. Fall, suspected of conspiring to dispossess the Pueblos of their ancestral lands.

The issue caught the public imagination when a bill was introduced in Congress in 1921 by Senator Holm Bursum of New Mexico, an associate of Fall who had succeeded to his Senate seat. The Bursum bill was addressed to a complex issue involving disputed claims to Pueblo lands occupied by several thousand non-Indians between 1876 and 1912. Opponents of the bill charged that most of the settlers on these lands were squatters. The bill would have placed the burden of proof of title on the Indians, an unusual procedure that would have been difficult and expensive, since the original titles had been granted by the Spanish and Mexican governments.

The plight of the Pueblos was an especially appealing cause to a growing community of artists and writers who lived near their villages, in Taos and Santa Fe, and who had contacts in New York, Los Angeles, and San Francisco. These intellectual exiles of the Harding era found the Pueblos an exotic and attractive people, altogether different from the materialist society of white America, and equally unlike the demoralized, half-assimilated Indians of Oklahoma and the plains reservations. The obvious Indian-ness of the southwestern tribes and their forthright defense of their own way of life also proved appealing to the wider American public. They were ideal symbols for a reform movement which sought to portray Indians not as a dying race but as a people whose vigorous culture was endangered by the machinations of crass and corrupt officials like Fall and Bursum.[26]

One of the leaders of this new reform movement, ultimately the most important and influential, was John Collier. A native of Georgia, Collier had attended universities in New York and Paris in the early years of the twentieth century, and subsequently was drawn into a movement among social workers and educators in New York and other large cities seeking to organize immigrant communities. These community organizations were viewed by their sponsors as the nuclei for a society that would respect cultural differences and promote citizen participation in public decisions. During World War I the community center movement benefited from support by the Council for National Defense (CND), which incorporated the organizations into its wartime mobilization program.

Collier was active in the New York community organizations, and established a National Community Center Association in 1917 to perpetuate the ideas and organizations established under the CND. His hopes proved short-lived, however, and in 1919 he left New York as the community centers were being dismantled and the movement collapsed. In California he worked briefly as a community organizer for the state government, but legislative hostility to his unorthodox notions forced him out a year later.

During his years in New York, Collier had made many friends in the intellectual and artistic community, among them Mabel Dodge Luhan, patroness of D. H. Lawrence and other writers, who invited him to her ranch near Taos, New Mexico, at the Christmas season in 1920. Here he encountered the Pueblos and was at once enthralled. It seemed he had found a truly stable, self-contained community that had for centuries resisted outsiders who sought to rule and exploit them. When he was asked a year later by Stella Atwood of the General Federation of Women's Clubs in Los Angeles to assist the Pueblos in their efforts to block the Bursum bill, Collier entered the fray with enthusiasm.[27]

Collier soon displayed formidable talents as a lobbyist for the Indians and emerged as the major figure in the American Indian Defense Association, one of the new reform groups established to fight the Bursum bill. He was well prepared and persuasive before congressional committees and proved skillful at exploiting academic and journalistic contacts to promote Indian reform and his own organization. His personality, however, was rather abrasive toward those whose opinions differed from his own, particularly other would-be reformers.

John Collier's background in community work and his encounters with the Pueblos influenced his ideas about the reform of Indian policy. Because he felt strongly about community organization as a means for changing and reforming American society as a whole, and because the Indians he first came in contact with exhibited the community cohesion he admired, it was easy for Collier to see tribal organization as the solution to Indian problems. He did not then recognize the difficulties of applying this approach to the allotted reservations. Both the strengths and the weaknesses of the Indian New Deal were the product of his enduring faith in tribal organization.

In 1923 the Bursum bill was defeated, and in the following year a Pueblo Lands Act established a board to untangle the maze of claims. The reformers, now organized in two new groups, the Indian Defense Association and the Eastern Association on Indian Affairs, joined eventually by the older Indian Rights Association, expanded their attacks, uncovering manifold schemes to defraud the Indians of their rights and property. After Fall's departure as interior secretary under the shadow of the Teapot Dome scandal, his successor, Hubert Work, reacted to the growing clamor against the Indian Service by summoning a Committee of One Hundred, a panel of distinguished citizens together with leaders of the various reform groups, to discuss future Indian policy. Because of the great variety of views represented at this assembly in New York City in 1923, most of its recommendations were ambiguous, and ignored long-range problems. Collier denounced the meeting as a fiasco and urged that a thorough investigation of the Indian Service be carried out by the Brookings Institution.

Work chose at first to rely instead on the Board of Indian Commissioners, a quasi-governmental body established in the nineteenth century and now largely defunct, to carry out an investigation. Predictably, the reformers regarded the board's generally favorable report on the bureau as a whitewash. Continued criticism forced Work to turn at last to Brookings in June 1926. During the following two years a team under Lewis Meriam carried out an extensive study of Indian policy. The Meriam Report, officially entitled *The Problem of Indian Administration,* was published in 1928.

The findings of the Meriam study have been discussed earlier. It criticized the government for inadequate appropriations, excessive centralization, and a lack of planning by the bureau, and charged administrators with emphasizing the management of Indian property over improvement of the quality of Indian life. While the report accepted assimilation as a basic goal of Indian policy, it acknowledged that there were alternative goals that deserved consideration. Bureau officials were urged to take "time to discuss with [Indians] in detail their own affairs, and to lead rather than force them to sound conclusions," and to "develop . . . rather than crush out all that is Indian." Specifically the Meriam study recommended the establishment of a planning division for "scientific use of Indian resources," decentralization of the Indian Service, the establishment of government loans in substantial amounts to Indians, eliminating boarding schools, and restricting allotments in order to develop a better-coordinated land use program.[28]

At the same time an equally comprehensive survey was undertaken by the Senate Committee on Indian Affairs. A subcommittee toured virtually every major reservation in the country between 1928 and 1933, investigating complaints about the Indian Service. Unlike the Meriam study, which eschewed attacks on bureau leaders, the Senate committee added its weight to the reformers' criticisms, forcing the resignation of the current Indian commissioner, Charles Burke, in 1929.[29]

Charles Rhoads, who was chosen to succeed Burke, was a Philadelphia Quaker and former president of the Indian Rights Association. Committed to implementing the recommendations of the Meriam Report and upgrading the Indian Service, Rhoads also held firmly to the idea that assimilation should be the ultimate goal of Indian policy.

The continuing congressional investigation benefited Rhoads in his quest for increased appropriations. Budget allocations for the bureau rose from $18 million in 1930 to $27 million in 1932. A large part of the new revenues went to improve Indian health and educational facilities. Under W. Carson Ryan, a member of the Meriam survey, the bureau's educational division began closing boarding schools and emphasizing vocational training geared to the current labor market and the needs of reservation life, adding a placement program for young Indians. The quality of Indian medical service was improved: new hospitals and clinics were built and the bureau coordinated its services with those of the U.S. Public Health Service.[30]

Rhoads also turned his attention to the problem of Indian resource management. In 1929, in a series of letters to Senator Lynn Frazier of the Senate Committee on Indian Affairs, he outlined some major changes. These included modifying the allotment system to encourage tribal landholdings by arranging for the exchange of allotments for shares in tribal corporations, and establishing similar Indian corporate bodies to manage tribal properties on unallotted reservations. He spoke of "passing over to the Indians themselves a collective responsibility for their tribal business" to be vested in tribal councils with authority to tax allotted lands leased to whites. Finally, he urged the establishment of an Indian claims commission which would operate more rapidly and efficiently than the regular Court of Claims. Rhoads recommended that these proposals be embodied in legislation, since any "such action of an administrative kind would be revocable by a succeeding administration."[31]

These proposals reflected a broad and growing consensus among reform groups that fundamental alterations were necessary in Indian policy; they had in fact been drafted by Collier and Matthew K. Sniffen of the Indian Rights Association, two men who were poles apart on many aspects of Indian reform. While the period 1930–33 was marked by bitter debates among reformers over the performance of the Rhoads administration, there was growing agreement on certain basic goals.

Despite these initial efforts and achievements, Rhoads soon encountered considerable criticism, not least for his failure to follow up on the 1929 proposals. They had been put forward cautiously and nothing more concrete or comprehensive was forthcoming from the bureau. In 1932 when the subject of tribal incorporation was raised again, in the case of the Klamath Indians of Oregon, who wanted a charter to manage their tribal timber properties, Rhoads counseled delay because of questions the proposal raised with respect to corporate tax liabilities, and because the bureau had "not yet evolved a plan that altogether meets the situation."[32]

Even before this, the bureau had become the target of reformers'

criticisms, and Rhoads was not helped by the growing unpopu-
larity of President Hoover. The most important factor in the
erosion of Rhoads's reform efforts was the Depression and its
effect on the Indians and on the attitude of Congress toward
Indian problems. Indian conditions, already bad, became worse,
but legislators, preoccupied with the problems of the rest of the
nation, gave Indians a low priority and ignored or criticized
Rhoads for his inaction. By 1933 the bureau was calling for emergency assistance from the Red Cross while Congress reduced
appropriations for the Indian Service by $5 million.

The Rhoads administration was not barren of achievement, but
the pace of reform slowed after 1930 as the Depression set in and
unanticipated by-products of administrative reorganization took
their toll. Rhoads was increasingly perplexed by the labyrinthine
connections of Indian problems with other issues involving western land and water use. As he became mired in the complexities
of Indian administration, his critics in Congress and the reform
movement enlarged on his failings. But even those who focused
attention on Rhoads's ineptitude were aware that the problem of
Indian administration required more than a change of leadership.
In the end the failure of the Rhoads administration reinforced
demands for the kinds of comprehensive changes in Indian policy
that Rhoads had outlined in 1929.

2
DESIGNING THE INDIAN REORGANIZATION ACT

The election of 1932, with the prospect of a new commissioner of Indian affairs and a new initiative in Indian policy, brought a semblance of unity to the reform movement which lasted long enough to provide the impetus for the passage of the Indian Reorganization Act, the major achievement of the Indian New Deal. This act marked a major departure from previous government policies toward the American Indian, and constituted a bold experiment to revive traditional tribal institutions and integrate them with a program for the economic rehabilitation of the Indians.

Much of the credit for this striking change of direction must go to John Collier, who directed the Bureau of Indian Affairs for twelve years, from 1933 to 1945; assembled a talented staff of reformers to help manage the agency; and energetically sought to make a reality of his dream of reviving Indian tribes and customs, thus restoring to Indians a sense of pride in their communities and themselves. Collier was not the obvious choice for commissioner in 1932. During the preceding years he had demonstrated skill as a lobbyist and publicist for the reform movement, but his abrasive manner and his intolerance of more moderate reformers, not to mention veterans of the Indian Service, made him a natural center of controversy. Despite his active manuevering for the position,

Collier was not assured of it until President-elect Franklin Roosevelt chose Harold Ickes, a Chicago Progressive reformer and former director of the American Indian Defense Association, to be secretary of the interior. Ickes gave his support to Collier partly to prevent the appointment of Edgar Merritt, a relative of the Democratic majority leader, Senator Joseph T. Robinson of Arkansas, and a veteran of the old guard in the Indian Service who staunchly supported the policies of allotment and assimilation.[1]

Despite his reputation for controversy, Collier's appointment was greeted with general approval. Senator Burton K. Wheeler of Montana, the Democratic chairman of the Senate Committee on Indian Affairs, endorsed it warmly, and even the Indian Rights Association offered "hearty support and cooperation," noting that the choice of Collier "was a case of an outstanding critic being . . . told in effect, 'Show us how it should be done.'"[2]

Collier brought with him to the bureau several colleagues from the Indian Defense Association, including Ward Shepard, Walter V. Woehlke, and Jay B. Nash. He moved quickly to meet disastrous situations on the reservations resulting from drought and blizzards in the winter of 1932–33. He acquired $5.8 million in emergency funds through the newly established Civilian Conservation Corps, establishing a separate Indian Emergency Conservation Works program under Nash, which was authorized to initiate projects at or near reservations so that Indian employees could remain with their families and the projects would benefit the Indians directly.[3] As a first step toward reversing past policies, Secretary Ickes declared a temporary cessation to further allotment of Indian lands. Meanwhile, groups in Congress, the bureau, and the reform movement began to develop a comprehensive program that would link land reform with fundamental changes in the administration of Indian affairs.

In the early part of 1933 several bills were presented for reorganizing Indian administration, some recommending the establishment of tribal councils similar to those proposed in the Stephens bill in 1912, while others simply proposed the termination of allotment. The most far-reaching bill was submitted by Representative Roy Ayers, a Montana Democrat, who proposed to remove all field positions in the bureau from the civil service and open them to Indians and to control by the tribal councils.[4] All these proposals remained in committee during the spring session of Congress while the emergency legislation of Roosevelt's "Hundred Days" took priority.

In the latter part of 1933 the Indian reform groups began to take a greater interest in the reorganization issue, stimulated by Commissioner Collier's first annual report, which called for an end to allotment and for "group organization and tribal incorporation" for the management of Indian resources. In November 1933, Allan G. Harper, Collier's successor as head of the Indian Defense Association, met with Oliver La Farge, president of the National Association on Indian Affairs (formerly the Eastern Association on Indian Affairs) to discuss a joint lobbying strategy for 1934.

In their discussions the two Indian reform leaders revealed a skepticism about the extent to which Indians were prepared for self-government, an attitude shared by Collier and the reformers now in the bureau. Harper and La Farge agreed that the Ayers bill would probably make the Indian Service a patronage plum for local politicians rather than helping the Indians, and that proposals for removal of superintendents by popular vote should be modified to allow for hearings before an appeal board. La Farge favored the idea of giving tribal councils a veto over the spending of tribal funds, but Harper argued that "this might result in the refusal by Indians to maintain important services, even such as health and schooling, for the sake of diverting all funds into head-right cash payments." In general, the two reformers agreed that tribal councils constituted "an important first step in the training of an Indian self-government and self-reliance . . . but if we advance too fast or fail to safeguard the exercise of these rights in a manner ensuring that . . . they will really be educational and beneficial to the Indians . . . the result will be only a reaction which will set back the whole process of freedom among our Indians. Care and caution are necessary."[5]

Harper and La Farge also concurred on linking administrative reorganization with land reform and some proposal for resource planning in a single bill. In order to ensure widespread support for such a proposal they initiated a call for a general meeting of all the Indian reform groups together with bureau representatives and other interested parties to discuss a new policy. The conference, held on January 7, 1934, at the Cosmos Club in Washington, D.C., was attended by the reformers and Collier and Ickes, with Lewis Meriam as the chairman. The conference agreed on a series of resolutions calling for an end to allotment, the consolidation of remaining Indian trust lands and heirship lands under community ownership, the establishment of tribal councils with certain defined powers, the replacement of the existing Indian court systems, which were widely regarded as instruments of bureau control over Indian domestic affairs, and the return of the Oklahoma Indians to federal guardianship.[6]

During this period Collier, along with Assistant Commissioner William Zimmerman and two members of the Interior Department's legal staff, Nathan Margold and Felix Cohen, had been working on a bill incorporating these reforms. A month after the Cosmos Club conference a bill was sent to Senator Wheeler and Representative Edgar Howard, chairmen, respectively, of the Senate and House Committees on Indian Affairs. The draft was long and complex, covering forty-eight pages, and divided into four titles concerning Indian self-government, education, lands, and the proposed court of Indian affairs. The most important sections of the bill, from the viewpoint of its sponsors, related to Indian self-government and land management.

Under Title I the secretary of the interior was authorized to issue a charter granting powers of local self-government and the right of incorporation for economic purposes upon petition of one-fourth of the adult Indians residing on a reservation and ratification of the charter by three-fifths of the residents. Under the charter the local government could establish ordinances and enforce them, contract with the federal government for public services, define and regulate membership in the community, and take over other administrative functions deemed suitable by the secretary of the interior. The bill also provided these chartered governments with important powers relating to tribal and individual property; the right to review bureau appropriations estimates for the reservation prior to their being sent to Congress; the power to tax and to condemn property; and the right to hold title to all individual property given to the tribe, or property transferred to it by the federal government.

The extent of these latter powers was further clarified by Title III relating to Indian lands. This title repealed the Dawes Allotment Act and provided for the classification of all allotted lands susceptible of consolidation into productive units. Those allotments could then be exchanged for shares in the tribal corporation, while heirship lands would be ceded to the community and the individual heirs compensated for improvements. Tribal funds would be used to purchase allotments, and the Interior Department could spend up to $2 million annually to purchase lands for Indian communities or for landless Indians who could form themselves into chartered companies.

Title II concerning Indian education would provide training for Indians to take over service positions in the bureau, financial assistance to individuals seeking further education, and measures to preserve and restore traditional Indian cultures. The Court of Indian Affairs, covered in Title IV, would complement the program of self-government by acting as a court of original jurisdiction, in cases involving the community itself as an interested party, to "protect the Indian community . . . against unnecessary obstruction and delay in carrying out of the program contemplated in this bill . . . [and afford] effective protection of the rights of individuals in the administration of the program."[7]

The Indian reorganization bill drafted by the bureau reflected the various and somewhat ambivalent objectives of the reform movement. In the sphere of internal political affairs it was extremely liberal, outlining in considerable detail the powers that the tribal government could exercise. In the area of economic affairs, however, where Indian groups necessarily had to deal with white society, the authority of the tribal organizations was less clearly defined. Most of the provisions relating to the acquisition of land vested ultimate power in the secretary of the interior, who would initiate land classification, the purchase of additional lands, and the transfer to the tribe of title to individual allotments. If the tribal government chose to use its funds for land purchases, the secretary must approve. Similarly, any leasing of community resources, such as mineral or subsurface rights, must also be approved. The secretary also had discretionary power over the conditions relating to the assignment of tribal lands to an individual, a power traditionally belonging to tribal governments. While the tribal councils could review appropriations, no tribal initiative in expenditures was proposed.

These limitations on the freedom of Indian communities to manage their economic affairs indicate a major ambiguity in the reformers' attitudes toward tribal self-determination. On the one hand, the bureau sponsors of the bill desired to promote self-government, but on the other hand, they were reluctant to relinquish the power of the purse to communities whose members had little or no experience with modern business practices. Like Harper and La Farge, the reformers in the bureau feared that a too rapid devolution of authority to the Indians would ultimately impoverish them beyond any hope of reconstruction. The temptations presented to the Indians for ready cash through per capita distribution of their tribal funds or the sale of their precious remaining resources would be too great to resist, particularly in a time of economic hardship.

Furthermore, the bureau wanted to retain control over the Indians' major productive use. This planning aspect of the program was not stressed by Collier in his presentation of the draft to Congress, but it was implicit in the allusions which he made to current programs for soil conservation and land use planning undertaken by the Departments of Agriculture and the Interior. The purpose of the bill was "to provide the Indian with a workable plan of land management and development . . . an indispensable means of putting Indian lands (especially forest and grazing lands) into units for profitable and conservative management. The land program of the bill fits in closely with the larger program of intelligent land use for white-owned and public domain lands now being worked out by this administration."[8]

There was a difference between the programs, however, that was not made clear. White landowners and holders of grazing leases on the public domain had to be exhorted and attracted to participate in land use planning through subsidies and ultimately a share in decisions. The Indian Service, under this bill, could exercise far greater control over the process of land consolidation and could anticipate fewer obstacles from local landowners who did not want to participate.[9]

A bill which proposed to expand the power of hitherto weak or nonexistent tribal organizations over local landowners, and the power of the bureau over the management of Indian resources, was bound to arouse opposition even in a Congress that had proved notably receptive to innovations. While the House and Senate Indian Affairs Committees reviewed the bill, the reformers sought to counter general attacks on their proposals in both Congress and the public press.

These criticisms focused on two issues. The first was the effect of the bill on the policy of assimilation. During the hearings before the House commmittee, Representative Theodore Werner of South Dakota questioned whether the effect of the bill would not be to "segregate the Indian and isolate him and make it impossible to ever become an assimilated part of the citizenship of our country." In Congress, Representative William Hastings of Oklahoma, a Cherokee Indian, attacked the proposal as a means of indefinitely perpetuating federal guardianship over the Indians.[10]

Collier and his aides attempted to reassure the skeptics that the ultimate goal of assimilation was not being abandoned. While not establishing any definite timetable, the commissioner sought to draw a parallel between the new bureau program and the Department of Agriculture. In the explanatory statement sent to Congress with the bill, he asserted that under reorganization "the Office of Indian Affairs will ultimately serve as a purely advisory body, offering the same type of service to the Indians . . . that the Department of Agriculture offers to American farmers." Later, during the House hearings, Collier added that "under the operation of the self-government features of the bill . . . many of the things that the government is now doing through paid employees would pass over to the individual communities, by co-operative voluntary effort."[11]

Collier's position on assimilation was deliberately enigmatic. He maintained that his policy was intended to benefit those Indians who wished for assimilation by preparing them for a productive life in white society while providing those who chose to retain their tribal ways with the means for continued communal life.[12] That was not quite the same thing as considering assimilation to be the goal of policy, and in practice Collier's interest was focused on those Indians who remained in or returned to the tribal relationship. Even the educational program outlined in Title II of the bureau's draft contemplated that most recipients of assistance would function within the environment of the tribal governments and the Indian Service. Collier admitted to Congressmen that full assimilation would be a matter of generations, not years.

To a certain extent Collier may have been misleading or misunderstood in presenting to Congress his concept of Indian reorganization as an instrument of assimilation. His basic orientation was toward groups and communities, not individuals, as the building blocks of society; and that was not necessarily clear to his questioners who were reared on older political theories. When asked by Representative Isabel Greenaway of Arizona if the proposed program would prepare Indians for individual responsibility, Collier responded, "I would expect . . . that there would be groups who would probably be very peculiar and different and would probably continue to be of peculiar interest and concern to the Government. . . . Unquestionably with other groups, the tendency would be to rise to the full stature of ability and personal responsibility." The concept of "personal responsibility," however, was placed in a communal framework, as Collier tried to indicate by citing the example of the Mexican agricultural communities, the *ejidos*, which were promoted by the Mexican government after the 1910 revolution.[13]

A second attack labeled the tribal organizations conceived by the bureau as Communistic. Flora Seymour, a former member of the defunct Board of Indian Commissioners, was most active in spreading this interpretation, which Collier sought to counter through the press, relying on such defenders as Oliver La Farge.[14] This attack was not used successfully in 1934, but the charge of promoting communism proved durable and was resurrected later in the decade by congressional critics of Collier and the Indian New Deal. It seems safe to say, however, that the western congressmen scrutinizing the reorganization bill in 1934 were less concerned about the prospective conversion to communism of the Indians than continued and expanded federal control of Indian resources.

Congressional attention focused on several elements of the bill that outlined the potential powers of tribal organizations. Of these the most controversial involved the relationship between the tribe and holders of allotments and heirship lands. The bureau draft made the exchange of allotments for shares in tribal corporations voluntary, but also provided for the automatic transfer of heirship lands to the tribe, gave the tribe the power of eminent domain over members' lands, and implied that the determination of fair compensation in all cases would be made by the tribal governments. Collier cited the experience of the Pueblo Lands Board since 1923 as justification for these provisions, noting that non-Indian landowners had delayed and obstructed its operation by refusing to accept reasonable offers of compensation for their lands. Unless the new tribal organizations had some reserved powers in this area, the whole program of land consolidation could be stymied.[15]

Critics of these aspects of the bill were not restricted to white westerners interested in acquiring Indian allotments. Anthropologists Franz Boas and Ralph Linton, two of the major figures in their field, having observed Indians in the Northern Plains and coastal regions, felt that holders of allotments in trust would be reluctant to part with them voluntarily in view of their previous experience with bureau maladministration.[16] Collier recognized the soundness of these suspicions and arranged a tour in March 1934 to meet with assemblies of Indians in the West and explain features of the bill. The bureau portrayed the tour as a novel means of bringing Indians into the policy-making process, but skeptical congressmen regarded it as a public relations effort intended only to spread propaganda among the Indians. Their suspicions were not allayed when Indians at each assembly were polled for their support of the bill and the results, which were favorable, were then presented as evidence of the Indians' endorsement. Collier's tour did have obvious publicity and lobbying overtones, but it also probably served as a desirable method of communicating with the Indians. The bureau sought to ensure that representatives chosen to attend the assemblies were elected rather than chosen by reservation superintendents.[17]

The bureau leaders discovered that a great deal of misinformation about the bill had spread among the Indians, for it was a complex proposal and few Indians had seen the draft. Some of the major points of the program were clarified and the appearance of consultation probably helped assuage some fears. At the same time, the assemblies had some unexpected aftereffects. The bill that was described to the Indians at this time was the unrevised bureau draft. Government spokesmen stressed the powers which the tribal organizations would exercise over tribal funds, individual property, and reservation employees. The subsequent Wheeler-Howard Act modified some of the provisions considerably, but for many Indians the differences between the bill explained to them in March 1934 and the act passed in June 1934 were never clarified.

Throughout the spring the reform groups and their critics debated the bill while the congressional committees reviewed it. By the beginning of May it was clear to the bureau and the reformers supporting the bill that major changes were necessary to get it through Congress. After President Roosevelt sent a letter to Wheeler endorsing the bill, representatives from the bureau, including Collier and Zimmerman, met informally with committee members from both houses to "salvage all the good points" of the bill.[18] By general consent, the Indian court section was jettisoned completely, as was the provision for the automatic transfer of heirship lands to the tribes. Exchanges of land for shares in tribal corporations were made completely voluntary for the individual landowners and a new section established a revolving credit fund of $10 million to provide loans to tribes. The section outlining the powers of the tribal governments was reduced to one short paragraph, and the whole bill was rewritten and reduced considerably.

There were still differences between the drafts submitted by the House and Senate committees. House chairman Edgar Howard introduced an amendment under which all Indian tribes would vote in referenda whether or not to come under the self-government provision of the act, the referenda to be held within one year after the act was approved. Howard appears to have been under the impression that under the original draft, tribes would have been compelled to accept charters. Collier objected that there was no compulsion contemplated, and pointed out that the effect of the new clause would be to deprive Indians who voted not to come under the self-government provisions of access to the credit and educational features of the act. Wheeler agreed with Collier, but deferred to the House committee, and the provision for referenda went into the final draft.[19] The House bill also included a new section relating to the chartering of corporations, allowing any number of members over ten of any recognized tribe to form a chartered corporation. The proposal was eliminated from the final draft by the Senate committee, presumably because it would have weakened the tribe's potential control over its resources.

In certain respects, the drafts proposed by the congressional committees were more liberal in promoting and protecting Indian self-government than the bureau's original draft, reflecting some members' feelings that the original proposal would have established a façade of Indian government behind which federal administrators could expand their control over Indian resources. In the bureau draft the charter of self-government would not have been ratified until approved by three-fifths of the Indians on the reservation or territory covered by the charter. The House bill changed this to a simple majority vote "of the adult members of the tribe, or of the adult Indians residing on the reservation," a confusing terminology, since it left unclear whether nonresidents could vote. Eventually a supplementary act was necessary to resolve the question so that "the vote of a majority of those voting" would be sufficient.[20]

The debate on the floor of Congress was an anticlimax after the months of preparation. On May 22, Wheeler submitted the amended bill to the Senate, and Howard sent the House bill to the floor on May 28. The Senate debate took place on June 12. Senator Pat McCarran of Nevada raised the specter of bureau manipulation of the Indians and succeeded in having the section dealing with corporate charters altered so that the petition for ratification required one-third rather than one-fourth of the adult tribal members. Senator Ashurst of Arizona introduced an amendment, much discussed in the Senate committee hearings, relating to Papago mineral lands, which was accepted with modifications. Wheeler effectively countered attacks by some other western senators, and the bill passed by a voice vote.[21]

The House debate took place three days later. Howard led the supporters, countering most of the opposition by pointing out that the House version made the whole program voluntary for the Indians. The bill passed by a vote of 258 to 88. Significantly, 80 percent of the opposition votes were from representatives of states east of the Mississippi River, and of the thirty Republican votes cast for the bill, nineteen came from western states. Clearly, western opposition had been virtually eliminated by the bill's revisions, and only those congressmen representing the demands of assimilationists held out against it.[22] A conference committee met on June 16, resolved the differences in the two versions, and reported back to Congress, where the final draft was agreed to without apparent opposition. On June 18, 1934, the bill went to President Roosevelt, who signed it into law.

The Indian Reorganization Act, or the Wheeler-Howard Act, as it was more popularly known, was much shorter than the bureau draft and had drastically revised certain key elements of Collier's proposals, but included most of the original ideas for a reorientation of Indian policy. The act repealed the allotment laws, permitted the restoration of surplus reservation lands to tribal ownership, and provided for voluntary exchanges of restricted trust lands for shares in tribal corporations. An appropriation of $2 million a year was authorized for the purchase of additional lands for tribal use. A $10 million revolving credit fund was established to provide loans to chartered tribal corporations, with additional appropriations of $250,000 a year for use in organizing tribal governments and to establish a loan fund for Indians seeking college or vocational education. Indians could be employed by the bureau without meeting civil service qualifications.

The final sections of the act dealt with tribal self-government. A referendum was to be called on every reservation included under the act within one year (subsequently extended to two years) to determine whether or not the tribe chose to come under the act. Those Indians who rejected the act would legally remain under direct bureau control. Those tribes which accepted it could then prepare a constitution, which must be ratified by a majority of the Indians on a given reservation and officially recognized members of the tribe. Next, a tribal council would be elected; it would have "all powers vested in an Indian tribe . . . by existing law" and other defined powers, including the right to employ legal counsel, prevent the sale or lease of tribal properties without its approval, negotiate with other governmental agencies, and review federal appropriation estimates relating to the tribe before their submission to the Bureau of the Budget and to Congress. If at least one-third of the tribal members petitioned favorably, a charter of tribal incorporation would be prepared. Once ratified by a majority vote, the charter would enable the tribe to manage its resources and purchase individual allotments or issue shares in the corporation in exchange for the transfer of allotments.[23]

The act in its final form resembled most closely the version drafted by the House committee. On the whole, it retained many of the basic features of the original bureau draft relating to the process of tribal incorporation and organization, employment of Indians by the bureau, and the termination of allotment. Furthermore, the act provided for the establishment of a credit fund for Indian tribes, albeit a relatively small one. On the other hand, the ability of the tribes and the Department of the Interior to acquire allotted lands for purposes of consolidation was considerably diluted, and the tribes were denied the power to take over heirship lands. Collier later lamented the loss of these features as "a major disaster to the Indians, the Indian Service, and the program."[24] The requirement of referenda on all Indian reservations within a time limit imposed an unexpected burden on the bureau and forced the reformers to move more rapidly toward tribal organization than they had intended.

There were two other elements in earlier drafts of the bill whose absence from the act may have vitiated tribal self-determination. First was the section relating to Indian courts. They had been expected to complement tribal councils by establishing a system for the efficient administration of Indian laws and for handling disputes involving individuals or groups and the new tribal organizations. Lacking this forum for the resolution of controversies, Indians used political opposition to the new councils and protests to Congress and the bureau, thereby placing a heavy burden on administrators, who had to spend a good deal of time settling these disputes and explaining them to curious and sometimes hostile Congressmen.

The removal of the House committee's proposal for the incorporation of Indian groups smaller than the tribe, which was apparently done at Collier's behest, also weakened the act in operation. The fact that business organizations could function only at the tribal level or be initiated by tribal councils reinforced a strong tendency by administrators to focus on tribal activities at the expense of more local, community-centered initiatives. It is not surprising that the original designers of the bill in the bureau regarded the tribe as the logical focus for organizational efforts. Few anthropologists or other students of American Indians had dealt much with Indian political organization. Nevertheless, the inability of Indians to organize politically or economically except through tribal auspices perpetuated and strengthened what were to be basically artificial units of Indian political and social life.

3
THE ADMINISTRATIVE
APPROACH TO
REORGANIZATION

The aim of the Indian Reorganization Act was defined in a variety of ways by those who sponsored and endorsed it. Felix Cohen, the leading legal architect of the original draft, described it as "the progressive transfer of municipal functions to the organized tribe," that is, to give the new tribal governments authority in such areas as law enforcement, public health and education, and similar services performed by county and municipal governments.[1]

Collier's interpretation was set in a broader focus. As he put it in retrospect, "The Indian New Deal . . . held two purposes. One was the conservation of the biological Indian and of Indian cultures, each with its special purposes. The other . . . was conservation of the Indian's natural resources."[2] The act would not simply replicate Anglo-American patterns of local government but would seek to promote forms of community self-determination enabling Indians to function in a modern economic environment within the framework of their own traditional cultural institutions. The program was directed toward economic development that would not disrupt the traditional society.

Achieving these goals would not be a simple task. The preservation or restoration of Indian material resources often required action of a drastic nature: the use of new and hitherto limited authority in land acquisition, and the introduction of new techniques of resource control and planning. At the same time, the preservation of Indian cultural institutions and group ties within this context of change demanded a good deal of caution, patience, and flexibility. Anthropologists Clyde Kluckhohn and Robert Hackenberg emphasized the concept underlying the program:

The Indian Reorganization Act was a deliberate attempt to induce certain kinds of changes in Indian society and to control other changes. In its inception the authors made use of the knowledge . . . [that] constructive changes must not destroy psychological security and must preserve continuity in both the group and the individual so that personality integration and stability may be maintained.[3]

In practice the reorganization program fell short of these goals. Framed as a compromise between the demands of the reformers and the interests of western landowners, the act, by making the transfer of lands from individual to tribal ownership voluntary, and by restricting the appropriations for land consolidation and purchases, provided only a limited degree of control to the federal agency in reshaping Indian economic resources.[4] The notion of reinstituting tribal organizations along traditional lines and providing for their gradual assumption of greater responsibilities was distorted by the requirement of immediate referenda among the Indians for inclusion in the program and by differences within the bureau over the range of authority that the new Indian governments should be granted and the pace at which they should develop. Some Indians were hurriedly pushed into a system of organization with which they were unfamiliar, while others found the powers that they were given more limited than they felt had been promised. Even Collier, who defended the Indian Service without qualification throughout his tenure as commissioner, later concluded, "We had pressed the democratic philosophy not too far; we had not pressed it far enough nor skillfully enough."[5]

Nevertheless, the Indian reorganization program in its conception and execution constituted an unusual, though not unique, attempt to generate significant social and economic changes administratively. In so doing Collier opened the bureau to new contacts with other federal departments in planning the development of Indian resources, and to new ideas about the goals of administration in a democratic society and the future of the Indian in the United States. Anthropologists were brought in as advisers. However faulty the administrators' ideas about Indian life may have been, they now at least acquired a greater appreciation of cultural differences among tribes and between whites and Indians. An effort to reorganize the Indian Service was made. More important in the long run, Indians were for the first time given positions of real responsibility in the bureau.

The Indian New Deal marked the first time in the history of the Indians' relations with the government that a conscious attempt was made to take the Indian point of view into account and to shape a program to meet Indian needs rather than to reshape the Indians. Yet it was also an experiment in social engineering, a "laboratory in ethnic affairs," to use Collier's words. To this extent it resembled earlier Indian policies in that it proposed to manipulate Indian behavior in ways which their white "guardians" thought best for them.

The sense of urgency generated within the bureau by the desperate economic situation on many reservations was reinforced by the provision of the Indian Reorganization Act that referenda be held by June 1935. Collier had opposed this proposal as unnecessary when the bill was under consideration; the reformers now made a virtue of necessity, proclaiming that "the principle of self-government was carried to a new phase when the Indians themselves were asked to vote on whether or not the law establishing self-governing powers should apply on different reservations."[6]

Collier did not intend to leave the outcome entirely to chance, however, in view of the local efforts being mounted among the Navajo and Sioux tribes, in particular, to block reorganization. Since he had not had time to build up a tribal reorganization staff, Collier had to depend on the agency superintendents, some of whom had openly opposed the new policy before it was enacted.[7] His strategy, as he described it to a field representative, was to "select those reservations which appear to be best informed and most favorably inclined towards acceptance of the Act" for an intensive "educational campaign" with assistance from the Washington office.[8] During the summer of 1934 the campaign was pushed on the plains reservations in Montana and the Dakotas, and in the Great Lakes region, where the first referenda were held, with gratifying results, in October and early November. Altogether during the first year of the act 263 Indian groups voted; 172 with a total population of 132,000 accepted reorganization and 73 with a total population of 63,000 rejected it.[9]

Many of the groups that voted against the act were small bands like the Mission Indians of California, while the large reservations generally favored it. There were, however, some prominent exceptions: the Klamath tribe of Oregon, which had been touted as a model for reorganization and which already had a well-established tribal government, rejected the act by a heavy vote in June 1935. The Crow Indians of Montana, regarded by anthropologist Robert Lowie as one of the strongest and most cohesive tribes in the plains region, voted against the act despite the efforts of their new Indian superintendent, Robert Yellowtail, to promote reorganization. Several other large plains reservations, including Fort Peck in Montana, Sisseton in South Dakota, and Turtle Mountain in North Dakota, voted negatively, as did the Iroquois tribes of New York, which had also sought exclusion from the bill while it was being considered by Congress.[10]

The most significant rejection of the Reorganization Act took place on the sprawling Navajo Reservation in Arizona and New Mexico on June 14 and 15, 1935. The margin of defeat was 384 votes out of 15,600 cast, almost 98 percent of the eligible voting population having participated. The bureau attributed the vote to "energetic campaigns of misrepresentation carried on by special interests," including local white businesses; but probably more influential was the coinciding of the referendum with a bitter controversy between the bureau and the Navajos over stock reduction.[11] The defeat was a major one, since congressional supporters of the bill had argued that if it "did not work among the Navajos it would not work anyplace." Moreover, Collier had devoted a good deal of attention to the ratification struggle, sending two of his key advisers, Felix Cohen and Ward Shepard, to meet with the Navajos, and seeking the aid of La Farge's organization and even the Indian Rights Association in securing a favorable vote.[12]

While the ratification campaign was proceeding, Collier had to deal with other pressing problems, notably an effort by the House Committee on Indian Affairs to abort the Indian Reorganization Act by denying necessary funds to put it into operation. Since the act had not passed until the end of the session in June 1934, no funds were available to finance tribal organization work and land purchases until Congress reconvened. In the new session, early in 1935, the House committee sought to cut the appropriations for these two programs to one-fourth the amount authorized in the act, and requested additional appropriations to maintain the boarding schools. These shifts would jeopardize any serious effort to redirect Indian policy.[13] Collier's lobbying managed to force the allocations up to one-half of the authorized appropriations for the credit and land purchase funds, and $175,000 of the allowed $250,000 per year for tribal organization; but it was a sobering experience and portended further difficulties from congressional critics.[14]

Collier also turned his attention to additional legislation. One of the defects of the original act was that under the referendum provision, once an Indian group had rejected the act, it could not subsequently ask for a chance to reconsider; and exclusion from the act meant not only that tribal organization would not occur, but also that the Indians would not be able to share in the credit or land purchase programs or receive scholarships for higher education. An effort to have this provision amended failed, but legislation was passed in June 1935 extending the deadline for referenda for another year. This amendatory act also clarified an ambiguity in the earlier measure by specifying that "the vote of a majority of those voting shall be necessary and sufficient to effectuate such exclusion or ratification."[15] The law in effect upheld a ruling made by the Interior Department's legal division earlier and prevented delays in balloting that might have arisen if a majority vote of all the enrolled tribesmen, some of whom were settled far from their original reservations, had been required.

Two additional measures were successfully lobbied through Congress by the bureau. Section 13 of the Indian Reorganization Act excluded the Indians of Oklahoma from those provisions relating to the establishment of self-government, although they could participate in the land purchase, educational, and credit fund programs under the act. The Alaskan Indians could draw upon those funds and also form tribal councils but were curiously excluded from Section 17 of the act, which provided for the establishment of tribal corporations.

Most Alaska Indians lived in small, isolated fishing villages; some of the more prosperous operated canneries for commercial fisheries. These Indians still claimed significant areas of land in Alaska that could not be defined as reservations, and their settlements were largely independent of one another. The Alaska Native Brotherhood endorsed the efforts of the bureau to extend the incorporation provisions of the act to them, but argued against a direct extension of the provisions, since they wanted to form corporations at the village level rather than at the broader "tribal" level.[16] This request was accepted and the Alaska Reorganization Act of May 1, 1936, included a provision that "groups of Indians in Alaska not heretofore recognized as bands or tribes, but having a common bond of occupation, association or residence within a well-defined neighborhood or community or district may organize to adopt constitutions . . . and to receive charters of incorporation."[17]

The Oklahoma Indians posed a different and more difficult problem. The Indians of eastern Oklahoma were members of the Five Civilized Tribes, whose governments had been destroyed and lands allotted in the late 1890s and early 1900s. They were relatively assimilated and lived scattered among the white population; many had lost their lands while others leased their best lands to neighboring white farmers. In the western part of the state were more isolated tribes, the Cheyennes, Arapahos, Kiowas, and Comanches, who still retained some tribal cohesion. The bureau kept a tighter rein on the properties of these Indians, although the basic policy of allotment was maintained, and their agents devoted more time to administering the properties of the wealthier Indians than to building up tribal resources.[18]

Oklahoma representatives to Congress, including Indians like William Hastings, had opposed the extension of the Indian Reorganization Act to their state, arguing that it would retard a well-advanced movement toward assimilation. Senator Edgar Thomas, a member of the Senate Committee on Indian Affairs, had been instrumental in excluding the Oklahoma Indians from the act. But during the fall of 1934 Thomas had visited the various reservations with Collier and was apparently persuaded of the benefits that the Indians would receive from an extension of the act. Thomas and Representative Will Rogers sponsored an Oklahoma Indian welfare bill, similar to the Indian Reorganization Act, which became law in June 1936.[19]

To meet the objections of assimilationists, the bill proposed to divide Indians into two categories, or degrees, allowing second-degree Indians to move more rapidly out of guardianship than first-degree Indians, defined as those of more than 50 percent Indian blood. The Indian witnesses at the hearings on the bill were critical of this proposal and expressed greater interest in the provisions relating to the acquisition of land for landless Indians and the formation of tribal corporations. All of the Indian reform groups supported the bill, but it was vigorously opposed by

Joseph Bruner's American Indian Federation (which had its head-quarters in Oklahoma) and by white businessmen and politicians who objected to the withdrawal of Indian lands and mineral deposits from state taxation.[20]

The final draft of the bill accommodated the critics by getting rid of the provisions relating to degrees of Indian-ness and allow-ing the state to tax the gross receipts from oil and gas leases on Indian lands. It also enabled Oklahoma Indians to draw on the revolving credit fund and provided for the establishment of tribal governments and corporations. In addition, the Oklahoma bill included the provision deleted from the final draft of the reorgani-zation act permitting groups of ten or more Indians to organize into cooperatives which could draw upon an additional $2 million fund for the purchase of lands or for other purposes. The potential for corporate business enterprise was thus extended below the tribal level. The designers of the bill recognized that for many of the eastern Oklahoma Indians, tribal organization would be a difficult if not impossible task.[21]

Under the Oklahoma Indian Welfare Act eighteen groups or-ganized under constitutions and thirteen under corporate charters. Most of these groups numbered only a few hundred people and the bulk of them were located in the western part of the state. A little more than half of the Indian population of 22,000 in Okla-homa organized under tribal governments. The governments of the Five Civilized Tribes were beyond restoration, although several of the Creek towns established councils. The Indians were reluc-tant to accept tribal organization for fear of being put on reserva-tions. At the same time, the cooperatives brought a good deal of needed money into the Indian communities of Oklahoma.[22]

Meanwhile the process of tribal organization was being pushed forward. There was no need for haste once the referenda were over, but Collier did not want to lose the impetus for organization that the ratification debates had stimulated among Indians, and his economic advisers wanted tribal governments established as the prerequisite to incorporation and the operation of the credit fund. By the middle of 1937, sixty-five tribes had established constitutions and thirty-two had also ratified corporate charters. Altogether between 1936 and 1945, ninety-three Indian groups set up tribal governments, and seventy-four of them also had busi-ness charters. All but seven of the tribes were organized before 1938, indicating the intensity of the effort in the intervening period.[23]

In its first efforts at tribal organization the bureau drew upon outside assistance, as it was also doing in the field of economic development. Collier had been able to call upon the support of several talented lawyers in the Interior Department, notably Nathan Margold and Felix Cohen, in drawing up the Indian Reorganization Act, and these men contributed their services and those of their assistants to the preparation of tribal constitutions and charters. A model constitution was prepared and teams of lawyers were sent around the reservations to meet with Indian delegates and agency officials to discuss the general format of the constitutions and particular provisions desired by the Indians. The use of model constitutions was not a completely happy arrangement, and one lawyer warned of "an incredibly high degree of standardization of the constitutions." Other field agents felt the language in the constitutions (and other bureau documents on tribal organizations) could use more "one-syllable words." But the lawyers in the field made a conscientious effort to tailor the constitutions to the particular tribal situations they encountered.[24]

Collier also brought in anthropologists, both from the Bureau of American Ethnology (a branch of the Smithsonian Institution) and from the universities, to work with the lawyers on tribal constitutions. Initially the social scientists were part-time consultants, their work loosely coordinated by W. Duncan Strong, on loan from the Smithsonian.[25] This approach seemed inadequate because the staff was "too small to gather basic facts for all tribes which are organizing," and in 1936 an Applied Anthropology Staff was established within the bureau under H. Scudder Mekeel, formerly of Harvard University. The new unit was assigned the task of making social surveys of reservations as well as continuing advisory work on tribal constitutions. The Applied Anthropology Staff was disbanded in 1938 because of reductions in the regular bureau budget, according to Collier. Anthropologists continued to work with the Educational Division of the bureau, however, training new employees on Indian cultural differences.[26]

In 1936 an Indian Organization Division was set up under F. H. Daiker to handle the administrative details of the reorganization program after the phase of preparing constitutions was completed. It was also directed to "assist . . . in what may be called long-term planning along social, economic and political lines." This rather vague authorization was in keeping with the premise that the political and the economic development of the Indians were closely related. The division was to operate on a district basis, primarily through a system of traveling field representatives with a small Washington staff. Most of the field force was to be composed of Indian employees of the bureau, and it included many of the Indians who were to rise to prominence in the bureau during and after the Collier era.[27]

By the end of 1936 the basic administrative framework was complete. New legislation had brought virtually all the Indian groups in the United States under the program, relatively formal procedures for tribal organization had been developed, and new units had been created to oversee the process and coordinate political and economic programs for the Indians. Even among Indians who had rejected the act, such as the Navajos, the bureau sponsored and supported the formation of tribal councils and sought to provide the Indians with the economic benefits available to them. The new Indian Organization Division not only worked with those tribes that were still in the process of preparing constitutions and charters, but also reviewed the operations of established councils, seeking in some cases to mediate disputes arising under the new governments, and in other situations to ensure that the tribal councils were given due consideration by other Indian Service and outside agency officials in the development of social and economic programs for the reservations.

The tribal organization effort was genuine, designed to integrate new approaches to Indian resource management with the best information available about laws relating to Indian affairs, and about the traditional institutions of Indian life. The shortcomings of this effort, which will be analyzed in the following chapters, were not the result of indifference on the part of bureau leaders toward the goal of Indian self-determination. The ultimate failure of the Indian New Deal was the result of circumstances that to a large extent were beyond the control of the Collier administration.

4

PROBLEMS OF TRIBAL ORGANIZATION: ASSIMILATION AND FACTIONAL RIVALRY

Underlying the Indian Reorganization Act were some basic assumptions about the character of traditional Indian life. The failure of allotment had revealed the gulf between white and Indian cultures, and the work of a generation of anthropologists like Franz Boas and Clark Wissler provided the background for an understanding of the varieties of Indian cultures. The new Indian policy was based on a conscious recognition of the separate cultural identity of Indians. The bureau leaders, nevertheless, faced grave difficulties in shaping the policy to fit the circumstances of Indian groups whose experiences of white contact had varied widely, in ways which even anthropologists were only beginning to investigate.[1]

The reformers had long before concluded that the failure of allotment and assimilation policies could not be attributed solely to corruption and mismanagement in the Bureau of Indian Affairs, but that faulty basic premises also played a part:

The Indian is not a "rugged individualist"; he functions best as an integrated member of a group, clan or tribe. Identification of his individuality with clan or tribe is with him a spiritual necessity. If the satisfaction of this compelling sentiment is denied him—as it was for a half a century or more—the Indian does not . . . merge into white group life. Through a modernized form of Indian tribal organization, adapted to the needs of the various tribes . . . it is possible to make use of this proverbial latent civic force.[2]

For Collier the traditional Indian tribe incorporated a spiritual element that European civilization had lost in the industrial era, an element that bound the group together far more effectively than the need for economic self-preservation. Indian tribes, like other nonliterate societies, transmitted their cultural heritage through rituals, symbols, and ceremonies involving the participation of each member. Through these ceremonies and through the intricate web of kinship and clanship, well understood by all tribesmen, group cohesion was reinforced. Despite years of white misrule, the potential for tribal organization remained, for it was ingrained in the thought patterns of Indians, in their ways of viewing one another and the world around them.[3]

It followed from this view that tribal governments did not operate, in the manner of American and European governments, through the conflict of organized interest groups or on the assertion of power by the dominant interest. "The principle of unanimity was not imposed but was reached only through discussion and acceptance by the entire tribe."[4] The traditional tribe, recreated, could be regarded as an entity because it expressed the wishes and interests of all its members.

The designers of the Reorganization Act recognized that the new policy had to be applied flexibly:

[The Reorganization Act] attempts to deal with situations as diverse as those exemplified by the comparatively isolated unallotted reservations of the Southwest, in which self-government has persisted in fact for centuries; and certain long-allotted reservations of the Northwest in which almost the last vestiges of Indian social and tribal organization have disappeared. It must deal with groups of Indians which, through intermarriage and assimilation, have taken on the social and economic habits and viewpoints of the surrounding white civilization and with other groups which have adhered proudly to the peculiar heritage of their own history.[5]

In practice the provisions of the amended act limited the flexibility of the program by requiring a referendum on every reservation and limiting access to the revolving credit fund to tribal corporations. The impossibility of achieving a satisfactory form of decentralization with the bureau and the chronic shortage of money for tribal organization work contributed to the problem. At the same time, the concept of the tribe as the most effective mechanism for improving Indian economic and social conditions was flawed; and this weakness would, in the long run, undermine the important economic achievements of the Collier administration.

Indian cultural groups had always varied widely on a range of characteristics, but by the twentieth century the main area of variation was the degree of acculturation, or assimilation, as it was generally called then. The Dawes Act and associated policies had not succeeded in integrating the Indian into white society, but had made significant inroads on traditional institutions, hastening processes that had begun at the earliest period of white contact.

Acculturation is in some aspects selective and adaptive; in the longer run the changes introduced are cumulative and affect the entire culture, particularly, as in the case of the American Indian, when the recipient group is outnumbered and its institutions are systematically under attack. Physical isolation and the indifference of whites had protected some Indians; others, more visible, had been subjected to the full force of government policy and only scattered remnants of their reservations remained in Indian hands. In still other cases, the Indian land base had been preserved but intermarriage and education had weakened traditional ways of life.

Table 1 shows the variations in the extent of assimilation among Indian groups. It is based on data assembled for forty-four reservations between 1930 and 1933 by the Bureau of the Census, the Civil Works Administration, and the National Resources Board. The forty-four reservations comprised more than 75 percent of the total Indian population and included almost all the major Indian tribal groups remaining in the American West.

While the sources of the data are not entirely satisfactory, they seem reliable enough to provide the kind of schematic arrangement used here. Patterns of assimilation or acculturation are complex and affect many aspects of a cultural group, so no simple categorization based on a few characteristics can be wholly accurate. But certain characteristics that have been summarized statistically for a large number of cases can at least reveal basic differences among groups.

The three characteristics summarized are (1) the extent of white intermarriage with the Indian group, based on the percentage of mixed-blood members of the population of each reservation; (2) the extent of at least rudimentary white education, based on the percentage of Indians over age twenty-one on each reservation judged to be literate by the standards of the census takers; and (3) the extent to which the tribal domain was broken up beyond

Table 1

ASSIMILATION AMONG 45 INDIAN GROUPS

Region	High Assimilation, Economic & Cultural	High Assimilation, Cultural	Medium Assimilation, Economic & Cultural	Medium Assimilation, Cultural	Low Assimilation, Economic & Cultural
The East & Oklahoma	Osage Five Civilized Tribes	Iroquois	Kiowa Pawnee		Cheyenne-Arapaho
Great Lakes	Chippewa	Menominee Ottawa			
Plains	Flathead Potawatomi Yankton Sioux Cheyenne River Sioux	Blackfeet Turtle Mt. Chippewa Ft. Belknap (Gros Ventres, Assiniboins) Rosebud Sioux	Ft. Totten Sioux Winnebago Standing Rock Sioux Pine Ridge Sioux Crow Creek Sioux	Ft. Berthold (Mandans, Hidatsas, Arikaras) Crow Northern Cheyenne	
Great Basin			Uintah-Ouray Ft. Hall (Shoshones, Bannocks)	Shoshone	Ute Paiute
Northwest		Spokane Colville Umatilla Klamath		Warm Springs	
The Southwest & California		Sacramento Mission			Apache Papago Navajo Pueblo Pima Yuma Hopi

restoration, based on measures of the percentage of land on each reservation which had been released to individuals in fee patent or otherwise alienated. This last characteristic does not constitute a direct measurement of assimilation but does indicate the most important aspect of that process (for our purposes), the decrease in potential tribal cohesion.[6]

The Indian groups examined for these characteristics are ranged into five rough categories, distinguished by variations in the economic and cultural (including racial) cohesion of the groups. The first category, High Assimilation, Economic and Cultural, comprises those groups in which (1) over 50 percent of the Indian population were of mixed blood; (2) over 75 percent of the Indians were regarded as literate; (3) over 50 percent of the allotted lands had been released on patents in fee to individual Indians. The second category, High Assimilation, Cultural, refers to groups whose racial and educational characteristics are similar to those in the first category, but whose allotted lands had never been released in fee patent.

The third category, Medium Assimilation, Economic and Cultural, includes reservations where mixed-bloods constituted between 25 and 50 percent of the population, the literacy rate was over 75 percent, and between 25 and 60 percent of the allotted lands had been patented. The fourth category resembles the third category except in the last characteristic, that is less than 25 percent of the allotted lands had been patented or allotment had never been introduced. The last category, Low Assimilation, Economic and Cultural, refers to reservations where less than 20 percent of the population were of mixed blood, the literacy rate was below 75 percent, and less than 25 percent of the allotted land had been patented, or allotment had never been introduced (as was generally the case in this category).

The regions used in the table correspond, not to the culture areas identified by anthropologists, but to the administrative districts established by the bureau in 1935, which do parallel natural culture areas in some regions such as the Great Basin and the Southwest, but do not in other regions. The plains districts embraced the largest number of reservations, but the heaviest concentrations of Indian population were in Oklahoma and the Southwest, which together accounted for about one-quarter of the total Indian population of the United States.

The regional dimension to this distribution is evident. Virtually all of the southwestern tribes were relatively unassimilated, living on reservations remote from white settlements and having escaped allotment. The heaviest concentration of assimilated tribes was in the northern Great Lakes, plains, and northwestern regions, and in eastern Oklahoma.

At the same time, there are peculiarities in these patterns which reflect the different experiences of Indian groups during the preceding generation. The classic case is Oklahoma, where the Five Civilized Tribes and the Osages in the eastern part of the state had been broken up by allotment in the 1890s and early 1900s and by extensive intermarriage with neighboring whites, while in the western section tribes like the Cheyennes, Comanches, and Kiowas had been left alone on isolated reservations. A similar but less obvious division existed in the plains states.

In some cases, like those of the Blackfeet in Montana and the Turtle Mountain (Chippewa) Reservation in North Dakota, the physical isolation of the reservations helped to keep full-blood Indians together despite their minority status, while the land base remained largely in Indian hands, although allotted. Of greater importance in affecting the pace of assimilation was the work of the bureau's competency commission of 1917–20, which, judging from the results, operated in a totally capricious and irrational fashion.

A good example of the bewildering legacy of the competency commission could be found on the reservations of the Sioux in South Dakota. At the Yankton Subagency of the Rosebud Reservation, more than 80 percent of the allotted land had been patented and 80 percent of the Indians enrolled there were landless, while on Rosebud itself and the neighboring Pine Ridge Reservation, less than 50 percent of the allotments had been released in fee patent and the proportion of landless Indians was correspondingly lower. There was little recognizable difference among the Indians at these agencies, in terms of their degree of assimilation, although that had been the presumed basis upon which the competency commission made its decisions.

There were similar anomalies throughout the reservations of the Northern Plains. Several, notably the Crow Reservation and Fort Belknap in Montana, had escaped the fee patent process altogether, despite the fact that they had large mixed-blood populations and the literacy rate was not substantially different from that of other plains Indian groups. The Menominee tribe of Wisconsin, which by white standards could be considered the most assimilated of Indian groups, also completely evaded patenting, while lands of neighboring Indians like the Chippewas were almost completely broken up as a result of decisions made by the competency commission.

These differences among Indian groups played an important role in the responses of the groups to the Indian Reorganization Act and the political divisions that were to emerge under the new tribal governments. Divisions were most evident and could be anticipated among the more assimilated groups; but even among the isolated, less assimilated Indians of the Southwest, tribal reorganization encountered formidable obstacles resulting from internal disunity.

The notion that Indians had traditionally lived in a state of domestic harmony was not simply the naive assumption of white reformers like Collier; the contemporaneous concept of the tribe as a historical entity that could be regarded as a unit concealed deep and lasting divisions within Indian groups, divisions which were no less important than the actions of whites in shaping Indian responses to white contact.

That the tribal connection counted for little among the semi-assimilated Indians of the Northern Plains in the 1930s was obvious even to the most optimistic observer, but it had been no less true among Indian tribes long before the era of white conquest. Factional struggles within the organized tribes and confederacies of the East were often manipulated by whites to their own ends, as in the case of the Muskogees or Creeks, whose internal squabbles eventuated in the Creek War of 1813. The sources of conflict, however, were unrelated to the issue of white influence. Among the less formally organized nomadic groups of the western plains, serious disputes generally resulted in a breakup of the tribe as the dissident minority would secede and set off on its own course. The advent of reservation life worsened the situation by forcing formerly independent bands to coexist; but the reservation was not in itself the only cause of tension within Indian groups. Its major effect was to bottle them up and allow petty conflicts to fester in frustration.[7]

Tribal organizers in the Collier era encountered some of these situations of ancient but enduring conflict, particularly among the less assimilated groups in the Southwest. On the Mescalero Apache reservation in the Sacramento Mountains of southwestern New

Mexico, Morris Opler of the Applied Anthropology Staff discovered that the tribal council was split between the Mescalero majority and the Chiricahua Apache band (remnants of the followers of Geronimo transferred there from Oklahoma, over the protest of the Mescaleros), who believed, with justification, that the districts established under the new constitution had been gerrymandered to keep them in a state of permanent underrepresentation. The two bands lived separately and differed on almost every issue.[8]

A similar situation of rivalry, though of a less serious nature, existed among the Jicarilla Apaches, whose reservation was on the border between Colorado and New Mexico. Here two clans which had previously existed completely independently had to be brought together on a tribal council; an earlier experiment with a unified council established in 1915 had broken down within five years. Consequently, the Indians were reluctant to endorse the Reorganization Act without assurances that clan autonomy would be preserved. The Jicarilla constitution that was drawn up in 1937 was not accepted until equal representation was ensured to each clan and the powers of the council over land assignments to individual tribal members were limited.[9]

Factional divisions of this nature existed on other southwestern reservations, although a more serious problem for tribal organizers in this region was the lack of any traditional tribal institutions. Oliver La Farge distinguished four factional groups in the Hopi villages, two based on religious differences, and two others on attitudes toward the assimilation policies introduced by the bureau in the previous decade.[10] On the Pima Reservation a faction had formed in the 1920s, inspired by the ideas of Carlos Montezuma, the Apache spokesman who had broken with the Society of American Indians in 1922 and advocated complete termination of bureau supervision of Indian affairs; this element resisted the introduction of new programs by the government.[11]

Even Collier's ideal Indians, the Pueblos, did not escape such internal strife. At Santa Clara pueblo on the Rio Grande a faction emerged soon after reorganization was introduced. Its leaders, most of whom were frustrated office seekers, lobbied extensively with local congressmen and pressure groups like the Indian Rights Association, charging the pueblo government with discrimination and interference in elections. Collier and La Farge responded to these allegations with countercharges that the dissidents were linked to local white elements and organizations hostile to the New Deal. This was a standard response by the bureau to critics of the program. But Elizabeth Sergeant, who had been involved with Collier in the struggle against the Bursum bill, observed that the divisions in Santa Clara pueblo between the traditional religious leaders and the proassimilationist "winter people" dated back more than a generation.[12]

A more serious rift surfaced at Taos pueblo in 1936 when the leader of the new council, Antonio Mirabel, sought to eradicate the peyote cult, which had spread throughout the pueblos since 1917, challenging the authority of traditional religious leaders. The situation was complicated by the fact that Mirabel was an associate of Collier's mentor in Indian reform, Mabel Luhan. Mirabel's actions, which included a raid on a peyote church and confiscation of the land of several convicted peyote users, posed a major dilemma for Collier. In a proclamation to all the Pueblo Indians in June 1936, he warned that continued persecution of the peyote users might drive them to seek the protection of the federal courts, which in the process of upholding their rights would undermine the authority of the traditional religious and civil government of the pueblos. In the aftermath, Mirabel was removed from office for exceeding his authority, and the All-Pueblo Council, an association Collier had helped establish in the 1920s to enhance cooperation among the Pueblos, attempted to establish a modus vivendi with the peyote church. Collier later wrote confidentially to a close associate expressing his respect for Mirabel's "desire to reintegrate the Pueblo's life," but emphasized again the dangers that might ensue if the contest were allowed to continue without intervention by the bureau.[13]

The Taos problem was not atypical. The pueblo governments were accustomed to exercising a large measure of control over their communities, particularly in religious matters. This claim to power infringed the civil rights of individual Indians as citizens of the United States, and in a similar case of suppression in 1922, the bureau had stepped in to force reorganization of the council at Isleta pueblo. The political leaders of the pueblos were naturally protective of their traditional claims to authority, and chose not to prepare written constitutions, which they feared would limit their powers, although they approved the Indian Reorganization Act. The bureau accepted this decision and dealt with the traditional pueblo governments as legal entities.[14]

Not all the divisions among the Indians of the Southwest were of a religious or cultural nature. Among several of these groups there were significant differences in property and income. The Indians of this region were either farmers on a small scale or herders, primarily of cattle, sheep, and goats. Among the latter, it was not uncommon that a few families would accumulate large herds which dominated the reservation grazing lands. Twelve families of the Papago Indians at Sells Agency in southern Arizona were reported to control more than 50 percent of the reservation range.[15] On the large Navajo Reservation, a small number of families which had established a prior claim to rich grazing land during the initial years of reservation life, or earlier, when the Navajos were a nomadic raiding people, set themselves up like feudal lords: "Poor young relatives gathered around them much in the manner of an ancient Scottish clan around its chieftain. They tilled the land of the headman and tended his sheep on shares."[16]

Under Collier the bureau adopted a somewhat ambivalent approach toward these wealthy herders, not only on the principle that they represented traditional social elements, but also because their opposition carried weight among Indians and congressmen. Papago tribal organization was held up partly because of the fears of the dominant herders that it was linked to a concurrent effort to establish a tribal cattle cooperative. The bureau delayed pushing for a tribal constitution in order to reduce opposition; meanwhile, the extended drought reduced the leverage of the large herders and made them more cooperative.[17]

The Navajo situation was more complicated. In 1934 the bureau and the Soil Conservation Service initiated a program of planned reduction of the Indian sheep herds, which had far outstripped the carrying capacity of their range. Despite his earlier criticisms of the Navajo tribal council, Collier decided to implement the stock reduction program through it. The wealthier stockmen balked, however, at the attempt of the council to introduce a sliding scale that would allow subsistence herders to retain their stock while taking a larger proportion from the larger herds. They forced the council to introduce an across-the-board 10 percent reduction in herds, which turned the smaller herders against the conservation program and the Collier administration in general. Nevertheless, the bureau continued to seek the support of the big stockmen like Chee Dodge and his son, Tom Dodge, in the hope that they could bring the other Navajos to accept the Indian Reorganization Act. The livestock issue exacerbated existing religious and sectional divisions among the Navajos and resulted in their rejection of the Wheeler-Howard Act.[18]

Factionalism was widespread among the Indians of the Southwest and played a sometimes crucial role in determining the position of these groups on tribal organization. The sources of factionalism were diverse, reflecting old and new issues and the widely varying religious, cultural, and economic conditions of these peoples. In this diversity the Indians of that region contrasted sharply with those of the Northern Plains.

Internal division was, if anything, more prominent among the Indians of the plains reservations than in the Southwest. One Indian correspondent described to Collier the range of factions at Pine Ridge among descendants of the followers of Red Cloud: "full bloods versus mixed bloods; progressives versus conservatives; Catholic versus Protestant; Democrat versus Republican; Chiefs versus Council; Sons of chiefs versus Sons of other chiefs" and so on, each group differing with the others on one or more issues.[19]

To some extent factionalism on this scale could be attributed to a culturally stimulated tendency toward political disputation that was particularly marked among the nomadic tribes of the plains. Collier asserted that the source of such conflicts lay in the years of powerlessness that had produced in groups like the Sioux a basically irresponsible attitude toward public affairs.[20] Certainly many of these differences among Indians were essentially irrelevant to their real problems.

The superintendent at the Rosebud Agency vividly portrayed the activities of the prereorganization business council on that reservation: each council member formed his own partisan organization and maneuvered constantly for a position of dominance, while periodically the other council members would combine for the purpose of impeaching the chairman. Resolutions passed at one meeting would be repealed or reversed at the next meeting, for no apparent reason.[21] Despite the likely bias of the observer, this is a fairly accurate description of the kind of volatile politics that pervaded the tribal councils on the Sioux reservations under the reorganization program. The influence of traditions of personal autonomy and informality seem evident. Where in earlier times discussions could have continued until all disputants were satisfied or minority secession occurred, now the unfamiliar device of decision by majority vote was interposed, making the debates all the more bitter but not altering the Indian politician's practice of changing his mind from one vote to the next.[22] Even the habit of impeaching council chairmen was not simply a reflection of political irresponsibility induced by reservation life; stable individual leadership had never been a particularly notable feature of tribal government among the nomadic plains Indians.

Overarching these contests for personal prestige and release of frustration was a basic division characteristic of all the Indians of the Northern Plains and Northwest, between mixed-bloods and full-bloods. Variations in degree of Indian-ness were not important in themselves, but they related to more significant differences. First, full-blood Indians were older than mixed-bloods (defined as anyone with two generations of non-Indian parentage on one side): in 1930 the median age for full-bloods was greater by more than six years. Second, the illiteracy rate for full-bloods was more than 10 percent higher than for mixed-bloods for Indians of all ages, and almost twice as high for Indians over twenty-one.[23]

Mixed-bloods also generally had a wider range of experience in dealing with whites than full-bloods, and that affected their orientation toward white society in general and the Indian Reorganization Act in particular. Even among the relatively unassimilated Indians of the Southwest this sort of division could assume importance: at the Mescalero Agency, for example, the Chiricahua Apaches, who had lived at Fort Sill in Oklahoma before being removed to the isolated reservation in Arizona, looked down on the Mescaleros as "blanket Indians" while the Mescaleros charged their unwanted neighbors with bringing venereal disease as their main contribution from white contact.[24] Feelings were all the more intense on the reservations of the Northern Plains, where full-bloods were declining in influence or had become a minority.

Before Collier's administration these divisions had been tacitly, and sometimes openly, encouraged by the bureau administrators, who would support the "progressive," or proassimilationist, factions, giving them jobs or excluding full-bloods from the business committees which were set up on many of the reservations in the 1920s.[25] Under Collier the bureau was committed to reversing, or at least discouraging, that sort of division. But the form of tribal government established under the Reorganization Act unwittingly exacerbated the situation.

The bureau leaders felt, justifiably, that the Reorganization Act could not simply resurrect ancient tribal institutions if the Indians were to learn to deal independently with white society; tribal corporations, in particular, must be organized on lines appropriate to enable them to enter into contracts with other companies and have legal standing in the courts. Consequently, the councils and corporations established under the act were all in some degree modeled along Anglo-American lines, with electoral districts, voting by secret ballot, tribal presidents, vice-presidents, treasurers, and committees. The paraphernalia of American legal and political tradition were transferred to a people whose experience of these institutions was remote or nonexistent.

Among the unassimilated Indian groups the introduction of these novel forms of organization could pose problems in communication. Among the Papagos, for example, anthropologist Ruth Underhill found that there were no equivalent words for terms like *budget* and *representative*, that the same word was applied to *president, Indian commissioner, reservation agent* and *king*; and that there was no linguistic distinction between the terms *law, rule, charter,* and *constitution.* The Papagos' understanding of the implications of the Reorganization Act could best be described as vague.[26]

This sort of difficulty could be overcome with patience and open discussion, so long as the problem **was** recognized by the white administrators, which was not always the case. On the allotted reservations the advent of reorganization raised more substantial issues: full-bloods, reluctant to participate in the unfamiliar structures and distrustful of yet another shift in bureau policies, remained passive. Younger men, often of mixed-blood background, predominated in the new councils. A field representative of the Washington office, John H. Holst, raised this point in a report on organizational problems on the Sac and Fox reservation in Iowa:

For a long time the old system of local government under headmen has been breaking down. Most of the old men have held tenaciously to the traditional system while the young, trained in school and in closer contact with the whites, have gradually adopted the new ways. Reorganization has tended to emphasize this cleavage and set up irreconcilable groups. This is not a new theory or one peculiar to this reservation. It is . . . a difficult problem among all real Indian groups.[27]

In such situations neither side seemed to comprehend the intent of the new bureau policy. Traditional leaders among the full-bloods resented the fact that the Indian New Deal did not return to them the prestige of the past, and they looked down on the mixed-blood councilmen as upstarts with no experience. A full-blood spokesman from Pine Ridge wrote to Collier complaining about the mixed-bloods: "They are white people, essentially, they are no more Indian than you. . . . [There] should be some separate provision excluding [them] from the benefits of the Act. They make too much trouble on the reservation."[28]

Mixed-bloods, for their part, were not necessarily any more enlightened. Some understood the needs of the full-blood leaders for prestige, or at least recognized the expediency of not unnecessarily alienating them. On several of the larger reservations where full-bloods were still in a majority or had a strong minority position, notably the Cheyenne-Arapaho Reservation in western Oklahoma and the Flathead Reservation in Montana, traditional chiefs were given permanent positions on the tribal councils, although there was no provision for succession after their death.[29] Other mixed-bloods, however, treated the full-bloods with a good deal less respect, exhibiting what Collier called "mixed-blood with a white-plus psychology."[30] To these Indians the difference between reorganization and earlier bureau efforts at forced assimilation was not evident.

This natural cultural tension between full-bloods and mixed-bloods was aggravated on reservations where the competency commission had left its mark. Here the full-bloods clung to their allotments tenaciously, having witnessed the results of earlier bureau experiments with Indian property, and resisted reorganization on the mistaken assumption (from which the bureau could never dissuade them) that the tribal governments would be empowered to strip them of their only means of support.

The condition of mixed-bloods on these reservations also reinforced the tendency of the full-bloods to regard them with contempt. As one observer noted of the Nez Percé full-bloods at the Colville Reservation in Washington: "They say, in effect, most of those [mixed-bloods] . . . got their fee patents, sold their lands, squandered their substance and have no right to come back and tell the older people what they shall do; they have exhibited their lack of business sense and are poor examples of 'leadership.'"[31] This was not an entirely fair charge, since many patentees had been defrauded of their lands or lost them through inability to meet tax payments, but it was an argument that carried weight with the full-bloods on reservations like the Yankton, Flathead, Turtle Mountain, Pine Ridge, Standing Rock, and Potawatomi, where there were large numbers of landless Indians and full-bloods were in a minority or where the proportions were evenly balanced.

Contempt was mingled with the suspicion that the mixed-bloods, having lost their property through incompetence, would use their control of the new tribal councils to take over the full-bloods' allotments and redistribute them to the landless.[32] One frustrated full-blood Sioux wrote to Interior Secretary Ickes: "Some of the Indians that have no land and are one-eighth white . . . took the Wheeler-Howard Act and the money that goes with it. And they don't let us Indians that have land [in] on it."[33] The ascendency of mixed-bloods on the councils did nothing to relieve the suspicions of full-bloods toward the entire program.

A more complex variation on this theme was played among the Chippewas of Minnesota. An eastern woodland tribe, the Chippewas of the Great Lakes traditionally lived in small settlements where they fished and harvested the plentiful wild rice that covered the region. During the early years of the twentieth century, most of the Chippewa settlements in Wisconsin and Minnesota, including the largest, White Earth and Leech Lake, were allotted, and large numbers of the allottees were judged competent to receive patents in the 1905–1907 period. The Chippewa lands were particularly attractive to local whites, who devoted considerable attention to extracting them from the Indians. Consequently, by 1915 many of the Chippewas had lost their property; in 1928 only 4 percent of the land of the original Chippewa reservations remained in Indian hands outside of one agency. The exception was the northernmost reservation, Red Lake, which was the only settlement in Minnesota where full-bloods constituted a majority of the population and which had escaped allotment.[34]

Whatever their difficulties as individual proprietors, the Chippewas proved to be gifted at organization. Under the 1889 law that established the Minnesota reservations a general tribal council of the Chippewas had been recognized. Annuities and other tribal assets were held in its name by the U.S. government. Unlike other tribes, the Chippewas endeavored to keep their council in operation, particularly after other Indian properties had been lost as a result of patenting. In 1916, however, friction developed between the Red Lake band and other Chippewas when some mixed-bloods on the tribal council proposed that Red Lake be allotted to provide land for Indians at the other Chippewa agencies who had lost their lands. In 1918 Red Lake seceded from the Chippewa general council and set up its own local government. Subsequently, the remaining bands sued the Red Lake band for $10 million which, it was argued, had been removed from the tribal assets as a result of the secession. In 1933 the case finally reached the U.S. Supreme Court, which denied a writ of certiorari to the Chippewa plaintiffs, thus providing Red Lake with legal recognition as an independent Indian group whose assets would be segregated from those of the other Chippewas. This was a serious reverse for the latter, since the Red Lake band held almost 10 percent of the total tribal assets and a large amount in tribal funds had been used in prosecuting the case. In 1934 the relations between the two groups were something less than amicable.[35]

Nevertheless, an effort was made to reunite the two elements under the new council to be established under the Indian Reorganization Act. In June 1935, after a majority of the Chippewas had agreed to come under the act, a general council of the Chippewas meeting at Cass Lake invited delegates from Red Lake to join them in drawing up a new constitution. Under it, each reservation would have an equal number of representatives and the powers of the tribal council, including the powers of taxation of tribal members, would be circumscribed. At the same time a proposal for the cooperative marketing of wild rice, still an important part of the Chippewa economy, was discussed.

The Red Lake leaders were initially receptive but continued to insist upon the segregation of their proportion of the tribal funds. The arrangement broke down after six months, however, as the majority of the Chippewa representatives on the council insisted that the assets remain consolidated; matters were not helped by the fact that the dominant figure on the new tribal council, John G. Morrison from White Earth, was believed to be promoting a rival mixed-blood faction at Red Lake, and was also regarded as the person who had been most responsible for the lawsuit against Red Lake. In March 1936, the Red Lake general council, the only recognized body functioning on behalf of that group, announced its intention to withdraw from the Chippewa tribal council and the cooperative marketing association as well, stating that it would not affiliate with "bankrupt tribes."[36]

Despite efforts by the bureau to bring Red Lake into the tribal organization (which was called the Consolidated Chippewa Council), and, failing that, to resolve the factional fight at Red Lake, neither of these aims was achieved. Red Lake finally organized under the act in 1958, but remained aloof from the other Chippewa groups. Since Red Lake was the only reservation with a substantial land base and since in addition the Red Lake band held tracts of wild rice fields on other reservations like White Earth, its refusal to participate either politically or economically with the rest of the tribe aborted to a substantial degree the bureau's attempts to develop a tribal economic program.

At the same time, it could hardly be said that the full-bloods at Red Lake did not have good reason to suspect the intentions of the mixed-blood Chippewas. Many of the fears of the full-bloods were exaggerated or based on misconceptions about the aim of the Reorganization Act or the powers it would grant to tribal councils. But there were cases in which the struggles were serious and the stakes substantial.

One such case was the Blackfeet of Montana. Located on the Canadian border, the most northern reservation in the United States, the Blackfeet Reservation contained what had once been the dominant warrior people of the Northern Plains. Like other groups in its situation, the Blackfeet were now predominantly of mixed blood, but because of the relative isolation of the reservation, the full-bloods remained an effective force. In 1912 the reservation had been allotted and 200,000 of the 1,200,000 acres allotted had been released in fee patent, often under suspicious circumstances.[37] During the 1920s the local bureau administration had established a five-year plan to promote dry farming by the full bloods on their allotments. By some accounts the program was a major success, but according to Allan G. Harper, it was "an unholy mess," having done little except aggravate the tendency of the Indians to lease allotments to white ranchers. The Blackfeet, like many of the plains reservations, was grazing country, and apparently the most enduring result of the five-year program was an increase in soil erosion.[38]

The major point of conflict between the two groups, however, was not land, but control of the proceeds from the leasing of mineral rights that belonged to the tribe. Oil was discovered on the reservation shortly before the advent of reorganization; and although substantial increases in tribal income from this source did not appear until the 1940s, the Indians were well aware of the prospect of prosperity. Full-bloods, who had taken a skeptical view of the whole reorganization program and proposals for land consolidation, were alarmed by the new constitution, which granted the tribal council authority to lease mineral rights on tribal lands and dispose of the royalties as it saw fit. This provision apparently pertained only to lands still under tribal control (approximately 300,000 acres) and William Zimmerman sought to reassure the full-bloods that the power of the council did not extend to the leasing of mineral rights on allotments.[39]

Their fears were not assuaged, however, particularly since the council did indeed fall into the hands of an ambitious group of mixed-bloods who had definite plans for the disposition of oil revenues. In a 1937 report H. S. Mekeel and C. E. Faris noted that the full-bloods were definitely underrepresented on the tribal council, and recommended a redistricting of the reservation to eliminate the grounds for the charges of deliberate gerrymandering which the full-bloods were making. The chairman of the council argued that the reason for underrepresentation was that the full-bloods tended to dissipate their votes on several candidates rather than concentrating on a few, and that they constituted a declining minority under any circumstances; and his opinion was supported by the observations of field representatives of the bureau.[40] He exaggerated their minority status, however, for full-bloods of voting age constituted 45 percent of the tribe but held only two of thirteen positions on the tribal council. By accident or design, full-bloods were inadequately represented in their local government.

Lines became more sharply drawn as revenues from leasing began to flow to the Blackfeet after 1940. Full-bloods demanded distribution of these royalties and other tribal assets on a per capita basis. Some of the revenues were distributed in this manner, but a larger proportion was withheld by the tribe and used to create a fund to provide small long-term loans to individuals. The council appears to have set up this program, administered by a tribal board, largely because they objected to the fact that loans made from the Indian Reorganization Act revolving fund had to be approved by the local bureau extension agent, a condition which they felt restricted their freedom.[41]

The decision of the council to consolidate leasing revenues for long-term loans to needy tribesmen could probably be characterized as a more intelligent use of the funds than dissipating them through per capita payments. As Zimmerman pointed out in 1944, had the latter course been followed, each tribal member would have received only forty dollars per year, based on current revenues. Full-blood members of the tribal council, however, charged that the loan board discriminated against full-bloods (which was perhaps understandable, since most of the loans were for land purchases and most of the landless Indians were mixed-bloods). They also asserted that the majority of the council was corrupt, spending far too much of the revenues for "administration," and that certain members had tried to push through a resolution authorizing them to approve the selective leasing of mineral rights on allotted lands still under trust, presumably to benefit oilmen who were suspected of bribing councilmen and influencing elections.[42]

The point is not that the full-bloods' solutions to their problems were more appropriate or less self-centered than the mixed-bloods', nor even that their charges against the council were completely accurate. But it is certain that their views were not being considered and that their minority position excluded them from a full share in the wealth acquired in the name of the tribe. One bureau observer in 1945 drew this harsh conclusion: "The advent of the IRA has placed a legal tool in the hands of the ruling clique, mostly mixed-bloods, that more or less formalizes the struggle for control on a plane that makes full-blood resistance almost an act of treason."[43]

The Chippewa and Blackfeet experiences are only examples of a pattern which appeared on all reservations where the processes of economic and cultural assimilation had taken effect. The conflict was sharper in some cases than in others, but it was apparent in all these situations and became more intense as tribal organization proceeded.

Despite the abundant evidence of full-blood–mixed-blood rivalry on the reservations of the Northern Plains and Oklahoma in the bureau's records of tribal organization, however, such aggregate data as I have been able to assemble on Indian voting behavior in the reorganization does not reveal a significantly strong correlation with that characteristic. This paradox must be investigated.

In order to test the thesis that the division between mixed-bloods and full-bloods influenced their responses to the Indian Reorganization Act, I assembled data on ethnicity for thirteen reservations in the Northern Plains and sought to correlate it with

Indian voting in the 1934–35 referenda on the act. The proportion of full-bloods was matched with the percentage of all potential voters who voted against the act. The correlation was positive, but at a very low level of significance (+ .08; see Appendix 2 for tables and sources). When expanded to include thirteen reservations in the Southwest where the mixed-blood population was very small, the relationship is even less evident (– .03). The most that can be concluded from this analysis is that the ethnic factor was more important on the Northern Plains reservations, but not significantly so.

To further test the argument, I introduced a second factor, related to the first, the proportion of landless Indians on each reservation, the presumption being that the majority of these were mixed-bloods who would vote favorably on the act. If this were the case, the proportion of votes for inclusion under the act would increase as the percentage of landless Indians increased. The result for twenty-six reservations was the opposite: the correlation was negative (– .16), indicating that, if anything, reservations with larger populations of landless Indians were more likely to vote against the act, although again the relationship is not very strong.

In this situation we are left with several options. First, we may accept the quantitative data as conclusive and the judgment of at least one contemporary Indian observer that mixed-blood–full-blood conflict was "just superficial politics."[44] In view of the kind of strong, enduring rivalry described earlier, however, this seems unsatisfactory.

It is also possible to question the validity of the measurement, given the "ecological problem" which is present in all aggregate measures of popular voting behavior.[45] It is quite possible that there is some degree of error in this correlation, but it is limited by the fact that in most cases the percentage of full-bloods was extremely large or extremely small: in only eight of the twenty-six cases examined did the proportion of full-bloods and mixed-bloods fall within ten points of one another. Furthermore, the strength of the relationship established in both measures is so small that only monumental errors of measurement would be likely to significantly alter the conclusions.

Another explanation for this peculiar divergence between Indian voting behavior and other manifestations of Indian political attitudes has been suggested from time to time by critics of the

Indian New Deal. The most recent restatement of this argument was made by Robert Burnette, a former tribal council leader of the Rosebud Sioux, in an essay on tribal politics entitled *The Road to Wounded Knee*. In this book he relates a traditional claim by the Sioux that the reason for acceptance of the Reorganization Act on their reservations was that the full-bloods refused to vote, on the mistaken assumption that withheld votes would be counted as negative votes. Hence the referenda did not represent the views of the full-blood Sioux, and they regarded the tribal councils established under the act as having no legal authority.[46]

Burnette's explanation was never offered at the time, even by Indian critics of reorganization who had ample opportunity to advance it to various congressional investigating committees. Burnette does not assert that it holds true for any of the other plains reservations. Nevertheless, it raises an interesting possibility, since the strategy of nonparticipation was plausible because the act required that at least one-third of the adult Indians on each reservation vote in the referenda before the results could be considered valid. If in fact this strategy was pursued, the total percentage of votes cast in the referenda would be expected to fall below 50 percent of the potential voting population on those reservations with full-blood minorities.

An analysis of Indian participation in the 1934–35 referenda indicates, however, that this was not the case. A sample of forty-three agencies shows an average 62 percent participation on reservations in the Northern Plains and the Southwest. This is somewhat higher than the national average of 58 percent (for ninety-six agencies); the difference is explained by the fact that on the plains reservations the average rate of participation was a remarkable 66 percent. At the Sioux agencies in North and South Dakota, the rate was 62.5 percent (although the rate at Pine Ridge and Rosebud, with which Burnette was most familiar, was only 49 percent). Since the contemporaneous national average rate of participation, based on the presidential election in 1932 and congressional elections in 1934, was only 60 percent, the Indians could not be considered less involved in public affairs than whites. If full-bloods on the plains reservations had sought to boycott the referenda, they were not notably successful. (See Appendix 2 for the data.)[47]

There are some other arguments that may provide a more satisfactory answer to this question. First, voting on reorganization may be a misleading indicator of Indian attitudes, which in some instances shifted radically once the program went into operation. Analysis of Indian support for constitutions, the second phase of the tribal organization process, reveals some interesting patterns. While the average vote favorable to ratification among ten sample plains tribes was 42 percent, this average was lower (36 percent) for the Sioux. The claim that full-bloods boycotted the referenda may be more accurate in this case, and certainly the tribal councils elected under these constitutions could justifiably be characterized as minority governments. (See Appendix 2 for data.)

The lines of division between mixed-bloods and full-bloods did not always cut the same way on the Reorganization Act. Some mixed-bloods saw the economic advantages offered by the act, while others were more influenced by the charge that it would revive full-blood traditions and take Indians "back to the blanket." There are indications that among the Sioux, Catholic missionaries sought to influence mixed-bloods against the act on these grounds, in retaliation against the Collier administration, which was removing federal aid from their boarding schools.[48] There is also evidence of missionary influence over the mixed-bloods on the Navajo reservation, although in the latter case the mixed-bloods constituted a relatively small element in the population.

On the Northern Cheyenne Reservation in Montana, divisions over reorganization were completely the reverse of the usual pattern. Here the population was predominantly full-blood, but a group of mixed-bloods dominated the existing tribal business committee, which had been in operation since 1910, largely because district voting split the full-blood vote. Not unnaturally, mixed-bloods opposed reorganization, which would displace them as leaders, while the full-bloods made no secret of their intention to disenfranchise the mixed-bloods once they acquired control of the tribal government. In the end, the full-bloods emerged as the dominant faction.[49] Yet another variation could be found on the Crow Reservation in Montana, where mixed-bloods and full-bloods enjoyed fairly good relations and combined, apparently influenced by local white propaganda that they would lose their property under reorganization, to reject the act by an overwhelming majority.[50]

It is possible to see some patterns in this mosaic of tribal politics, although they are never clear or self-explanatory. The sharpest conflicts occurred on reservations where the mixed-bloods constituted a slim majority or where factions were evenly balanced and where the land base had been significantly reduced by the patenting of allotments, as, for example, at Pine Ridge and Rosebud in South Dakota and Colville and Umatilla in the Northwest. Where mixed-bloods were in a firm majority, friction might develop, as among the Chippewas or Yankton Sioux, but the outcome was less in question. On reservations where full-bloods were in a solid majority, such as the Crow and Cheyenne reservations, divisions were hard to predict and might as likely have the mixed-bloods in opposition to reorganization as in support of it.

There were cultural variations that must be taken into account. The Sioux reservations, in particular Yankton, Pine Ridge, and Standing Rock, the scene of some of the most sustained bickering, may simply have reflected a tradition of internal disunity. By contrast, the near unanimity of the Crows in Montana was probably influenced by the close-knit tribal organization, which was carried over from earlier times. At the same time, there were immediate issues of economic and political power which influenced attitudes toward tribal organization. The full-bloods who opposed the act and the tribal councils to be established under it because they feared the loss of their allotments may not have had legitimate misgivings, but they were correct in suspecting that a tribal government dominated by mixed-bloods would pay scant attention to their interests.

During the hearings on the Wheeler-Howard bill, Robert Yellowtail, the Crow leader, expounded at length on the divisions among his people and the obstacles that factions would raise to the success of reorganization. Collier responded, rather laconically, that "those are simply difficulties inherent in life." Congressman Peavey (R., Wis.) added the observation that factional divisions are "typical of the ordinary white community; and we are trying by this bill to raise the Indian people up to the level of white communities in their affairs."[51]

These are certainly valid points. Factionalism is an inescapable feature of representative government (or probably any form of government, including totalitarian ones). In liberal political theory it is an essential element in public affairs, ensuring representation of all points of view; although James Madison warned that the spirit of faction could undermine the stability of government.

Certainly in American and European experience, factionalism has been closely associated with the concepts of civil liberties and democratic participation.

Perhaps it was also fair to say, as one bureau leader did, that the full-bloods had only themselves to blame for not asserting their point of view more strongly by taking a more active part in tribal affairs and learning to play the game of politics, American style.[52] On the other hand, the full-bloods could hardly be expected to take readily to political practices with which they had no prior acquaintance.

The prevalence of factionalism stimulated or exacerbated by reorganization had some undeniable ill effects. Morris Opler found among the Mescalero Apaches that the men regarded widely as the most appropriate leaders were reluctant to run for the tribal council, not from indifference but because they "are alive enough to the realities of native sentiment to see the disadvantages of speaking boldly for a group who understand representation in a sense vastly different from that of the average white community. The candidate hesitates to become the surrogate of an electorate which sends him out with as many mental reservations."[53] Perhaps this attitude was peculiar to Apaches; certainly among other groups like the Sioux there was no reluctance to take strong public positions. But few, if any, of the tribal councilmen in these early years enjoyed the respect of many of their fellows, and the lack of support reduced their leverage in confrontations with the bureau over the limits of tribal authority.

On a more basic level of concern, Collier's offhand dismissal of factionalism, albeit realistic, seems rather strange. No doubt it was politic of him not to debate openly Congressman Peavey's conception of the aims of reorganization, but certainly Collier did not see them to be "raising the Indians up to the level of white communities." Indian communities differed from white communities; that was a central premise of Collier's approach to Indian affairs. Part of this difference arose from the fact, according to Collier, that Indian tribes had been divided traditionally, not into "partisan combat organizations," but rather into groups linked by shared needs and values. That situation no longer prevailed, but if the goal of the program was the restoration of individual integrity within a tribal context, the problem of factionalism could not be ignored or casually disregarded.

5

PROBLEMS OF TRIBAL ORGANIZATION: COUNCILS VERSUS COMMUNITIES

What is a tribe? The Indian Reorganization Act did not seriously face this question, although the tribe was a central feature of the new program. In the last section of the act, tribe was defined as "any Indian tribe, organized band, pueblo or the Indians residing on one reservation." This definition was flexible but not neces sarily helpful to administrators.

As we have discussed earlier, during the nineteenth century the tribe became the category most commonly used by white officials in distinguishing Indian groups. Tribes made treaties, ceded land claims, were awarded annuities, and ultimately were assigned to reservations. The American public read of warlike tribes like the Sioux, Comanches, and Apaches, while historians wrote of the exploits of the Iroquois and novelists of the "last of the Mohicans." When a reform movement repudiating assimilation emerged in the twentieth century, it was natural for the reformers to regard the tribe as the focus of the traditional Indian life whose restoration should be the goal of government policy.

But the meaning of tribe to most Indian groups differed markedly from the notions accepted by government representatives and the American public generally. The noted ethnologist A. L. Kroeber drew attention to this point in an influential essay published in 1955:

What are generally denominated tribes are really small nationalities, possess-
ing essentially uniform speech and customs and . . . an accompanying sense
of likeness and like mindedness. . . . The genuinely political units were smaller
units—corresponding rather to what it is customary to loosely call "bands"
or "villages." They were de facto self-governing and it was they that each
owned a particular territory rather than the nationality owned the over-all
territory. Ordinarily the nationality, miscalled tribe, was an aggregate of
miniature sovereign states normally friendly to one another.[1]

To be sure, some tribes exhibited a greater degree of political integration than others. The Cherokees and Creeks in the Southeast,
for example, and the member tribes of the Iroquois Confederacy
had developed formal structures of tribal government during the
historical period. Even among the relatively decentralized hunting
and warrior tribes of the plains, some, notably the Crows and
Cheyennes, had tribal councils which exercised more than nominal
authority over their fellow tribesmen. But with a few exceptions
such as these, Kroeber's proposition seems plausible.[2]

"The tribe," according to a recent study, "is a constellation of
communities and relations between communities." A key point
in this definition is the absence, in a tribe, of any formal institutions "specially constituted to maintain 'law and order' . . . struc-
turally separated from the underlying population and set above
them." Among "civilized" communities, "the right to control
force has precipitated from the society at large to rest exclusively
with the government"; in tribal systems the maintenance of order
within and among communities instituting the tribe remains informal and the task of all the members of the society through
the acceptance of customary relationships and patterns of individual and group behavior.[3]

This concept is not entirely satisfactory, since it implies the
absence of any kind of legal institutions distinct from the kinship
groups which form the basis of most aboriginal communities. As
E. A. Hoebel has indicated, in most tribes there is a structure of
law that applies to all tribesmen regardless of kinship affiliations,
and there are the functional equivalents of courts to determine
disputes and enforce decisions; they may not necessarily be tribal
institutions, but they uphold those values that are the shared
consensus of the tribe.[4] Nevertheless, Marshall D. Sahlins's formulation provides a useful line of approach to the analysis of the
relationship between traditional Indian communities and the tribal
organizations established in the Indian New Deal.

The imposition of formal institutions of government upon tribal systems like those described by Kroeber might reinforce existing cultural tendencies toward "national" self-identification. At the same time, it could have the contrary effect of arousing tensions among communities which had hitherto coexisted in a state of relative autonomy. The fact that for more than a generation before tribal organization the Indians had been subjected to a policy intended to suppress any form of cultural identity whatever further complicated the situation. Had tribal organization been encouraged or even permitted during the 1880s, the integration of communities into the larger structure might have proceeded with little difficulty. But while forty-odd years of reservation life and assimilation had not eradicated Indian cultural identity, it had not strengthened the sense of tribalism either.

In these circumstances, the tribal governments established under the Indian Reorganization Act constituted a totally new and unfamiliar level of organization for many Indian groups. One major result of reorganization was that control of those elements of Indian life that had not been taken over earlier by white authorities now passed from the hands of the communities to institutions which were nominally representative of the Indian view, but with which the communities had little contact or sense of identification. Where the traditions of community control were still relatively strong, as was the case among some of the southwestern Indians, the establishment of tribal government was the occasion for much bickering over local autonomy, and tribal officials engaged in continuous struggles with their constituent communities over the scope of their powers.

Bureau administrators responsible for tribal organization were not unaware of these problems and were constantly seeking ways of better integrating the local communities into the new tribal system and ensuring that the tribal councils were genuinely representative bodies. But they also felt constrained by the wording of the law and the goals of the program as a whole, particularly the establishment of viable tribal economies, to make the tribe the focus of attention, to channel federal funds through the tribal government, and to plan and implement development projects with tribal officials. Only when they were faced with an immovably hostile tribal council or when the whole process of tribal organization had been stymied did federal officials work closely with community groups. By emphasizing the tribe, the Collier administration in many cases created and sustained an essentially artificial institution in Indian life.

This crucial point was made by Archie Phinney in 1942 in a critique of Ward Shepard's proposal for transferring major administrative responsibilities to the tribal governments as part of his plan for decentralization within the Bureau of Indian Affairs. Phinney, a Nez Percé, had studied with Franz Boas before entering the bureau and serving as a field adviser in the Great Lakes region, where he worked primarily with the Chippewas of Minnesota and Wisconsin. After noting that for the Chippewas, as for many Indians of the Northern Plains, tribal unity had no relationship to the actual situation, Phinney went on to point out that the bureau had failed to recognize or exploit the potential for spontaneous and enduring participation at the community level:

A study of the relations between the elected representatives and their constituents will show a growing democratic centralism which kind of detachment can never lend itself to the creativity of wide community participation in tribal affairs. . . . The efforts of the Indian Reorganization staff in the past years have been directed mainly toward the strengthening of tribal council government. . . . But this achievement is empty of the result most needed— the reinforcement of community life. . . . The basic problem is how to stimulate development of initiative and responsibility on the community level, within local groups, for only on this level, below the council, can there be any real Indian participation and any real exercise of whatever new powers the Indian Bureau may want to transfer to the Indian.[5]

Control of the process of tribal organization and economic development was not entirely in the hands of the bureau, although Collier and his aides proved skillful at devising ways around legal obstacles. The Wheeler-Howard Act specifically identified the tribe as the focus for organizational efforts and the recipient of any authority and money the federal government would be willing to cede to the Indians. The tribal council could negotiate with other governments, employ legal counsel, arrange for the tribe's incorporation, and so forth. The only provisions of the act that refer to Indians in other than tribal status are those authorizing the Secretary of the Interior to purchase lands for landless Indians and to appoint Indians to the bureau without regard to civil service laws, and the one making education loans available to individual Indians.

An amendment offered in the House version of the bill in 1934 would have permitted the incorporation of Indian groups below the tribal level, but it was removed from the final version.

Recognition that the deletion of this provision from the Wheeler-Howard Act was a mistake seems indicated by the fact that the Oklahoma and Alaska organization bills both allowed for the incorporation of Indians in villages and cooperatives. A substantial number of the constitutions for the larger tribes organized under the Wheeler-Howard Act authorized the tribal councils to charter economic organizations like livestock cooperatives or housing projects, but such groups did not have equal status with tribal corporations under the law, nor did they have direct access to federal funds.

Given the relatively open definition of tribe in the act, it might seem logical for the bureau to have encouraged communities to be designated as tribes where it appeared appropriate. That was done in Oklahoma under the Thomas-Rogers Act. In 1937, Morris Opler of the Applied Anthropology Staff submitted a report on the Creek Indians (part of the Five Civilized Tribes settled in eastern Oklahoma) which indicated historical and sociological reasons for organizing these Indians into chartered towns, the traditional center of Creek political life. Collier accepted his view and the Creeks were urged to follow that course.[6] Similarly, in Alaska, villages became the basic unit of organization not only because this was the traditional pattern but also because the Indians themselves were reluctant to be grouped into tribes since that would entail the designation of reservations, limiting their mobility and their claims to Alaskan lands. When the Interior Department under the authority of the Alaska Reorganization Act did undertake to establish tribal reservations in 1944 and 1945, the Indians rejected three reservations and accepted six.[7]

Objections were raised within the bureau and the Interior Department to the fact that these localized organizations would have difficulty functioning effectively as economic entities because the resources available to any one community were simply not sufficient to support a tribal government and a development program. In the case of the Creek Indians of Oklahoma, F. L. Kirgis, the acting solicitor of the Interior Department, noted that the aim of the Thomas-Rogers Act was "the creation of organizations of Indians capable of handling common credit and land problems . . . it is obviously necessary that the Indians to be organized must be those with common problems . . . who can and will work together to effect a properly functioning unit."[8] This criterion was applicable to tribal organizations at any level, and larger tribal entities often failed to satisfy it. But it is noteworthy in the Creek case that in 1944, a Creek tribal council was established with representation from forty-four Creek towns and that it operated independently of the bureau's program.

Of the ninety-three tribal governments established under the Wheeler-Howard Act between 1935 and 1945, thirty-one could be characterized as representing constituencies small and cohesive enough to be considered communities. For the most part, these community organizations (which were given that title in eleven cases) were composed of scattered remnants of bands in areas like California, Nevada, Michigan, and Minnesota where there was virtually no remaining reservation land base, even in the form of allotments.[9] Where a potential land base still existed on a reservation in the form of either tribal lands or allotted land held in trust, the bureau apparently preferred to encourage reservation-wide tribal organization.

Occasionally the question arose whether community groups could be organized under the act on reservations where tribal organization was possible. At the Yankton Subagency of the Rosebud Reservation in South Dakota, the process of tribal organization was delayed throughout 1935 by full-blood opposition to a proposed constitution. In 1936, a group of landless Indians at Yankton petitioned the bureau to be allowed to draw up their own constitution so that they could apply for loans from the revolving credit fund. Kenneth Meicklejohn of the Interior Department's legal staff ruled that it would be contrary to the intent of the Wheeler-Howard Act, since the landless Indians could not be considered a tribe different from the other Yankton Sioux.[10] Similarly, at the Colville Agency the bureau discouraged efforts by both mixed-bloods and full-bloods to hold referenda excluding their rivals, even though such referenda were practicable since the two groups lived in separate sections of the reservation and could have been organized into two different "tribes." Again the rationale seems to have been that it would have obstructed future land consolidation programs as well as creating a bad precedent for other tribes wracked by factionalism.[11]

Once tribal organizations were in operation, however, bureau officials proved more flexible on this issue. In 1936, a tribal council had been established on the Uintah-Ouray Reservation in Utah, bringing together three hitherto separate Ute bands that had disputed over allotted lands since the 1890s. By 1942, the bureau was willing to admit that the experiment was not working and suggested that one of the bands, the Uncompahgre, be allowed to secede from the larger group and form its own tribal council.[12]

Simultaneously an alternative approach was recommended which would leave the existing tribal organization intact but amend the tribal constitution to give local communities the maximum authority possible, reducing the general powers of the tribal council. This approach became increasingly popular with local bureau officials responsible for tribal affairs as time went on and the weaknesses of the tribal council system became more apparent. This orientation toward community organization never became bureau policy, although it was tacitly accepted as necessary in situations in which there was no tribal tradition, as was generally the case with Indian groups in the Southwest. But only belatedly were the promptings of Oliver La Farge and Archie Phinney for a general and sustained effort to make the local community the focus of Indian economic and political rehabilitation given serious attention. By the time their view acquired influence with bureau leaders, money for such "nonessential" activities had diminished, while the tribal councils themselves, with aspiring Indian politicians, provided an additional obstacle.

Few of the Indian groups of the American Southwest, either nomadic, like the Apaches and Navajos, or settled agriculturalists like the Pimas, Papagos, and Pueblos, had any tradition of tribal organization. The Pueblos had formed an All-Pueblo Council in the seventeenth century to oppose the domination of Spain, but it had remained dormant thereafter until revived in the 1920s to oppose the Bursum bill and the Dance Order, an effort by the bureau to suppress traditional Indian religious ceremonies. Some other latecomer groups like the Comanches were developing an embryonic form of tribal organization at the time of white contact; with these exceptions the focus of organization among these Indians was the village or the band.

Within this framework the patterns of organization were quite intricate, although generally unknown to white observers except anthropologists and specialists in Indian affairs in the region. The Pueblos of the Rio Grande valley had perhaps the most complex form, with a religious leadership, the Caciques, superimposed over the civil government, nominating all officials and exercising the power of veto over their actions. A basically sedentary agricultural people, the Pueblos allotted farming rights to individuals while retaining communal title to lands, and had (like most other village Indians of the Southwest) escaped allotment.[13] The desert Pueblos—Laguna, Acoma, and Zuni in New Mexico, and Hopi in Arizona in the center of the larger Navajo Reservation—were if anything more remote from white influence and more village-oriented. Significantly, the All-Pueblo Council comprised the eastern, or Rio Grande, Pueblos, with little or no representation from the western groups. The interlinkages of kinship or clan groups with the distribution of religious and political control were much stronger in the western Pueblo communities.[14]

Another, even more isolated group, the Papagos, functioned with less formal systems of government. Located in the mountains and desert of south-central Arizona, the Papagos lived in villages which in fact constituted two separate settlements. During the summer rainy season they raised corn and other vegetables in the plain, retreating in winter to the hills to hunt, but retaining permanent houses and lands in each area. The original villages spawned "daughter villages" that held allegiance to their progenitors and kept aloof from other villages. Within this constellation of villages linked by kinship but no more formalized system of association, a council of men ruled, with a headman chosen to manage religious affairs and other routine civil matters.[15]

Most of the more nomadic groups of this region seem to have followed the same pattern in varying degrees. Bands had headmen, often senior members of the kinship group that made up the band, and there was little contact among bands, which in some cases spoke mutually unintelligible dialects. Indians in the Great Basin region had more rudimentary forms of organization, lacking clans or any form of association beyond the extended family unit.[16] Until the coming of reservations they had no experience of sustained interaction, and on the reservations the existing groups were broken up.

Before 1934 the bureau had experimented with tribal organization of a sort, although generally in order to ease the burdens of local administrations rather than to instill any sense of tribal self-determination. As we have noted earlier, a council composed of the leaders of the different clans had been established on the Jicarilla Apache Reservation in New Mexico around 1915, but it had broken up because of internal squabbling by 1920.[17] At the San Carlos Apache Reservation in Arizona, a business council had been set up by the agency superintendent about the same time, and a vigorous Apache leader, Henry Chinn, had emerged as spokesman for the council. In 1923 the new superintendent, James Kitch, dissolved the council, apparently because he preferred to run the reservation without Indian interference. For the next decade the Chinn faction, constituting about 50 percent of the Indians, had petitioned the bureau to reestablish the council, but without effect, since Kitch's administration was regarded as effective and productive.[18] The lines drawn in this clear-cut contest between Indians and administration were to carry over into the reorganization program.

Probably the most extensive, and most controversial, experiment with tribal organization in the Southwest before the New Deal occurred on the Navajo Reservation. Prior to 1923 there had been no Navajo tribal council, although superintendents at the various agencies would occasionally summon several headmen together to approve the leasing of mineral prospecting rights on Indian lands to a prospector or company that wanted legal standing in the event of a successful strike. In 1921 oil companies anticipating a possible bonanza on the Navajo lands urged the Interior Department, then under Albert B. Fall, to authorize the establishment of a Navajo tribal council for this purpose, and in 1923 the bureau initiated the creation of the first tribal organization in Navajo history, with one delegate from each of the six subagencies. Unlike earlier councils, this one was allowed to continue in operation, and the number of delegates was expanded, although the Interior Department retained the right of appointing delegates in the event that the Indians did not elect them.[19]

To Collier, this Navajo council was nothing more than a puppet government set up at the behest of would-be exploiters of the Indians to rubber-stamp the demands of Fall and his successors. In 1931 before the Senate Committee on Indian Affairs he made that charge, expanding on it in 1934 during the hearings on the Wheeler-Howard bill, when he asserted that Fall "smashed the Navajo tribal government . . . he wiped it out and dictated a new Navajo tribal council . . . to turn over to him unlimited power of attorney to represent the tribe. . . . Any American community that was at the mercy of such things would move out or rise in rebellion."[20]

Collier's view of this situation has generally been accepted, but one recent historian, Lawrence Kelly, has argued that his criticisms were wrong on two counts: first, there had been no previous

Navajo tribal council, so this step, no matter how wickedly conceived, "bound all the Navajo together in one deliberative body"; and second, after 1923 the council emerged as "an articulate and outspoken, if not always representative organ of the Navajo people."[21] This view had in fact been put forward at the time by Oliver La Farge, who in 1933 wrote to Collier that "the present Navajo council is effective and . . . must be regarded as the true government of the tribe."[22] All of these judgments are subjective in their evaluation of the evidence, but an examination of the records of the discussion between Collier and the Navajo tribal council on the stock reduction program in 1934 and 1935 indicates that the council was anything but submissive to the wishes of administrators.

Also during the 1920s, local bureau agents introduced community chapters, which seem to have been intended to supplant the headmen with local organizations more in keeping with white notions of representative government. Again, opinion is divided on the viability of this innovation in Navajo life. Anthropologists Clyde Kluckhohn and Dorothea Leighton regarded the community chapters as "entirely artificial," noting that each chapter was expected to elect a president and secretary and to use proper parliamentary procedures, thus making it "inevitable that 'educated' Navajos took a leading role." In the end, they maintain, the chapters collapsed when they lost the support of the bureau.[23] La Farge, however, in 1933 asserted that the chapters were representative of local constituencies, and urged that they be made the unit of representation for any reorganized tribal council.[24] A recent study of the Navajos by David Aberle concludes that the chapters did in fact prove durable, forming the centers for Navajo resistance to the stock reduction program during the Collier years, and that "the chapter provided a well-defined unit for the agent to deal with which at the same time . . . did not depart from the Navaho pattern of prestige leadership."[25]

Possibly both arguments are partially correct. The community chapters did flourish and certainly were closer to local people than the tribal council, whose members were elected on the basis of larger district units. At the same time, the rise of the chapter weakened the role of the traditional headman and to that extent represented a break with traditional patterns of organization. Chee Dodge, one of the traditional leaders (and a wealthy herder), complained in 1940 that "today the power and influence of the headman is broken. The present set-up is entirely too complicated to run smoothly and the Indian doesn't understand what is expected of him."[26]

Whatever the reasons for its establishment, the Navajo tribal council anticipated the tribal organizations of the Indian New Deal in its impact on traditional local patterns of government and in the growing assertiveness of its members as they came to regard themselves as the spokesmen for the tribe. By its very structure and mode of procedure the Navajo council was not representative of the scattered, isolated settlements of unassimilated full-bloods who constituted the majority of the Navajo people. They did not pay much attention to the council until it became the focus of the stock reduction struggle in the 1930s. Nevertheless, the council approached its work conscientiously and believed itself able to see beyond the parochial concerns of the communities. This was to be the experience of many of the reorganization councils: there was a certain amount of self-serving in the form of inflated administrative budgets, and councils often disregarded the views of minorities, but they also tried to cement their position as the legitimate depositories of tribal authority.

The eastern Pueblos of the Rio Grande valley were a classic example of the decentralized village oriented Indians of the Southwest. Collier, having worked with them extensively in the 1920s, recognized this aspect of their political system, and the bureau focused organizational activities at the village level. When the necessity of stock reduction on the Pueblo lands was perceived, the bureau made separate arrangements with each pueblo for community participation in determining the pace at which the program would be introduced, in contrast to the Navajo situation, in which only the tribal council was consulted and stock reduction was pushed through without much consideration of the objections of the Indian communities. As a consequence the conservation program met with considerably less resistance, although objections were raised to herd reduction at Laguna pueblo, which in 1938 sent a delegation to Congress to protest the program on the ground that they were being reduced to poverty through the elimination of their best stock.[27]

At the same time Collier encouraged the All-Pueblo Council to move beyond representing the villages in a legal capacity in the courts and before Congress, as it had largely done in the previous decade, and take a more assertive role in internal matters affecting the pueblos generally. A case in point was the conflict at Taos between the peyote church and the Mirabel government, discussed earlier. Economic and administrative requirements also created some pressure for greater centralization of control. In May 1935 the bureau reorganized the Pueblo agencies, consolidating three separate jurisdictions into one under the general supervision of Sophie Aberle, an anthropologist. Within this new framework the villages would be component units for administrative coordination as well as Indian government, but the overall effect was to underline the common elements of Pueblo economic life rather than the political differences among villages. Similarly, a Rio Grande Board established in 1936 to coordinate economic development of the watershed, involving the efforts of the Bureau of Indian Affairs, the Soil Conservation Service, and the Farm Security Administration, accentuated the common tribal economy of the Pueblos and reinforced the tendency to view them as a tribe rather than a group of independent city-states.[28]

The westernmost of the Pueblos, the Hopis of Arizona, were treated as a separate group, but the village context of their political organization was, as a result of the careful work of Oliver La Farge, given perhaps the fullest recognition accorded any of the Indian groups. Like the other Pueblo societies, the Hopis were an agricultural people, isolated by surrounding desert from white and other Indian influence, and hence retaining very strong religious and social ties to ancient traditions. Subjected to the gradual encroachment of Navajo raiders in the seventeenth and eighteenth centuries, they were completely surrounded by that large group after 1869, when the Navajos were removed wholesale to the Arizona desert where the two reservations exist today. Unlike their new neighbors, however, the Hopis clung to their village way of life.[29]

Within the villages, government was the function of an overlapping system of clans and secret religious societies which together could control individual behavior without using overt force; hence the Hopi pueblos were very cohesive but did not exhibit the characteristics of formal government. Nevertheless, white authorities since the era of Spanish rule had been accustomed to treating them as a unified tribe, which they were not; like other Pueblo Indians, they shared a common language and religious practice, but their "sense of unity," as La Farge pointed out, was "as against the outside world." There was no corresponding sense of internal unity.[30]

Although there had been a certain amount of outside influence in the years since the Hopi Reservation was established in 1882 (the Mennonites had made converts at some of the villages and there was a minute assimilationist faction), on the whole the Hopis preserved more of their traditional cultural system than virtually any of the other Indian groups involved in the reorganization program. Persuading them to establish a formal system of government, and even more novel, a tribal government, required a good deal of understanding of Hopi culture and a good deal of patience, since these Indians, according to La Farge, "in solving problems . . . go back to the beginning of things," recapitulating the chain of events from the creation of the world to the present situation, in the process of reaching a decision.[31] Partly because of his contacts with Collier and other bureau leaders, La Farge had a good deal more leeway in the preparation of a Hopi constitution than anthropologists were generally allowed. Throughout the winter of 1935–36, La Farge met and talked at length with representatives from each of the villages, preparing and revising a constitution that, in the words of its preamble, would "preserve the good things of Hopi life, and . . . provide a way of organizing to deal with modern problems."[32]

Under the Hopi constitution the tribal council was for the most part restricted to representing the Hopis in their relations with the federal, state, and local governments and adjudicating disputes among villages. All other power, including the regulation of inheritance of property, the assignment of use of land, and the regulation of family relations, were left in the control of the villages. The village could decide its own mode of organization and its method of choosing representatives to the tribal council. In short, the basically localized system of Hopi self-government was preserved and the informal systems of social control exercised within the villages were not reduced by incorporation in a written constitution.[33]

The Hopi tribal organization resembled on a smaller scale that of the eastern Pueblos of New Mexico. The Hopi constitution in particular has been lauded as a classic example of the successful integration of traditional and modern systems of government.[34] But the Hopi system was in some ways an aberration among constitutions written under the Reorganization Act; even among the quite similar Papago Indians there was far less tendency toward decentralization. To say that the Hopi (or Rio Grande Pueblo) form of tribal organization was typical of the Indian

Reorganization Act, even in the Southwest, would be an exaggeration.

Furthermore, the La Farge constitution perpetuated traditional Hopi forms and practices without laying the groundwork for a governmental structure that could deal effectively with the need for tribal economic development. Collier in later years asserted that the Hopi constitution "never worked" because it "did not take into account . . . the conscious and unconscious motivations and accompanying resistances of the several quite diverse Hopi societies."[35] What he seems to have meant is that the constitution did not generate any sense of shared tribal values and goals. The Indian Administration Research group made a somewhat related observation in its final report in 1951, noting that because of the paucity of natural resources in the area the only workable plan for land management would require a coordinated program for the entire agency, an unlikely development under the existing decentralized Hopi system.[36] In stark terms the dilemma of the Hopis clarified a basic problem of the Indian New Deal: how to generate real community participation in the framework of a program which for economic reasons must be oriented toward larger units of organization. Unlike that of the tribes of the Northern Plains, the Hopi land base had not been broken up by allotment, but the psychological barriers that kept the villages apart operated as effectively as the checkerboarding of allotments to inhibit tribal economic development.

Very similar to the Hopis in their desert habitat and form of social organization in villages were the Papagos of southern Arizona on the Mexican border. As noted earlier, the Papagos subsisted on hunting as well as dry farming, and their villages were in fact geographically and seasonally separated. Otherwise there were strong parallels. Isolated from both white and external Indian influences, these distant relatives of the Aztecs preserved their ancient patterns of village government, communal landownership (cattle herds were owned by families, some of whom were relatively prosperous), and traditional religious practices. After 1915 oil prospectors in the eastern part of the Sells Reservation extended white contacts and aroused considerable controversy among the Indians; but for most of the seventy-odd villages composed of extended kinship groups scattered around the agency, the traditional localized ways of life remained predominant.[37] Although the sense of tribal unity was no more developed among the Papagos than among the Hopis, their experiences under reorganization were to have a markedly different pattern.

During 1935, after the Papagos agreed to accept the Reorganization Act, the superintendent at Sells Agency, an energetic man named Theodore Hall, pressured the Indians to organize a tribal council and a cooperative cattle association, the latter an attempt to redevelop a self-sufficient economy since during the depression years more than 60 percent of the Papagos' income had come to be based on wages, earned mostly from the Indian Emergency Conservation Works (IECW) projects and from temporary work in local mines. When he encountered strong resistance to both programs, Hall was inclined to lay the blame on the handful of cattle herders who had acquired a critical monopoly over Papago grazing lands.[38]

Ruth Underhill of the Applied Anthropology Staff, however, found more deep-seated reasons for Papago resistance. Having no tradition of tribal organization, they reacted with suspicion toward the centralization envisioned in both the tribal organization and tribal livestock cooperative proposals. She found Indians believing that the cooperative would take their herds away from them as well as "make rules" for them and bring them "into subjection." Both plans involved the establishment of districts, based on types of land, which did not correspond to traditional village boundaries (keeping in mind that villages included the lands lying between winter and summer settlements). Hence to the Indians the two proposals were linked and both appeared to constitute threats to the Papago way of life, even though, as she pointed out, communal cooperation and self-government were traditional among the Papagos.[39]

Underhill recommended a slower pace of reorganization to give the Indians a chance to reexamine the issues at length, and also an emphasis on the villages, as in La Farge's approach to the Hopis, in proposing a Papago constitution. John Holst and Kenneth Marmon, the field advisers sent to work with Hall on tribal organization, supported these recommendations and emphasized the traditions of direct democracy that seemed to prevail at the village level and the relative absence of any concept of representative government. Given this situation and the fear of the Papagos that tribal organization was a scheme to get their lands, the advisers felt that Hall was pushing too fast for the establishment of a tribal constitution. Collier, however, supported Hall and a constitution was ratified by a substantial majority in December 1936.[40]

An effort was made by the designers of the Papago constitution to introduce some measure of community representation on the council, but it was rather halfhearted. Villages presumed to be related were grouped into eleven districts, each of which, in addition to electing two representatives to the tribal council, would have a district council and could "govern itself in local matters in accordance with its old customs." But control of tribal lands (substantially all lands not allotted, including the lands owned communally by the villages), the regulation of family relations and matters of inheritance, and the disposition of property were all in the hands of the tribal council, which could also change district boundaries and intervene in "any matters involving more than one district."[41] Contrary to the implications of the wording in the constitution, the districts were no more traditional than the tribal council. In any case, the basic structure differed radically from that established by the Hopi constitution. The "old laws and customs," the informal network of rights and obligations which dominated village life, were retained, but in a new, wider context in which they were unlikely to function without formal clarification and substantial change.

In this situation, relations between the local communities and the new tribal government did not develop smoothly, and the atmosphere of suspicion between the Indians and the white administration was not dispelled. When survey teams from the Soil Conservation Service, which was undertaking a joint economic development program with the bureau called Technical Cooperation–Bureau of Indian Affairs (TC-BIA), arrived at Sells Agency in 1937, they encountered resistance from the Papagos, who recalled that previous surveys had resulted in their losing land and, more recently, control over mineral deposits on their lands. The most recalcitrant communities were those which had also refused to participate in the district council scheme set up under the 1936 constitution. The immediate tension was reduced somewhat by the "social and economic" teams, including Ruth Underhill and several other anthropologists, that went in before the technical surveyors and discussed the purposes of the survey with village groups.[42]

This particular problem was not resolved so easily, however, for the Papago Reservation plan eventually proposed by the Soil

Conservation Service as a result of the surveys recommended a permanent reduction in existing Papago cattle herds and the removal of about half of the Indians to the Pima and Colorado River agencies, where construction jobs were available.[43] At least one local official challenged the data of the TC-BIA survey, arguing that they underestimated the available forage land; while another pointed out that there had been little communication with the local villages, which had existed at an adequate subsistence level in that inhospitable region for years, and that any plan for herd reduction should center on the villages to avoid inequities, particularly against outlying villages.[44] A cattle reduction program was established along the lines proposed, but in 1940 the outbreak of a disease known as equine syphilis forced the bureau to reduce the horse population rapidly, alienating the Indians further.[45]

Meanwhile, disputes arose over the powers of the tribal council and the districts. In 1938 the tribal council agreed to allow the districts to lease their guano deposits and keep any profits for their own use. Superintendent Hall vetoed this action and was supported by the Washington office on the ground that the deposits were tribal property and should be used to provide revenues for tribal council administrative expenses, since sources of such revenues were scarce.[46] In this extraordinary situation reflecting the localist orientation of the Papagos and the centralizing momentum which the bureau had introduced, the bureau was forcing the tribal council to assert greater authority than it actually desired.

In 1940, Kenneth Marmon of the Tribal Organization Division reviewed the development of the Papago tribal council and concluded that it "more nearly carries out the idea intended by the Indian Reorganization Act of Indian participation in tribal affairs than any of the other organized tribes in California and Arizona."[47] The council had established a law and order code in 1938 and had set up on its own initiative a Contributed Loan Fund for small loans, its capital based on contributions from the wages of all Papago IECW employees on the reservation. The Indians had also initiated a Crafts Board to market Papago handicrafts at the San Francisco Fair, and a Rodeo Association. As a working council the Papago tribal government proved active and highly motivated.

At the same time, there were weaknesses. Council meetings

rarely included all of the representatives, some of whom had to travel long distances: the two delegates from Gila Band, which was more than one hundred miles from Sells Agency, had never attended the tribal council meetings. Some of the district representatives chose to stay away because of grievances against the whole program of centralization, and Marmon recommended continued delay in trying to get the Papagos to form a chartered tribal organization.[48] Part of the reason for the apparent efficiency of the council, it later developed, was the presence of an educated secretary-treasurer who was also head of the loan board and became the dominant figure, but was found to have been siphoning off funds.[49]

The Indian New Deal had mixed results in promoting tribal unity. The IECW and other projects brought together villagers who had previously had little contact, and the district councils, although limited in powers, served the same function for village leaders. A bilingual Papago newspaper sought to instill a sense of shared Papago achievement by recounting tribal political and economic activities. Nevertheless, the village traditions remained strong: district and tribal council representatives were regarded by their constituencies as messengers between the different levels of government rather than as spokesmen clothed with authority to act on behalf of the villages. Resistance to coordinated range management and cooperative cattle marketing associations continued throughout the period.[50]

In organizing the Indian groups of the Southwest, the bureau recognized the traditions of local village or band autonomy and made some effort to accommodate this orientation to the centralizing format of tribal economic programs, notably in the case of the Hopis. But the effort was limited, and even in the Hopi situation the tribal council was unable to meet the requirement that it represent Indian communities and at the same time integrate community interests into a tribal economic and political system. The councils worked hard to establish themselves in the minds of bureau officials and their own people as the legitimate spokesmen for a tribal point of view; and in general Collier and his associates felt that the southwestern councils were among the best products of the Indian Reorganization Act. Many Indians, however, saw them, not necessarily accurately, as only another tier of alien officials, at best ineffective, and at worst the red puppets of white bureaucracy.

In the Southwest and the Great Basin, Indian groups were traditionally organized into villages or bands, and this pattern held also for the Indians of the Northern Plains. Some, like the Mandans and Arikaras, were settled in agricultural villages and supplemented their economy with hunting and trading, while others, like the Teton Sioux and Cheyennes, were basically buffalo hunters and traveled in small bands.[51] During the period of white contact, however, some of these groups, notably the Northern Cheyennes and the Crows, had developed a more cohesive tribal organization that exercised a degree of control over the members of the constituent bands.

The Northern Cheyennes of Montana had one of the more elaborate of these tribal structures. A council of forty-four chiefs was chosen every ten years and sat in judgment of disputes among tribesmen and made decisions relating to the general welfare of the tribe, such as the time and place for the annual buffalo hunt. To enforce decisions there were six military societies, which drew their members from different bands. The leaders of these societies were elected by the members, and no chief of a society could simultaneously be a member of the council of forty-four. In addition to policing the annual hunt and fighting battles with rival tribes, the military societies tended to reinforce the unity of the Cheyennes by suppressing would-be secessionist bands and factions, and thus acted as one of the strongest elements binding the tribe together.[52]

The Cheyennes were unusual in their degree of tribal organization. Other plains tribes exhibited similar features but had not integrated them to that extent. The Crows, Mandans, and Teton Sioux had military societies which served essentially the same function as those of the Cheyennes, but the tribal council, if one existed, met only sporadically and had no well-defined powers. Among the Crows the chief of the military society might also be chief of a band, but the duties of the societies extended only to policing the hunts and fighting other Indians.[53] Other groups like the Comanches lacked even this unifying element and seem to have been held together mainly by the need for mutual assistance in fighting other Indians. Their leaders, civil and military, were not chosen in any formal way but acquired temporary influence through persuasion and prestige. For the most part they operated only at the band or community level.[54] Nevertheless, those groups were all moving toward a form and scale of organization similar to that of the Cheyennes during the historical period; variations among their political systems were a matter of degree and the ancient tradition of village autonomy typical of the southwestern Indians did not develop. The Indians of the Northern Plains in the nineteenth century were in a state of transition to a more formal system of tribalism.

The imposition of white domination halted these processes. The attempt to force assimilation on Indians by downgrading their traditional chiefs and parceling out their lands in individual allotments failed, but it still eradicated vestiges of tribal unity except among those Indians like the Cheyennes who had developed an integrated internal structure. Strong leaders like Red Cloud and Spotted Tail of the Sioux held their followers together for a time by force of personality, but by the second generation of reservation life only a few older full-bloods recalled the political traditions of earlier days.

The bureau had further impinged upon tribal integrity and unity by its policies of settlement on reservations in the plains. Some reservations had originally been established for the exclusive use of single Indian groups but subsequently became receptacles for remnants of smaller groups who had nowhere else to go. That was the case at the Flathead Reservation in Montana, which had been established in 1855 under the Hell Gate Treaty for the Flathead, Kootenai, and Upper Pend d'Oreille Indians, who were collectively designated the Flathead nation for treaty purposes although they had constituted different groups in the past. Beginning in 1889 the Flathead Reservation was opened for settlement by residues of other, smaller groups, and the entire reservation was subsequently allotted.[55] The Fort Belknap Reservation was established for the Gros Ventres, a branch of the Blackfeet, in 1855, but in 1874 it was opened to the Assiniboins under the terms of an 1868 treaty that the Gros Ventres regarded as illegitimate. Later, allotment broke up the unity of both tribes although they remained hostile toward each other.[56] Similarly, in Oklahoma the Kiowa Reservation, established in 1867 under the Treaty of Medicine Lodge Creek, included Comanches and, later, Plains Apaches. The three groups remained completely apart and the reservation was allotted in 1900.[57]

Other reservations were set aside by government decree rather than treaty, and became dumping grounds for unrelated groups. At Fort Berthold in North Dakota, J. H. Holst noted that the tribes assembled there, the Mandans, Arikaras, and Hidatsas, were unrelated and their "main reason for proximity in the past had been defense against the Sioux." While their historical contacts may have been greater than Holst was aware, they spoke no mutual language, and there was little intermarriage among them.[58] A Montana reservation, Rocky Boy's, was established specifically for remnants of former tribes or bands who had nowhere else to go.

During the 1920s most of the plains reservations, on orders from Washington, set up business committees to represent tribes for purposes of legal transactions such as leasing tribal lands and mineral rights. The councils also presumably served as liaisons between the local officials and the Indians, but there were no uniform procedures for the selection of committee members. Sometimes they were simply hand-picked by the superintendent; in other cases an effort was made to establish a representative electoral system based on administrative districts, but the districts rarely corresponded to existing Indian communities. The functions of these committees were likewise ill-defined and they existed almost entirely at the whim of the superintendent. Few, if any, records were kept of their proceedings, and when the bureau sent out a circular in 1934 requesting information from the agents about the history of tribal organization on their reservations, most of the responses were pieced together from interviews with Indians and long-term agency employees.

Collier and his associates were well aware of the destructive effects that allotment and the bureau policy of shared reservations had on tribal integrity among the plains Indians. The program of land consolidation in the Wheeler-Howard Act was based on the premise that political organization of the tribes would be ineffectual without the establishment of an adequate economic base. At the same time, bureau administrators viewed political and economic reorganization as concurrent processes and felt impelled to promote and sustain tribal governments despite the absence of tribal unity on many of the reservations.

One of the first tribal councils to be established under the Reorganization Act was that of the confederated Salish and Kootenai tribes (which included Pend d'Oreilles and other smaller groups) on the Flathead Reservation in Montana in 1935. Representation was based on districts which corresponded roughly with the divisions among tribal groups on the reservation. On the

mountainous perimeter of the reservation were the districts of the
two major groups, the Salishes and the Kootenais, who were predominantly full-blood, while in the interior the districts were
composed of mixed groups, many of them of less than full blood.
One observer believed that "the lines of division on [the] reservation are based upon degrees of hybridity rather than upon tribal
affiliation," and contrasted the spirit of cooperation between the
full-blood groups with the "suspicion and distrust" between
mixed-bloods and full-bloods. But he also noted the clear-cut
tribal divisions among the districts, which had been determined
by the Indians, and the fact that the tribal council was composed
largely of mixed-bloods, who represented the central rather than
the peripheral districts.[59] A later observer of the council in operation noted that the Salishes and Kootenais spoke mutually unintelligible dialects, requiring interpreters at all council discussions,
and that there was "a tendency apparent for council members to
think and act in terms of the interests of their particular districts."[60] Again, the situation was complicated by full-blood–
mixed-blood rivalry, but there was a geographic dimension to
these divisions which also reflected intertribal differences.

During 1936 and 1937, the Flathead council sought to deal
with its difficulties by introducing a measure of decentralization.
In 1936 the council sponsored district councils that would meet
with their tribal council representatives to discuss matters relating
to both tribal and local welfare. Later the tribal council established a tribal loan fund based on income from the leasing of tribal
land for a damsite and power station as well as the revolving fund
set up under Reorganization Act, and endeavored to channel loans
to individuals through district committees rather than a tribal
council committee.[61] The community organizations were also to
be a means of acquainting Indians in outlying areas of the operations of the tribe.

These early efforts to develop a sense of tribal interest among
the different groups appear to have atrophied, however, for after
1940, complaints, particularly from the full-blood Kootenais in
the perimeter districts, began to flow into Washington, and the
Bruner movement, an Oklahoma-based effort by dissident Indians
to repeal the Wheeler-Howard Act, made increasing headway on
the Flathead Reservation. Martin Charlo, one of the traditional
Kootenai chiefs (and an honorary member of the tribal council),
and others from his district maintained that the council had

ceased communicating with the districts and was making decisions about the loan fund without consulting community groups.[62] In 1943 the bureau sent John Holst to investigate the situation.

Holst's report emphasized the history of disunity on the Flathead Reservation and noted that despite an "earnest effort to attain self-government and management of their own resources . . . they could not get a council eligible to represent the widely scattered and disintegrated tribal residues." He then raised a more fundamental issue:

They cannot operate a tribal enterprise because there is no tribe. When they attempt to do so . . . such enterprise becomes a political football. Associations of individuals in economic enterprises have little relation to tribal government. . . . But the tribe's extremity is the Bureau's opportunity, and it attempts to operate all of the tribal resources for the benefit of the tribe which is protected against itself by being required to agree to a program for the expenditure of its income. . . . The fact of the matter is that they are controlled by various Bureau divisions in every phase of their civic and economic life.[63]

Admittedly, Holst's argument was biased. He had by that time become a convert to assimilation and recommended that federal control of the Flathead Reservation be ended and "tribal" resources distributed among the Indians, a solution similar to the proposals for termination of bureau regulation of Indian properties made in Congress in the 1950s and applied with devastating results to the Klamath and Menominee Indians. Nevertheless, the problem which Holst raised was important, for it challenged some basic premises of the Indian reorganization program. The whole concept of tribal organization, he argued, became meaningless when there was no tribe and when the local communities in which Indians lived, and to which they felt some sense of loyalty, were ignored or assigned only a subordinate role in the tribal scheme. When the communities were not involved or interested in "tribal" matters, the council, no matter how well intentioned, became a branch of bureau administration and the programs for tribal economic development were, as critics asserted in 1934, nothing more than the continuation and expansion of federal bureaucratic control under the guise of Indian self-determination.

To some extent the argument may be misdirected because of a lack of perspective. Many of the councils did not go into operation until 1937 or later and, as of 1945 when Collier resigned as commissioner, had not yet developed a full comprehension of their function. "The intent of the new policy was to develop Indian leadership," Edward Spicer has observed, "but it became clear that such leadership was not going to develop within a few years."[64] Consequently, until after 1945 the councils were given only a limited role in managing reservation affairs, undergoing a phase of tutelage in a sense. But if the councils were not really representative of the existing Indian communities, the progressive transfer of new responsibilities and powers would not alter the fact that they were an artificial creation of an alien government and could not instill in the Indians a sense of tribal loyalty. Many of these councils worked diligently to assume obligations of government and sought to expand their powers vis-à-vis the bureau administrators. But like the Flathead council in the 1940s, they represented a minute constituency, sometimes less than 10 percent of the reservation population.[65]

In any case, the legal and economic advisers of the bureau seem to have followed rather consistently a different line of argument, that the demands for greater community control over reservation affairs might, if carried too far, undermine the goal of economic and political organization of the reservation as a whole. The plains reservations, the argument ran, were already badly fragmented by allotted and alienated lands, and the first priority must be the reintegration of some semblance of centralized authority over the remaining resources.

We have already noted this viewpoint in the case of the landless Indians at the Yankton Agency in South Dakota and the Colville Agency in Washington. A similar dispute emerged at the Tongue River Northern Cheyenne Reservation in Montana. The Cheyennes had been one of the most integrated tribes in prereservation days and the Indians at Tongue River, who were predominantly full-bloods, responded with alacrity to the opportunity to reestablish a self-governing body. By 1936 a tribal council was operating, apparently with the full support of all but a minority of mixed-bloods on the reservation.

Tongue River was one of the fortunate reservations that had escaped the worst ravages of allotment and fee patenting, and it was good rangeland. In 1937 the Cheyennes embarked on a program to develop a tribal cattle herd and drew the largest single loan of all the tribes from the revolving credit fund, arranging for a commitment of over $2 million.[66] The program involved the purchase of breeding cattle to ensure the full use of both the

summer and winter ranges of the reservation. The herd was to
be managed by a livestock cooperative and the beef marketed
through a tribal corporation.[67]

The tribal council in its discussions of the organization of the
program with bureau officials emphasized their desire to decentralize the management of the range and the herds, turning it over
to community units. The livestock cooperative would be organized
on a community basis and would carry out functions of range and
herd management. Concurrently the council decided to administer
an individual loan program (which would provide money to Indians to produce breeding stock) through district committees
elected at the community level rather than through a tribal loan
committee.[68]

Kenneth Meicklejohn, legal adviser to the bureau, had no objections to the latter proposal, which was already being introduced
on other reservations and would prevent the friction aroused by
tribal loan committees such as the Blackfeet operated. But he
raised the point that the decentralized cooperative "would have a
very definite tendency to substitute the association for the organized tribe. . . . Its powers would be all those which the tribal council . . . are authorized to exercise. The work which the association
would do is work which I believe the council should do. Unless
the tribal authorities are to take responsibility for themselves for
the development of the tribal resources . . . self government
doesn't mean very much."[69]

A similar dispute over the proper division of powers between
tribal and community organizations arose in the case of the Chippewas of Minnesota. As discussed in the previous chapter, the
Chippewas had drawn up a constitution for a decentralized government to meet their peculiar situation of fragmentation and to encourage the Red Lake band to join. Despite Red Lake's withdrawal in 1936, the constitution was ratified. There was some
feeling, however, that too much authority had been given the
tribal council, and in 1938 Archie Phinney and M. L. Burns of the
bureau's regional office in the Great Lakes region worked with the
Indians on a plan for band organizations that would become an
integral part of the tribal system. Under this plan the scattered
reservations would be designated as bands (larger reservations like
White Earth would be divided into community districts). The
bands would be assigned any lands purchased for the Indians by
the Interior Department and the Resettlement Administration and

would handle individual loans from the revolving fund under the Indian Reorganization Act. Each district or community would also elect representatives to a reservation executive council, which would constitute the tribal executive committee of the Minnesota Chippewas. The bands would thus be responsible for most administrative duties, while the tribal council would act principally as a legal representative of the tribe and as a conduit for funds provided under the act.[70]

During the latter part of 1938, Phinney held meetings with local community groups to discuss the plan and the Indians proved generally favorable to it, although some were apparently under the impression that the new band organizations would take the place of the tribal council. Some Chippewas felt that all the resources of the Chippewas should be under local control, but Phinney and the tribal representatives argued that certain resources, like the wild rice fields, should remain under tribal control for the management of harvesting and storage.[71]

Despite general support for decentralization on the part of the Indians, bureau officials in Washington were concerned that the plan might dilute tribal resources to the point where the tribe would no longer serve any purpose whatsoever. The lack of taxing power was cited as a weakness of the tribal organization which would ultimately force it either to draw on the tribal funds or go under. Similarly, the ceding of control over the lands acquired under the submarginal land purchase program of the Resettlement Administration would prevent the tribal council from exercising any coordinated management over lands that legally were its responsibility.[72]

The plan envisaged for the Chippewas resembled the existing pattern of government of the Rio Grande Pueblos in New Mexico and, to some extent, the Hopi constitution drawn up by La Farge. From the point of view of the Tribal Organization officials in Washington, however, there were significant differences in the conditions of these Indian groups. The Pueblos had a tradition of village organization, and their land, even though eroded and overstocked, was relatively intact. The lands of the Chippewas, like those of many of the plains tribes, had been completely broken up and many members of the tribe were desperately poor, having no source of support. Some kind of overall control was needed, if only for administrative purposes, to coordinate programs for land acquisition and the establishment of new enterprises for these

Indians. Since Indian participation was considered a necessary component of the program, it was logical that it should focus at some central point; fragmented community groups simply could not be fitted into this scheme.

Differences over community and tribal organization were sometimes determined by expediency rather than principle. An example of this situation developed on the Sioux reservations in South Dakota. Among the Teton Sioux, historically the basic political group was the band, or *tiospaye*. Bands might gather for hunts or dances, but there was no system of tribal organization such as the Cheyennes had. Tribal councils had been established on the Sioux reservations during the 1920s, but representation was based on the farm districts that had been set up for administrative purposes a decade before, rather than on the *tiospaye*. Most of the full-bloods, as noted earlier, ignored these business councils and supported a council of treaty chiefs which included headmen of the traditional bands.[73]

The tribal organization team sent to the Sioux reservations included H. S. Mekeel, an anthropologist who had earlier written at length to Collier about the potential for community organization among the Sioux.[74] Mekeel's enthusiasm about the *tiospaye* was shared by the superintendent at the Rosebud Agency, W. O. Roberts, who had been encouraging local community groups there to elect leaders to act as intermediaries with federal officials and handle the distribution of relief and the maintenance of law and order.[75] At the other agencies, however, local officials were less accommodating. W. F. Dickens, superintendent at Cheyenne River, objected to the abandonment of the districts, arguing that the Indians were "used to" that system and adding, "While I understand the desirability of a group organization, yet if we were to elect a delegate from every group our council would be far too cumbersome and costly."[76] The Pine Ridge agent raised similar objections, and Ben Reifel, himself a Sioux Indian and a lawyer with the team, also urged that the attempt to reorganize electoral districts to correspond to community groups was likely to arouse friction among the Indians. In the case of Pine Ridge at least, he believed, it was best to work with existing representational units. Mekeel reluctantly gave way in both cases.[77] Subsequently, however, a local bureau observer attributed the incessant squabbling and general ineffectiveness of the Pine Ridge tribal council to its failure to represent Indian communities that might otherwise take a serious interest in tribal matters and the quality of people being elected to the council.[78]

When Roberts was transferred to Pine Ridge, he brought with him ideas about developing community groups and, after a period of continual quarreling with the mixed-blood tribal council, proceeded to promote a model community at Red Shirt Table. In 1938 community meetings were held and a local committee composed of full-bloods and mixed-bloods was established. Advisers were brought in from the Agricultural Extension Service, the Soil Conservation Service, and other federal agencies to help design a community resource use plan. To prevent friction between full-bloods and mixed-bloods the community projects were divided: full-bloods established a livestock cooperative, while mixed-bloods designed and developed an irrigated gardening project and a housing construction enterprise.[79] Red Shirt Table and several other community groups were able to acquire special representation on the tribal council.

Bureau leaders took note of the Red Shirt Table experiment in the context of the otherwise dismal record of tribal reorganization among the Sioux. There was no systematic effort to expand the approach, but the Indian Organization Division took an increasingly flexible position on the relation of community groups to tribal organization in the plains region.

Roberts's earlier activities with *tiospaye* groups at Rosebud had been praised by Reifel in reports to the bureau in Washington; and after tribal council organization efforts bogged down at the nearby Yankton Agency, local officials sought to work around the situation by channeling relief and rehabilitation funds through community organizations. Subsequently the community groups were given a role in making land assignments, which under the Wheeler-Howard Act was supposed to be a major function of tribal government.[80] By the middle of 1938 the community groups were managing loan committees drawing on the revolving credit fund and exhibited little interest in diverting their energies to establishing a tribal council. At a congressional hearing on the Yankton situation in 1940, the leader of the faction that had blocked tribal organization there charged that the bureau was using the community committees to carry out the basic duties of a tribal organization without going to the trouble of holding a referendum on a tribal constitution. Superintendent Whitlock somewhat disingenuously declared that the community groups had been formed only for "economic improvements," but it was clear that the charges were more than slightly accurate. Many of the functions of the tribal council had been assigned to the *tiospaye* groups, but only after tribal organization was stymied.[81]

6

TRIBAL GOVERNMENT IN
THEORY AND PRACTICE

Perhaps the most enduring legacy of the Indian New Deal was a by-product of the tribal organization effort: the beginnings of a code of Indian law and tribal constitutional powers, initiated in 1934 by Nathan Margold, solicitor of the Department of the Interior, and carried forward by Felix Cohen during the next eight years. Working their way through the scattered documentary sources of U.S. government treaties with Indian tribes, congressional and administrative references to tribal legal rights, federal court cases, and written Indian constitutions like those of the Cherokees, Choctaws, and Chickasaws, Cohen and his aides assembled the first relatively complete treatise on Indian rights and systems of government in American history.[1] Meanwhile the Indian Organization Division of the bureau worked with Indian groups in preparing new constitutions which enumerated in detail the powers and duties of the governments established under the Wheeler-Howard Act.

The affirmation that Indian political systems existed in their own right and possessed powers that no external authority, including Congress and the Bureau of Indian Affairs, could abridge was an important step in reestablishing Indian self-determination and was long overdue. But affirming that such powers existed was not the same thing as ensuring that they were consistently recognized and upheld. In the latter area the record of the Collier administration was not so impressive.

To a certain extent Collier and his reformer colleagues in the bureau were limited by the organization they inherited and by their inability to combine administrative decentralization satisfactorily with strong control from Washington in the crucial areas of tribal political and economic reorganization. Many of the local officials upon whom the burden of these changes depended regarded the new tribal councils much as they had the business committees of the preceding decade, as at best a meaningless addition to the agency and at worst an obstacle to the efficient administration of the reservation. Disputes between the Washington divisions and local agents over the scope of tribal authority and the role of the councils in decision making were frequent and abrasive. During the twelve years of the Collier administration some of the more authoritarian representatives of the old guard were replaced, but the basic divergence in viewpoint between Washington and some local officials remained in 1945.

The reform leaders themselves were prepared to grant only a limited amount of autonomy to the new tribal organizations. Two considerations determined their stance. First, they recognized that, in order to achieve any real decentralization, the local agents must be given some leeway in dealing with their Indians; to overrule agents arbitrarily in too many cases would demoralize them or arouse further antagonism toward the reform program. Furthermore, Indian political leaders, who often represented a minority within their own communities, were not always averse to feathering their own nests, discriminating against other Indians, or attacking bureau policies and employees on ill-considered and unfair grounds.

The second and more basic consideration was that the highest priority had to be given to salvaging Indian economies, and from the viewpoint of the bureau leaders, that task required the continuation of maximum administrative control over Indian resources. Consolidation of Indian lands in the form envisaged in the original version of the Indian Reorganization Act was not allowed, so emphasis was placed on protecting existing resources. Indian tribes were not deemed competent to manage their economic affairs without substantial guidance. The harsh lessons of allotment and fee patenting seemed applicable to Indians collectively as well as individually.

In these circumstances it would not be surprising to find that the tribal councils were nothing more than adjuncts to the local administration, placidly rubber-stamping the decisions made by the bureau. And in fact many of the councils, particularly those praised for their "cooperative spirit," were precisely that. But this picture can be misleading. Even the most turbulent of the tribal councils would sit, listen, and accept the proposals of the hosts of advisers sent to aid them in their economic programs. In part they may have genuinely agreed with the ideas presented to them; or, having experienced an endless series of experiments and reforms, they may have regarded the economic programs of the New Deal as another well-meaning but probably short-lived enthusiasm of white administrators. At the same time, the councils engaged in continuous, angry debate with bureau officials, locally and in Washington, over other issues: the hiring and firing of agency employees, determination of tribal membership, salaries and perquisites of council members, and the handling of restricted tribal funds. Given the opportunity, the Indian politicians attempted to get control over these areas, and when frustrated, as they usually were, they complained bitterly and persisted in their efforts.[2]

The Collier administration has been charged with failing to carry through on its promise to the Indians of genuine self-determination by imposing constitutional limits on the powers of the council through routine decisions on reservation policies. Defenders of Collier have responded by citing the more imperative requirements of economic rehabilitation and administrative coordination: without these economic measures the Indians would have fared far worse. In any case, the tribal councils were not equipped at this early stage to handle the complex problems with which the bureau struggled.[3]

Yet, in a left-handed way, the Indian Reorganization Act did succeed in arousing a remarkable degree of Indian political activism, much of it futile, much of it self-centered and self-serving, but an important new element in Indian affairs nonetheless. The tribal councils were rarely representative of their constituencies and included opportunists and timeservers as frequently as serious spokesmen, but Indian politicians are not necessarily any more paragons of civic virtue than any other group of politicians.

One recent commentator has made some interesting observations

on the present tribal councils which are equally applicable to those
of the New Deal era in many respects:

As in most communities there are strong tendencies to regard the local government as a source of benefit for local factions and interest associations;
very few regard it as an instrumentality for community developments and
changes benefiting the general populace. Most of the local folk derogate the
tribal government and its politicians except when they can extract some favor
. . . and most [councilmen] regard election to office as a reward to be be-
stowed upon senior men, friends and kin rather than as a choice among competent men with competitive policies. In these, as in many other respects,
tribal . . . governments are not too different from national and local governments elsewhere.[4]

It is certain that this result is not what Collier had in mind when
he envisioned tribal regeneration. His expectation about Indian
political behavior may have been unrealistic; but, again, that the
councils became the arena for political opportunists and bastard-
ized versions of white local government may also reflect the fact
that they did not have a direct connection with Indian communities.

Still, the tribal councils, for all their weaknesses, did represent
a step away from the kind of total bureaucratic control under
which most Indians had lived in the pre-Collier era. Their demands
might continue to be ignored, but there were now forums where
they could be expressed. While Collier and his adherents lamented
that the Wheeler-Howard Act had severely limited the potential
economic powers of the tribal organizations and made them less
consequential in the programs for economic reconstruction, a
recent student of the subject has noted that the act "opened the
way for an era of tribal politics and tribal self-determination which
could not have been as extensive under the original Reorganization
bill."[5]

In October 1934, Nathan Margold, solicitor of the Interior Department, rendered an opinion on the derivation of tribal powers
of self-government and the scope of the "powers vested in any
Indian tribe or tribal council in existing law" that provided the
basic framework within which the tribal constitutions under the
Wheeler-Howard Act were established. Basing his opinion on the
rulings of the U.S. Supreme Court in *Worcester* v. *Georgia* and
subsequent decisions, Margold asserted that while Indian tribes
had lost their "external sovereignty," that is, the right to independent recognition under international law, they retained

"internal sovereignty," the right to organize their own local self-government, except where the latter powers were limited by express act of Congress. Among the inherent powers retained by Indian tribes were the power to adopt a form of government of their own choosing, to define the conditions of membership in the tribe, to exclude nonmembers from their territory, to regulate the domestic relations of tribal members, to regulate the disposition of all tribal property, to levy taxes on tribal members (and others resident in their territory), and to prescribe rules of inheritance with respect to real and personal property, except where limited by U.S. law. In addition, the tribes could regulate the conduct of federal employees and other non–tribal members, on their territory, to the extent that they were allowed to do so under federal law and the determination of the Department of the Interior.[6]

To these inherent powers of Indian tribes the Wheeler-Howard Act added several explicit ones: the right to employ legal counsel; to negotiate with federal, state, and local governments; to prevent further alienation of lands and tribal assets; to review all bureau appropriation estimates relating to the tribe; and to establish tribal corporations. Legal restrictions were placed on several of these powers. The choice of legal counsel must be approved by the secretary of the interior; and tribal organizations could not sell, mortgage, or lease any land on the reservation for a period of more than ten years.

These elements formed the basis of most tribal constitutions. There were additional provisions in specific constitutions and variations in the electoral districts of tribal councils and the distribution of powers between the tribal and district or community levels, but the description of powers of tribal councils followed a relatively uniform pattern.

During the early stages of tribal organization, the Interior Department's legal division prepared a model constitution that was supposed to form the basis for discussion between Indian delegates and bureau advisers in preparing specific tribal constitutions. This step was probably necessary, owing to the ignorance of both Indians and bureau officials of the inherent legal powers of Indian tribes, and to confusion over the actual provisions of the Reorganization Act, but it provided critics of the Collier administration with evidence that the Indians were being manipulated into a sham self-government.

A 1944 report by the Senate Committee on Indian Affairs recommending the repeal of the Wheeler-Howard Act characterized the constitutions in this fashion:

The Indians were supposed to write their own constitutions but they had no experience in such matters; besides they did not know what the Bureau wanted them to want. The only way to organize them was to offer them model constitutions acceptable to the Indian Bureau and allow them to accept such drafts, revise them within limits set by the Bureau or else reject them. Using standard forms a constitution could be pieced together in a conference with the Indians by allowing them to fill in the blank forms as suggested, between the items required by the Bureau. Some constitutions when completed contained more Bureau required or suggested matter than matter that was used to fit them to the actual situation.[7]

Collier's response to this charge was that "a written constitution is a more or less formalized instrument. Its possible variations are limited by a number of circumstances—legal, economic and cultural. Nevertheless, no two of the 106 constitutions accepted by Indian groups in the United States or of the 44 adopted by native villages in Alaska are alike."[8]

Collier's statement that no two constitutions were alike was accurate in a technical sense, since there were variations in the number of councilmen provided for, the manner of holding elections, and similar matters. As we have seen earlier, particular tribes such as the Hopi and the Minnesota Chippewas chose to devolve many powers of the councils to more localized bodies. Among some smaller groups, such as the Ute Mountain tribe, whose reservation bordered Colorado, New Mexico, and Utah, the constitution provided for a general council of all members of the tribe in addition to the regular tribal council, although the specific powers of the general council were not clarified.[9] About two-thirds of the constitutions included provisions for referenda on council ordinances upon the presentation of a petition of 25 percent of the enrolled voters, and one-third of the constitutions included a bill of rights, generally a shortened form guaranteeing civil liberties, equal economic opportunity, the suffrage, and protection of the rights of those accused of crimes before tribal courts.[10]

At the same time, there were substantial similarities among constitutions in the enumeration of powers of the tribal councils and provisions relating to the management of tribal lands and resources. These sections were based largely on the model constitution, which in turn was based on Margold's description of tribal powers

and the provisions of the Wheeler-Howard Act. The major variation in these areas related to land management: on reservations
where allotment had broken up the tribal land base there was a
long section on land including elaborate provisions for the voluntary exchange of allotments for assignments of tribal land, the
conditions under which heirship lands could be transferred to
tribal ownership, and the circumstances under which the tribal
government could take over private lands under the powers of
eminent domain. Among tribes whose land base was relatively
unaffected by allotment, as was generally the case in the Southwest, or where there was not enough tribal land left to make
reconsolidation plausible, the section on land was relatively short,
simply providing that no existing lands should be allotted and any
lands acquired in the future would be held by the tribe and assigned to individual use.

Except for this general variation, the constitutions followed
closely the pattern of the model. The basic format consisted of
nine articles devoted to territory, membership, governing body,
powers of the council, election, removal from office, referendum,
land, and amendments. Some tribes dropped sections that seemed
unnecessary; some added sections on community and bill of
rights; and some dwelt at greater length on certain subjects than
others. But the fundamental elements remained the same.[11]

Collier's argument that some degree of uniformity was necessary because of the limitations which the Wheeler-Howard Act and
other congressional measures placed on tribal autonomy was certainly defensible. It is also probable, and hardly cause for criticism
of the Collier administration, that few of the Indians had any clear
notion of what a written constitution ought to contain. But in the
process of preparing the tribal constitutions the bureau in several
instances ignored or actively opposed initiatives coming from
Indians or from sources outside their administrative control. The
reasons for opposition were usually legally justifiable, but the
rejections helped create in the minds of the Indians the convic-
tion that tribal reorganization was a game in which the bureau
made all the rules.

At the San Carlos Apache Reservation in Arizona, a dispute
involving rival constitutions erupted while the reorganization bill
was still under consideration by Congress. A tribal council under a
Tonto Apache named Henry Chinn had been dissolved in 1923
by superintendent James Kitch, who was later characterized by

Senator Lynn Frazier as "one of the old school of autocratic superintendents who . . . take the attitude that the Indians' wishes are not worth considering, and that they do not know what they want." Under Kitch, economic conditions at San Carlos had improved, but Chinn's faction continued to grumble, petitioning the bureau frequently about Kitch's arbitrariness. Apparently sensing the way winds were blowing from Washington, Kitch early in 1933 reestablished the tribal council, hand-picking its members. On the recommendations of Moris Burge and Oliver La Farge, the bureau agreed to recognize Kitch's council on a temporary basis, for the purpose of preparing a new tribal constitution.[12]

While Kitch's council prepared a constitution with the advice of Burge, Chinn and a lawyer from Phoenix drew up a rival constitution. The two constitutions were brought before the Indians in November 1933, and the Chinn version won handily. In January 1934, however, Collier wrote to Chinn that his constitution was unacceptable to the bureau for several reasons, in particular, that it gave complete authority over reservation affairs to the tribal council, and that it arbitrarily directed the exclusion of white traders and ranchers (some of whom owned or leased land there) from the reservation.[13] A subsequent constitution prepared by a local missionary and believed to be acceptable to both sides was also rejected by the bureau as administratively unworkable.

Later in 1934 a battery of bureau specialists, including F. H. Daiker, Walter Woehlke, and even Felix Cohen appeared at San Carlos to prepare the tribe's constitution. The new constitution, which was drawn up on the basis of the model one, was accepted by a majority of the Indians in October 1935. The dispute between Kitch and the Chinn faction did not cease, however; after Chinn was elected to the new council, Kitch excluded him on the ground that he had not been elected by a district populated by Tonto Apaches (under the constitution the Tontos and Mohaves were considered separate bands from the rest of the agency population). The same rule was not applied to other Tonto Apaches. Chinn was not reinstated to the council and Kitch remained superintendent until 1940.[14]

This particular dispute related only peripherally to the Reorganization Act, and the constitution designed under the law was apparently satisfactory to most of the Indians, including Chinn. But the issue under debate, the range of powers of the council, must be noted, and also the attitude of the bureau, which for legal reasons consistently appeared to side with an authoritarian official against what can only be characterized as a spontaneous effort on the part of the Indians to assert their rights.

A more difficult situation developed at the Yankton Agency in South Dakota and blocked tribal organization throughout the Collier era. The Yankton Sioux were interested in tribal self-government: only 17 percent of them voted against coming under the Reorganization Act in 1935. But a faction led by Clement Smith, apparently composed largely of full-bloods holding allotments, were suspicious of what they perceived as an alliance of the bureau and landless Indians on the reservation. A constitution prepared by Ben Reifel and the members of the business committee that had been established in 1932 was rejected by a close vote in November 1935. This constitution had been based on the model and resembled closely the tribal constitutions ratified at the neighboring Pine Ridge and Rosebud agencies.[15]

The Smith faction then presented its own version of a tribal constitution, prepared by R. T. Bonnin, who was seeking appointment as tribal attorney for the Yanktons.[16] In December 1935, the Smith-Bonnin constitution was sent to the bureau for review, together with a petition signed by about three hundred Indians (30 percent of the total voting population) urging its acceptance.

Some Indians expressed doubts about the validity of the signatures on the petition;[17] but the bureau had other reasons for objecting to the constitution. It held the constitution for review for almost nine months, then returned it with extensive criticism. The major grounds for rejection were that the president of the tribal council was given too much power to act without consulting the council and held a veto over council actions; and furthermore that the terms of office of the president and council were not clearly established. No provision was made concerning the exercise of tribal powers over tribal property, including the power to assign unallotted land to landless Indians. The council was given the power to enact ordinances even over the veto of the secretary of the interior; and the president of the council was empowered to fill all positions on government projects on the reservation.[18]

The reasons for rejecting the constitution were plausible. The provisions relating to presidential powers would have set the stage for the establishment of a political machine, replete with extensive patronage and free of any limits on the disposition of whatever funds were made available to the tribe. The lack of any provision concerning land assignments would have negated a basic purpose of the Wheeler-Howard Act, for the Yanktons had suffered the ravages of allotment and the Depression probably worse than any of the other Sioux. More than 80 percent of the allotted lands had been alienated and the majority of the Indians had no source of income except relief. People were living in abandoned automobiles, and those fortunate enough to have horses were reported to be eating them, a sign of desperation among the Sioux, for whom horses were symbols of prestige and wealth.[19] The Smith-Bonnin constitution would hardly have benefited these people.

But if the Smith faction represented a minority of selfish politicians and suspicious full-bloods, it was a well-organized group and its leader was articulate and persuasive. In November 1936 the anti-Smith elements called for a general council to discuss a constitution modeled on the bureau draft, but the meeting was taken over by Smith and his followers and Smith presented a convincing argument in behalf of his constitution. The council concluded by rejecting Zimmerman's objections and calling for bureau acceptance of the Smith-Bonnin draft.[20]

At that point the bureau abandoned the effort to organize a Yankton tribal government and began promoting the community organization, as discussed in the previous chapter. Reifel drew up a new draft with the Yanktons in 1938, but it was not pushed by the bureau and a tribal organization never developed, although the charter of the business committee established in 1932 was later regarded by the bureau as the equivalent. However justified its position was, the actions of the Collier administration in this episode did not redound to its credit. Even Kenneth Meicklejohn of the Interior legal staff observed that the bureau had intervened so consistently against the Smith-Bonnin group that it could hardly claim to have been impartial in the matter.[21]

Furthermore, Zimmerman, in rejecting the constitution, had based his argument not on the obvious opportunities for political corruption which it would have permitted, but rather on the ground that the powers assigned to the president and council would infringe upon the administrative prerogatives of the secretary of the interior. Again, that was a legally correct argument, but it could not have reassured the Indians that the Reorganization Act was intended to encourage genuine self-government.

The tribal constitutions prepared under bureau auspices were in fact heavily loaded with qualifying phrases, devices to ensure that tribal action would be subject to administrative review. In the case of some provisions these safeguards were required by the Indian Reorganization Act (but had been present in the original draft of the Wheeler-Howard bill and so represented the view of the Collier administration); in other cases they were simply added to the constitutions because administrators wanted ultimate control over possible rash acts by tribal governments, and because the secretary of the interior had been assigned legal responsibility for Indian interests since 1849.

In some constitutions a distinction was made between powers of tribal councils which were subject to review by the secretary of the interior and those which were not; in other constitutions the powers were simply listed without such distinction. But there was a general uniformity to these provisions in virtually every constitution under the Indian Reorganization Act.

Among the powers not subject to review were those to negotiate with federal, state, and local governments; to review federal appropriation requests for the tribe; to regulate the domestic relations of tribal members; to "cultivate native arts and crafts"; and to regulate the procedure of the tribal council itself. In addition, there were two powers of limited extent: the tribe had the right to employ legal counsel, but the choice of counsel and the amount to be paid in fees were subject to review. The tribe could approve or veto the sale, lease, or other disposition of tribal lands or other property by administrators, but could not approve the lease or encumbrance of its property for a period exceeding ten years.[22]

Virtually all other powers, except for those enumerated by Margold in 1934, were subject to review by the secretary of the interior. These included the establishment of civil and criminal codes by the tribe; levying of taxes on tribal members and nonmembers residing on the reservation; licensing of traders; issuance of permits and setting of fees for hunting, grazing, and fishing; appropriation of tribal funds not under the control of Congress; assignment of tribal lands and resources; regulation of inheritance of property by individual tribal members or descendants of tribal members; chartering of subordinate economic or political organization such as cooperatives; and excluding nontribesmen from the reservation. Tribal membership was to be based on the official census rolls of the tribe, but any revisions of the roll or regulations concerning the induction of new members into the tribe were subject to review. Boundaries for electoral districts could likewise be altered only with approval by the secretary of the interior.

This is a formidable list, including all the powers that could have consequence in the regulation of the economic and political affairs of Indian tribes. Furthermore, the ratification of the constitution itself and any amendments was subject to review. Cohen in 1941 (by which time most of the reorganization constitutions were in operation) maintained that in no case had Interior Secretary Ickes vetoed a tribal constitution and that in fact "the chief threat to the integrity of tribal government" had been "the willingness of certain tribal officers to relinquish responsibilities vested in them by tribal constitutions," which the department had consistently refused to approve.[23] But the department did intervene on occasion to block what were regarded as ill-considered actions by tribal councils; and as we have seen in the case of the Yankton Sioux, it also acted to prevent constitutions from reaching the ratification stage.

Provision for review in some instances derived directly from the Wheeler-Howard Act. That was the case with the review of constitutions and amendments; the choice of tribal legal counsel and setting of fees; and the regulation of such matters as land assignments, the exchange of allotments, and the disposition of kinship lands. In other cases the power of the tribe to determine its own membership, access to certain tribal funds held in trust by Congress, and the licensing of traders—the power of review derived from previous acts of Congress and treaties relating to specific tribes. But under the Reorganization Act constitutions, the department established as general rules what had hitherto, in law at least, held for only some tribes. In still other cases, such as review of ordinances relating to taxes on traders, inheritance, and the establishment of criminal codes and courts, powers were assumed by the department which had no basis other than past practice.[24] Again, the reviewing power was rarely exercised arbitrarily or unreasonably in the Collier era, but the implicit limits on tribal action surfaced on occasion and made the Indians aware that self-government for them remained a strictly controlled affair.

The issue of control over tribal membership was a problem that cropped up among tribes in which mixed-bloods and full-bloods were hostile. One of the inherent powers of Indian tribes was the right to determine their own membership, but it was qualified by the U.S. Supreme Court in 1907.[25] During the nineteenth century, Congress had asserted this power largely for the purpose of establishing who was qualified to receive annuities under treaties or a share in tribal lands during the allotment process. As reservations were allotted in severalty, tribal rolls were prepared. Under the Indian Reorganization Act, membership continued to be important, but more for determining who was entitled to vote in tribal elections than in dividing tribal property, since the use of that property was to be transferred to the tribal governments.

We have seen in the case of the Blackfeet discussed in Chapter 4, the kind of difficulties that could develop when a full-blood minority was (or felt it was) deprived of a fair share of the benefits derived from tribal property because of the gerrymandering of electoral districts. This was basically a political issue, but a more far-reaching constitutional issue arose on the Northern Cheyenne Reservation for much the same reason.

Before 1935 the Tongue River business council had been dominated by mixed-bloods, but under reorganization the full-bloods, who constituted a numerical majority of the tribe, established control of the new tribal council. In the Northern Cheyenne constitution the council was authorized to revise the existing tribal rolls to bring them up to date with the most recent census. The committee appointed by the council, composed exclusively of full-bloods, submitted a report in 1937 recommending that several hundred mixed-bloods be dropped from the rolls.[26] This move aroused some debate in Washington, since it could set a precedent that would exacerbate already bad relations among Indians on the allotted reservations. Even the council was reluctant to endorse the proposal, and appointed a new committee.

Meanwhile, J. M. Stewart of the bureau's Land Division urged that this kind of action be firmly suppressed and that the term *revision* of tribal rolls be interpreted to mean only the addition of names of persons born on the reservation, new residents, and adoptions authorized under constitutional procedures, and that only deceased members or nonresidents be dropped from the rolls.[27] Kenneth Meicklejohn argued that that would be an "unnecessarily narrow construction" of the membership provision, and that the council should have the power to investigate and determine the legitimacy of membership in specific cases.[28] No action was taken on the issue, since the Northern Cheyenne council did not present it as an official measure, but the general position of the department on the subject can be gleaned from Cohen: "The general trend of the tribal enactments on membership is away from the older notion that rights of tribal membership run with Indian blood. . . . Instead it is recognized that membership in a tribe is a political relation rather than a social attribute."[29]

Another controversial area was the power to license traders and set fees. This was an area in which Congress had conferred full authority on the commissioner of Indian affairs. Presumably, the power could have been delegated to Indian tribes without restriction, and in practice licenses were not issued without the approval of the tribal council. The tribal constitutions, however, generally made action relating to taxes and fees on traders subject to departmental review, although they were not required to do so because the tribes had an inherent right in this area, upheld by the U.S. Supreme Court in the case of *Buster* v. *Wright* in 1906.[30]

In 1937 the Cheyenne River Sioux council in South Dakota passed an ordinance setting arbitrarily high licensing fees on traders at the agency, with provisions for discrimination among traders in setting fees. The local superintendent objected that the measure interfered with private business and was open to obvious abuses. Some bureau officials in Washington were inclined to agree, but Meicklejohn defended the action of the council, drawing an analogy with state and local legislatures, which were allowed to set any fees they chose. McNickle agreed with Meicklejohn, adding, "We are certainly not encouraging home rule among the tribes if we are to require that they post with the Secretary [of the Interior] (and have his approval on every detail of this license business). There may be good and proper reasons why the tribe will want to discourage a particular trader by charging more than a set fee. . . . There may be abuses too, but why should we anticipate them?"[31]

As can be seen in the examples cited, members of the Indian Organization Division and the Interior Department legal staff under Collier and Ickes sought to give the tribes the maximum degree of freedom possible in matters of internal regulatory powers. The weakness of this system was that it depended on the attitudes and flexibility of bureau officials in interpreting the limits of tribal constitutions; and it was this dependence on the good will of administrators that the Reorganization Act was supposed to eliminate by providing Indians with clear statutory autonomy. The limits on autonomy incorporated in the constitutions were designed as safeguards during the early stages of tribal self-government; but they remained to be interpreted more narrowly by later officials of the Interior Department who did not share the views of Collier and his associates on Indian self-determination.

One area of special complexity and difficulty involved the access of tribes to their revenues and control over their expenditures. Oscar H. Lipps, a bureau field representative, raised this general issue in the course of a report on tribal council operations at the Flathead Agency in Montana in 1937:

Under the provision of the Indian Reorganization Act we have entered upon the policy of what the British statesmen call "indirect rule." The vital point in this system is said to be the assumption of responsibility by those whom we are attempting to rule—the Indians. We are inclined to be reluctant to extend this principle to its logical end when it comes to putting financial responsibility on the tribal councils. The Indians feel that if they are not to be permitted to handle at least a reasonable part of their tribal income on their own responsibility the so-called Indian New Deal is a sham; . . . that if they do not have the chance of making mistakes they cannot enjoy real responsibility.[32]

The point was well made and was a source of continuing discussion within the bureau during this period. But transferring fiscal responsibility to Indian tribes was not a matter of single administrative action. There were different kinds of Indian revenues, and each kind had a different set of controls established prior to the Indian New Deal.

A substantial part of the liquid assets of Indian tribes, commonly called tribal funds, in the form of annuities due from treaties, proceeds from the sale or leasing of tribal resources, and the like, were held in trust by the U.S. Treasury and could not be disbursed except by act of Congress. Except in certain cases those funds could not be appropriated without the consent of the tribe, but the tribal government likewise did not have access without the consent of Congress. The principle was established in federal law and buttressed by provisions in virtually all tribal constitutions.[33] During this period both the Department of the Interior and Congress were reluctant to use these trust funds, which had been badly depleted in the Depression years, thus reducing the total assets of the tribes. Between 1933 and 1945, a total of $17 million from tribal funds were included in bureau appropriations, or an average of $1.5 million per year. By contrast, the

Rhoads administration had drawn an equal amount in only four years.[34]

Congress had provided in 1916 and 1926 that tribal trust funds could be used for certain purposes without specific legislation. These purposes included expenditures for Indian education, insurance on tribal property, equalization of allotments, and per capita payments to individual tribal members, with the authorization at the discretion of the Department of the Interior.[35] The Reorganization Act made the per capita distribution of tribal assets subject to tribal consent, but that posed a serious problem to the bureau, since its basic policy was to discourage the dissipation of tribal moneys, which would undermine the intent of the tribal organization program. A large number of Indians, however, regarded per capita payments as their right in the desperate circumstances created by the Depression.

Demands for per capita distribution of tribal assets and income from leases of tribal property were particularly strong among the plains Indians. Their unrest was encouraged by Joseph Bruner's American Indian Federation, which for a time acquired a substantial number of dues-paying members by proposing to lobby for a congressional bill to "detribalize" the trust funds and guarantee each Indian three thousand dollars a year. Interior Secretary Ickes denounced Bruner's scheme as a "swindle" and the bureau attempted to convince the Indians that the notion was unrealistic and Bruner's group was simply bilking them of their money; but a subcommittee of the Senate Committee on Indian Affairs, now hostile to Collier, held hearings on the proposal in 1939. The bill never had a serious chance of passage, but it provided the senators with a forum before which they could summon Indians in order to discredit the Indian New Deal.[36]

Although this scheme came to naught, pressure remained strong on tribal councils to authorize per capita distributions of revenues throughout the 1930s. When the councils, on the recommendations of bureau advisers, refused to act on these demands or released only a small portion of the revenues in per capita payments, internal friction increased. Most of the $17 million in trust funds appropriated in the Collier era went for per capita payments, but it did not alleviate the feeling among some Indians that the New Deal had little to offer beyond new programs and more administrators, and it resulted in charges that the councils were hoarding funds to defray their own extravagant expenditures.[37]

The bureau took the position publicly that the councils were not misusing their revenues, but among themselves administrators expressed some concern that the councils were less than frugal when meeting their routine expenditures and in keeping accounts. For the most part, revenues for tribal operations came from tribal organization funds appropriated under the Wheeler-Howard Act, which were subject to administrative discretion, supplemented by revenues acquired by tribal taxes, licensing fees, and proceeds from leases, which were not. Although bureau control over these moneys was consequently less than complete, administrators felt it necessary to exercise some degree of management. In 1939, for example, after several bad experiences with tribal treasurers keeping inaccurate books or even misappropriating tribal revenues, Joe Jennings of the Indian Organization Division recommended that the bureau collect all revenues on behalf of the tribes and deposit them in individual money accounts to the credit of the tribes.[38]

One extravagance that the bureau sought to curb was the persistent desire of tribal council representatives to travel to Washington, D.C., to air their grievances or just generally look around. During the first years of the reorganization program Congress proved niggardly in appropriating funds for tribal organization, and Collier sought to hold down unnecessary expenditures by limiting those trips. Tribal council members or representatives of other organized groups who wrote to the commissioner proposing a meeting were often urged to work out their problems with local officials; where that solution was impossible, individual investigators like Cohen or Woehlke would go to the reservation.[39] Administrators discovered, however, that in some situations a timely trip to the head office would reduce local friction. During 1936 the Salish-Kootenai tribal council expressed misgivings over what they felt was a failure by the bureau to follow through on earlier promises of autonomy in managing tribal credit funds and similar matters. When the tribal council was brought to Washington, it met with various divisional heads and Collier himself, who explained the reasons for limitations on tribal control. Upon their return the council conveyed its finding to the Indians while the bureau worked with them on a plan to develop a tribal loan fund that would be more directly under their authority and would not be subject to the delays in the revolving credit fund.[40] In situations such as these the cooperation which resulted from direct communication more than made up for the expenses of travel. Furthermore, tribal council representatives were sometimes brought in to appear as witnesses before congressional hearings to refute the testimony of Indians hostile to the Collier program.

Another, and major, source of money for tribal use was the revolving credit fund established by the Reorganization Act. Like that of the tribal organization money, the disposition of loans in this fund was entirely in the hands of the bureau, and overall control of the credit fund was assigned not to the Indian Organization Division but to the Agricultural Extension Division of the bureau. According to Margold's interpretation of the act, the bureau could assess the applications of tribal corporations only in terms of the proposed use of the money, the tribe's capacity to repay the loan, and the conditions relating to advances. For the bureau to supervise the administration of the loan once the contract was in operation would be "a serious invasion of tribal responsibility and initiative" and an assumption of "political control of matters internal to the tribe."[41]

To administer the revolving fund, the Extension Division established a Credit Unit and drew up a set of general regulations for use by its agents in judging loan applications. Tribal corporations, once they had acquired money, established loan boards to supervise collections and routine processing. A critical Senate report in 1944 charged that in practice the regulations respecting loans had become so complex that only the most experienced credit agents understood them and that the tribal loan committees allowed agency employees of the bureau to serve on the committees and "do all the actual work." The report also maintained that the administrative expenses of the loan fund were excessive, and that the loans were too restrictive, being permitted only to "productive enterprises which . . . have every assurance of being able to reimburse the credit fund."[42] Collier took the report to task for distorting the record in relation to specific loans, but tacitly admitted that the administration of the credit fund did require more bureau supervision and greater cost than may have been intended initially, adding, "In view of the fact that Indian tribes have had little experience in lending and financing activities and require a good deal of assistance, this overhead is not out of proportion."[43]

The Credit Unit clearly exercised a good deal of caution in authorizing tribal loans from the revolving fund. This was necessary because Congress did not appropriate the full amount allowed under the Reorganization Act, so additional funds had to come out of repayments on earlier loans.[44] As of 1944, loan commitments of $5.5 million had been made to eighty-two tribal corporations and $3.4 million of that sum had been advanced. The two largest loans had been to the Northern Cheyenne tribe in Montana and the Mescalero Apache tribe in Arizona; together they had drawn 31 percent of the total loans under the Reorganization Act. Of the other eighty corporations, the average loan amounted to $30,000; over 63 percent of the loans went to individuals rather than corporations or cooperatives, and over 50 percent of all the loans were for sums of less than $1,000.[45]

The Collier administration laid great emphasis on the larger corporate programs like the Tongue River steer enterprise and the Mescalero housing project in discussing the accomplishments of the credit fund program, but it seems clear that the large volume of loans to individuals, totaling over $2.8 million, was equally significant. Most Indians had never had access to credit of any kind. Private lenders were reluctant to extend credit to them, and an earlier government loan fund, the Industry among Indians Fund, had experienced considerable difficulty in collections: in 1940, more than 50 percent of the total amount loaned since 1911 was still outstanding. The record of the reorganization fund was quite different: as of 1945, less than 1 percent of the loans were in default, and 95 percent were paid in full. The Indians had put their loans to productive use: over 50 percent of the loans were used to purchase livestock and another 16 percent for the purchase of machinery; 10 percent had been applied to home improvements, 8 percent for boats, and another 8 percent for seed and feed grains.[46] Through its administration of the revolving fund, the bureau could legitimately claim to have provided Indians with an opportunity they had never had before and of which they were able to take maximum advantage.

But only 8 percent of the adult male Indians in the United States had access to this credit. The high rate of repayment also implies a certain degree of conservatism in lending, with an emphasis on security. In this respect the reorganization credit program did not differ markedly from other New Deal lending programs such as the Farm Security Administration's tenant purchase loan fund.[47] By setting extremely rigorous standards for participation and requiring that the tribal government provide a full and detailed description of its proposed individual loan program (which in turn would conform to the standards of the Credit Unit's regulations), the bureau exercised a high degree of control over the administration of funds. This is not surprising, since Congress never appropriated the full amount allowed under the act, and hostile congressmen would have been quick to cut the fund still further if the number of delinquent and defaulted loans had been at all significant. But in setting these standards and carefully screening applications, the bureau substantially limited the extent to which tribal corporations managed their funds from this source.

Some tribal councils raised objections along these lines. The Salish-Kootenai confederated tribe, as we have seen, was among the most vociferous. The Indians at the Flathead Agency had been among the first to organize under the act for the express purpose of getting access to the credit fund. To ensure access they pledged their anticipated income from the leasing of the Polson dam and power site as security against a $65,000 loan. By 1936, however, the council and the Indians were irked by what they felt were delays by the credit agents in processing individual loan applications which they had approved, and by the implication that "the Government still [wanted] to treat them as incompetents."[48]

Following the tribal council's Washington visit in 1937, a plan was marked out whereby a portion of royalties from the leasing of the power site would be set aside to provide loans to individual tribesmen for the purchase of land, livestock, and machinery and these funds could be handled in a less restrictive manner than the Wheeler-Howard credit funds. A similar arrangement was made with the Blackfeet, who used revenues from the leasing of oil lands to establish a loan fund completely under tribal council control. Unfortunately, this kind of dual loan program was feasible only where the Indians had substantial revenues to which they had direct access, and few of the tribes possessed the resources to make such a plan worthwhile. Even the Blackfeet and Salish-Kootenais had to depend largely on the supplementary reorganization credit, and in 1944 the council spokesmen for both those tribes lodged complaints before Congress that there were too many delays in processing the loans, and that the Credit Unit did not allow the Indians to take the initiative in determining the qualifications of applicants and the amounts allowed to individual borrowers.[49]

Whatever the intentions of Collier and his associates in the bureau, they did not, in practice, promote the development of tribal self-determination in the crucial area of fiscal responsibility. In other areas, such as regulation of the use of tribal resources, determination of tribal membership, and the establishment of law codes, the bureau allowed and even encouraged Indian initiative, but always in the context of a system in which the federal administration retained the ultimate authority. Their reasons for exercising such caution in permitting Indian autonomy in the spirit suggested by the rhetoric of the Indian New Deal were generally based on legitimate considerations: the inexperience of Indians in managing their resources, the desperate economic situation of most Indians, and the danger that a few incidents of corruption or bad judgment on the part of Indian councils could discredit the entire program.

Their dilemma was real and should not be viewed simplistically. It would be easy to portray the Indian New Deal as a fraud in which puppet councils danced to the tune of hypocritical administrators mouthing worthless slogans about Indian self-government. But it is hard to accept the view that men like Collier, Cohen, Woehlke, Harper, Zimmerman, and all the others who labored to make the program operate effectively were simply arrogant megalomaniacs so enraptured by theories and visions of the future that they ignored the real needs and demands of the Indians they were supposed to serve. Certainly, Collier's combative instincts led him at times to dismiss all criticism as unjustified and sinister in intent. Fellow administrators often became exasperated by the carping of Indians and the indifference or hostility of Congress and the public, welcoming more pliant tribesmen as "cooperative" and dismissing opponents as self-serving or ignorant. At the same time, they were trying to lay the groundwork for genuinely independent Indian tribal communities. They were probably too conservative on vital issues of Indian autonomy and too willing to accept the status quo, which they had helped establish, as representing the fulfillment of the goals they had proclaimed, which it was not. But, psychologically as well as legally, the range of choices open to the reformers in the bureau was limited by their perception of immediate necessities and the haunting and all too justified fear that their work would be undone by those who followed them.

The inability of the Indians to achieve substantial self-determination under the Collier administration did not go unnoticed as the years passed, and supporters of the Indian New Deal cast about for explanations. One theory which acquired a certain amount of acceptance, particularly among anthropologists, was that the goals of Collier and the reformers had systematically been undermined by the old guard within the bureau, particularly the reservation superintendents, who were in a peculiarly strategic position to do so.

In 1944, H. S. Mekeel, former chief of the Applied Anthropology staff of the bureau, argued that since "those men appointed prior to 1934, which would include a majority of those in executive field positions, have been brought up to fulfill an entirely different policy, their resistance to the Reorganization Act was inevitable even though most . . . [were] loyally trying to readjust themselves to the new policy."[50] This view was also advanced by Clyde Kluckhohn and Robert Hackenberg in 1951:

[A] great deal of what . . . Collier and his associates planned in a sophisticated way in Washington was not put into effect because insufficient attention was paid to the two habitual ways of thinking . . . of the group out in the field. It was not that the Indian Service field representatives were irresponsible or insincere or unintelligent, by and large. It was simply that their own subculture screened the instruction they got from Washington and their appraisal of the local situation.[51]

In part these arguments reflect the bad relations that had developed between anthropologists and field agents during the implementation of reorganization; Mekeel, in particular, believed that the Applied Anthropology staff had been disbanded by Collier under pressure from the old guard in 1938. Collier's response to Mekeel was a vigorous defense of his bureau, including the pre-1934 field service, whose record under him had been "exemplary" and who had worked hard to improve Indian economic and health conditions.[52]

Evidence is abundant, however, that there was a deep gulf between the bureau leadership and the field force in their view of Indians and the purposes of the Reorganization Act. Vocal opposition to the Wheeler-Howard bill among field agents was apparently strong enough to induce Ickes to impose what critics called a gag rule on them in 1934. Even after reorganization was in operation, muted complaints continued, among not only field agents but also some of the staff and divisional officials. The Indian Rights Association, which maintained a constant barrage of criticism of the Collier administration in its journal, *Indian Truth*, for abandoning assimilation, received occasional letters of support from bureau staff, including Oscar H. Lipps and John Holst, as well as reservation officials. In 1937 a correspondent wrote to M. K. Sniffen, executive secretary of the Indian Rights Association, "During recent field trips I have had several Indian Service superintendents tell me how much they appreciate *Truth*. At several jurisdictions they pass the copy of *Truth* around to the heads of different departments so as to make sure that each one has a chance to read and ponder."[53]

All of this did not add up to a conspiracy to subvert the Indian New Deal, of course, and many superintendents, whatever their inner reservations, loyally supported bureau policy, writing laudatory reports on reorganization achievements for *Indians at Work*, the in-house journal established by Collier to counter the sort of influences that *Indian Truth* and other journals might have on bureau employees and the interested public.[54]

The gap between the Collier group and the field force was nevertheless real. Some agents not only took an authoritarian and patronizing view toward the Indians but expressed their view openly to bureau leaders with no self-consciousness. The superintendent at the Cheyenne River Agency blandly announced his intention, in 1934, to hand-pick a committee to draw up a tribal constitution, since an electoral process would result in the choice of "reactionary Indians who are incompetent." He promised to select "level-headed" men who "are not anxious for too much authority."[55] Another agent objected to the concept of tribal corporations handling Indian resources, asserting, "We would be optimistic indeed to expect any of the Indians . . . with their limited business experience, to develop and maintain an enterprise with success, even with the assistance of a government loan," and recommended instead leasing the resources to a local firm, the traditional practice.[56] Generally, local officials with these attitudes were more circumspect in making them known to the Washington office, but reports of highhanded actions by local officials flowed into the Indian Organization office during the early years of tribal organization.

Misconceptions about the Indian reorganization program were not restricted to authoritarian remnants of the old guard, however; even the more conscientious local officials did not fully assimilate the new orientation toward Indians that Collier wished to encourage. The experience of William O. Roberts provides an example of this problem. Roberts, who was superintendent at the Rosebud Agency before 1933 and was later transferred to the neighboring Pine Ridge Agency, was one of the most energetic and creative of the agents in the Sioux country. He had encouraged the development of local community organizations (*tiospaye*) even before the advent of Collier's administration, and continued to promote a community involvement approach to economic development that culminated in the establishment of the Red Shirt Table Development Association at Pine Ridge, widely regarded in the bureau as a model for coordinated planning at the local level. Unlike other agents, who treated reorganization as simply another routine administrative task, Roberts was interested and involved from the outset, sending in a stream of recommendations to the Organization Division in Washington. Roberts was highly praised by Mekeel, Reifel, and other bureau staff representatives who worked with him during the early years of the Indian New Deal.[57]

But from the moment he came to Pine Ridge in 1936 Roberts was embroiled in a running battle with the tribal council, which was dominated by two mixed-bloods, Frank Wilson and George Pugh, who also had political contacts outside the reservation. Disputes arose over the range of council authority in the areas of hiring employees, the administration of relief funds, and the leasing of reserved lands. In these matters the bureau generally sided with Roberts and urged Wilson to "sit down and discuss problems" with him rather than complaining publicly. When Wilson resigned in 1937, relations between the agent and the council became less heated, but in the meantime Roberts had further alienated the mixed-bloods at Pine Ridge by openly soliciting the support of the full-bloods in an effort to get a tribal charter ratified, working with, in Wilson's words, "known reactionary factions on the reservation" (meaning the treaty chiefs).[58]

During the next few years tensions relaxed somewhat, but when Congress reduced and eventually stopped relief funds after 1940, Roberts became the target of new complaints, the dispute culminating in a series of vetoes and a deadlocked struggle with the tribal council in 1945. A Pine Ridge Indian wrote to the National Congress of American Indians later that during Roberts's years at the agency, he had managed to alienate the full-blood conservatives and the mixed-blood majority which had originally supported reorganization, as well as the tribal council, which had the support of only 25 percent of the Indians at this point. Roberts, distracted by the protracted illness of his wife, reacted with increasing bitterness toward the Indians.[59]

The bureau sent D'Arcy McNickle to investigate the situation. McNickle was sympathetic to Roberts's situation, noting that "the Sioux are a vigorous people and left with time on their hands . . . will make trouble for themselves and for every one around them." He also praised Roberts's "accomplishment with respect to the intelligent use of Indian resources." But he went on to discuss what he regarded as a crucial weakness of the agent's approach to the tribal council:

> He has never fully understood or been in sympathy with the idea of self-government for the Sioux people . . . [although] in a vague way he thinks that he believes in tribal government. The secret is that he has not in any way coordinated his work with the council; he has offered it no leadership in any direct or indirect way; he has not helped it to find jobs for itself.[60]

The situation at Pine Ridge was in some respects the result of circumstances beyond the control of any administrator; in particular the cutting of emergency relief funds had raised animosities which were naturally turned against the resident representative of the federal government. Still, McNickle's assessment is significant, for it was this kind of inability by local agents to grasp the idea that Indians should be allowed to assume responsibilities in administration that posed a greater obstacle to reorganization than the open animosity or quiet subversion of the old guard in the bureau. As Ben Reifel stated in 1939, "The biggest task . . . is to get the agency personnel to look upon the I.R.A., the constitutions and charters and resolutions and ordinances under them as being as much a part of the procedures that govern their administration as the regulations of the Indian Office and . . . other laws of Congress."[61]

Roberts's case was unusual in that he was an exceptionally conscientious administrator in the conventional sense. Reports of a similar breakdown in communications between local agents and tribal councils were submitted constantly by bureau observers during the early years of the reorganization program. With obvious relief one such report noted the work of a Montana agent: "This is the first time in my experience that a superintendent has actually demonstrated the desire to take the council, and the Indians on the reservation, into his confidence to the extent of advising them as to what is really being done on the reservation, and why."[62] Even this open-minded approach fell short of actual encouragement of Indian initiative in making policy for the reservation.

While the local officials may have had difficulty in determining a role for tribal councils in the management of reservation affairs, the councils themselves frequently advanced their own notions of what their functions ought to be. We have noted earlier the complaints of councils, even those considered cooperative by the bureau, that they were not being allowed enough responsibility in managing loans and tribal land assignments, levying taxes and licensing fees, and participating with federal technical advisers in planning the long-range development of reservation resources. In the latter area, A. G. Harper, coordinator for the TC-BIA program, found that the technical staffs of the bureau and the Soil Conservation Service habitually gave low priority to economic projects that would encourage Indian participation, preferring instead to draw up more orthodox and ambitious plans in which the Indians would play no part.[63]

A problem of particular difficulty involved the power of tribal councils in the appointment and dismissal or transfer of reservation employees, including superintendents. The Stephens bill of 1912 had envisioned this power as essential to any policy promoting genuine Indian autonomy. The original draft of the Reorganization Act had included a provision allowing the tribal government "to compel the transfer . . . of any persons employed in the administration of Indian Affairs," subject to conditions laid down by the commissioner to protect the rights of employees, and in hearings on the bill Collier asserted that this power was fundamental, "otherwise the whole thing is [a] fraud."[64] The provision was eliminated from the final draft of the legislation, but in fact the secretary of the interior had the power under the General Indian Act of 1834 to give to the tribes "the direction of . . . persons engaged for them" by the federal government. That power had been upheld by federal courts although it was rarely exercised.[65]

This provision had been introduced to the Indians by Collier during his tour of the reservations in March 1934 as an inducement for their support of the reorganization bill, and many Indians believed that it was part of the act. Some of the tribal constitutions included provisions authorizing the tribal council to make recommendations concerning the appointment and removal of reservation employees. But Indian expectations went further: councils wanted to replace white employees at the agencies with trained members of their tribes, and that had certainly been an underlying aim of the educational support provisions of the Wheeler-Howard Act. By the 1940s several of the councils were proposing to emulate the example of the Crows of Montana, who in 1933 had chosen one of their own leaders, Robert Yellowtail, to be agency superintendent.[66]

These various demands by tribal councils posed a dilemma for bureau leaders because of their desire to decentralize the administrative system, which would necessarily involve relying on the local officials. In 1936 the general issue of council-agent relations was brought to a head by the attempts of certain councils to by-pass the superintendents in filing complaints about agency conditions and by the action of the Cheyenne River council, which was summoning local bureau employees and subjecting them to a "roasting," in the words of Ben Reifel.

In a meeting of the commissioner and division heads, Extension director A. C. Cooley complained that the actions of those councils were demoralizing employees and that the position of the superintendents was being undermined. Collier agreed, and linked the developments to the decentralization issue, stating, "The superintendents' prestige and responsibility for the . . . program is not to be broken down but rather to be built up. . . . We must think of our superintendents as the representative of the entire Indian Organization. Things coming here from the council should come through the superintendent and Washington should not have independent dealings with the tribal councils."[67] On the matter of councils summoning employees for investigation, it was agreed that a procedure should be set up under which all complaints about employees should go first to the superintendent, and only then to a special committee rather than to the whole tribal council.[68]

This policy was adhered to in most cases thereafter and the powers sought by the councils were effectively limited by administrative decision. The handling of local employees was left to the reservation agent, and only in circumstances of chronic abuse of power, clearly determined by an investigation by the Organization Division, were superintendents removed or transferred.

7

THE ECONOMICS OF THE
INDIAN NEW DEAL

Most of the limitations of the tribal organization program were linked directly to the economic aspects of Collier's policies. Indian economic problems were complex and serious. In this respect Indians differed little from other Americans in the dark years of the Depression. But their problems were more deep-rooted, the result of generations of exploitation and sometimes well-meaning but disastrous government policies. The mere return of general prosperity would do little to alleviate their situation.

Ironically, the Depression itself did not affect Indians as harshly as it did other Americans. Only a relatively small number of Indians were involved in the commercial economy, and while they suffered, like the Red Lake Chippewa and Menominee tribes, whose mill operations were reduced by the business slump, other Indians already at subsistence level or on relief remained much as before, poor and demoralized. The reforms in health and educational services initiated by Rhoads improved the situation of some Indians, while New Deal projects like the Indian Emergency Conservation Works helped Indians by providing jobs where none had existed before.

Of far graver significance to Indians in the Depression years was the collapse of agricultural prices and the rapid deterioration of the lands of the Great Plains and Southwest. These were problems that had emerged long before 1929, but conditions reached a crisis point in the first years of the Collier administration when blizzards and drought severely damaged western lands and decimated livestock herds. White farmers and range users who had leased Indian allotments and tribal grazing lands departed, so many allottees who had subsisted on their rental income were forced on relief. This situation was particularly noticeable on the checkerboarded reservations of the Northern Plains.

In the Southwest a crisis of a different sort developed. During the 1920s the Navajos, Pueblos, and other tribes of that region had been encouraged to increase their sheep and cattle herds, and the carrying capacity of their range was approaching, indeed surpassing, the saturation point, a situation aggravated by the erosion of their grazing lands.

The Indian Reorganization Act was originally intended to deal primarily with the first crisis, by promoting the consolidation of Indian lands under tribal ownership on the allotted reservations, to be operated cooperatively. This program resembled the subsistence homesteads projects established in the Interior Department and later consolidated under the Resettlement Administration, an agency with which Collier maintained close and fruitful relations.[1]

The Collier administration soon recognized the second problem and, after several years of piecemeal efforts at range control, inaugurated a planning program in conjunction with the Soil Conservation Service, the TC-BIA surveys. Eventually the bureau sought to integrate measures to salvage Indian resources into regional development programs, most notably in the Rio Grande area, where an interdepartmental planning board was established. This movement from individual agency-level efforts to coordinated regional operations reflected a broader trend among New Deal agencies responsible for rural economic reconstruction which culminated in the Land Use Planning program of 1938–42, an ambitious though short-lived attempt to integrate social and economic development measures on a regional basis and to promote the participation of local communities in planning the use of their resources. Ultimately the onset of war and growing congressional conservatism doomed this wide-ranging effort as well as Collier's Indian program.[2]

The land reconsolidation program was only partially successful, hampered by the suspicions of allottees and legal restrictions on the powers of tribal organizations. More than two million acres were added to the Indian land base, largely in the form of transfers of land from the public domain, and some tribes, like the Northern Cheyennes, took advantage of the opportunity to operate their lands on a cooperative basis to increase general tribal prosperity. But the problem of checkerboarding of allotted reservations remained unresolved, as did the bewildering issue of control of heirship lands.[3] At the same time, the loan fund initiated under the Wheeler-Howard Act provided credit to thousands of Indians who used it wisely and productively to improve their individual situations.

In the Southwest, herd reduction was executed with considerable success and range conditions were improved. During this period grazing acreage for Indians increased through land transfers and purchases while the range used by non-Indians was decreasing.[4] Establishing long-term range control and development proved more elusive. The TC-BIA surveys (which focused on general resource use and potential as well as rangelands) were completed for fifty reservations between 1937 and 1941, but the recommendations of the survey reports were not systematically implemented. The whole project came to a halt as the war channeled funds away from the Indian Bureau and associated domestic programs. The momentum for a general coordinated Indian economic program slowed after 1941, although specific reservation operations were developed. At the Navajo Agency, Allan Harper, former head of TC-BIA, worked through the 1940s to improve communications between the Indians and the agency bureaucracy in promoting plans for the use of Navajo resources and the income from leases on oil lands.[5]

Congressional niggardliness, legal restrictions on administrative action, and the coming of World War II all had a marked impact on the progress of the economic program of the Indian New Deal, as Collier's defenders have pointed out. At the same time the failure of the bureau to develop strong, independent tribal organizations with widespread community support ultimately undermined the economic as well as political reforms of the Collier era. Collier himself pointed out in his 1934 annual report, "The efforts at economic rehabilitation cannot and will not be more than partially successful unless they are accompanied by a determined simultaneous effort to rebuild the shattered morale of a subjugated people."[6] The effort was made, but the determination to strengthen Indian community control was continually at odds with the desire to improve Indian economic conditions before the inevitable day when an administration hostile to the Collier policies (and from the viewpoint of bureau leaders therefore hostile to the Indians themselves) took control in Washington.

If indeed there was, as Collier optimistically proclaimed, "a great spiritual stirring" among Indians in 1935 in the wake of the Wheeler-Howard Act, it did not last. Full-blood Indians with allotments soon concluded that tribal organization was for "school-children" (tribesmen who had attended boarding schools and shed their Indian views) and not for them, and refused to cooperate; mixed-bloods interested in building up tribal councils discovered that their opportunities for exercising real power were limited and left those institutions in the hands of the politically ambitious minority. Lacking the respect or even the interest of most Indians, the councils could not induce them to accept voluntarily the economic policies recommended by the bureau; and when the federal money and corps of advisers began to diminish, the councils could not sustain or regenerate Indian support.[7]

An essential element in the original draft of the Indian reorganization bill was the regrouping of scattered allotted and kinship lands into usable units, primarily for grazing under tribal control. This was to be accomplished by provisions for the automatic transfer of title to kinship lands to the tribal corporations, with heirs receiving shares in the corporation instead of otherwise useless parcels of land. Lands held in trust for the original allottee could be purchased by the tribe or relinquished by the allottee in exchange for shares in the corporation or for lands of equivalent size and value, called exchange allotments, within the consolidated tribal land units. In addition, the secretary of the interior would be allowed to purchase privately owned allotments or lands owned by whites on the reservations where these lands were determined to be necessary for a viable tribal land consolidation program.[8]

The bureau in its memorandum in support of the bill maintained that it would not disturb any "vested right" in private property of allottees and would guarantee "to allottees and their heirs every equity which they now possess." By extension, the implicit powers of eminent domain would not be used arbitrarily against non-Indian landowners on the reservations. Still, it was clear that the government would exercise its authority under this proposed act where it was deemed necessary for tribal economic recovery.

Naturally, the implications of these provisions troubled western congressmen and those who suspected Collier of planning "socialistic or communistic" experiments on the Indian reservations. Collier sought to quiet such suspicions by comparing the bill to the Taylor Grazing Act, which authorized the establishment of large grazing units on western public lands under the control of stockmen's associations. "The Taylor bill is . . . occasioned by the breaking up of the public domain through homesteading so that erosion is washing it away," he argued. "We have an analogous condition on the Indian reservations."[9]

Nevertheless, the congressional revisions of the Wheeler-Howard Act eliminated or limited the powers of the Interior Department and tribal corporations over kinship and allotted lands and adjoining non-Indian lands. The secretary of the interior could purchase surplus lands for Indian use from the remaining public domain, but the purchase of non-Indian lands, a key element in any land reconsolidation program on the checkerboarded reservations of the Northern Plains, was not mentioned. Allottees and heirs could exchange their lands for shares or exchange allotments, but only on an entirely voluntary basis.

Despite these disappointments, the bureau labored manfully to persuade allottees to relinquish their land voluntarily for exchange allotments. Most of the constitutions provided for the mechanics of exchanges and Indians were encouraged to use them. Money from the revolving credit fund was made available to tribal corporations for land purchases and was used extensively by several tribes, including the Blackfeet, Cheyenne River Sioux, and Paiutes in Idaho. In at least one case, that of the Jicarilla Apaches, the entire tribe proposed to transfer all allotments to tribal ownership without requiring exchange allotments, only shares in the corporation. That this was a rare situation was indicated by Allan Harper's comment, "I wish more tribes saw the wisdom of such a course, instead of insisting on specific assignments of land in exchange for allotted land."[10]

Even the use of exchange allotments was limited. Of the 2,755,019 acres added to the Indian land base between 1934 and 1940, only 20 percent was purchased by tribal corporations or exchanged. Almost half of the land added, over one million acres, was drawn by the secretary of the interior from the public domain, and 43 percent of that land was in Arizona and Nevada rather than in the region where allotment had been most extensive, largely because the public domain was considerably diminished in the Northern Plains. An additional 211,959 acres came from surplus reservation lands, which were now closed to homestead entry, and the Resettlement Administration purchased some 900,000 acres for Indians between 1936 and 1940 under its sub-marginal land purchase program.[11] At a conference with representatives from agencies of the Department of Agriculture in August 1938 to discuss Indian land problems, bureau spokesmen admitted that "precious little had been accomplished in either arresting the creeping paralysis of the fractionating land process in Indian inheritance or in bringing about the consolidation of the scattered parcels in useable units."[12]

The problem of management of heirship lands was the subject of much grumbling in annual reports by bureau staff, who singled it out as an administrative inconvenience as well as a formidable obstacle to land consolidation. The settlement of inheritance of sometimes ludicrously small pieces of allotted land was reported to take up to 40 percent of the office time of bureau divisions in Washington, and cases in which the cost of administering these parcels far exceeded their value were not unusual. Most of these lands were leased and the proceeds had to be subdivided among numerous heirs in paltry amounts, sometimes amounting to less than a penny a year. The National Resources Board survey of sixteen Northern Plains reservations in 1936 found that almost a quarter of the heirship lands lay idle.[13] Without the consent of all the heirs, some of whom did not live on the reservation, the lands could not be transferred to tribal management. Even tribal purchase was limited by the sheer bulk of lands in question. More than 7 million acres of Indian land were in heirship status in 1937 and another 17.5 million acres were held by the original allottees but due eventually to pass on to heirs. If the Indian tribes could acquire control of these 25 million acres, they would have the basis for productive self-support, according to the National Resources Board, but the cost at existing purchase prices would exceed $100 million.[14] Indian tribes acquired only one-tenth of their total land needs during the New Deal.

Bureau leaders like Collier and Harper lamented the limitations of the Wheeler-Howard Act but do not appear to have discerned the link between the political program of tribal organization and the economic objectives they sought. Tribal councils dominated by mixed-blood minorities, unrelated to existing Indian communities and restricted by bureau policy in areas where they had popular support, could not summon forth the energies of their people or persuade full-blood allottees and their heirs to pool their resources in an effort to improve their conditions on a collective basis. Certainly that was not wholly the fault of Collier and his aides who believed Indians had a tradition of communal welfare which could be restored. Some allottees had imbibed wholeheartedly the Anglo-American notions of individual proprietorship, and others simply distrusted any policy introduced by white officials. The defects of the tribal organization program, however, precluded the possibility of any widespread movement for voluntary action by Indians to support and participate in the development of their resources on a shared basis.

More than three-quarters of Indian reservation lands were estimated to be suited primarily for grazing, and livestock ranching of one sort or another was a far more logical transition for formerly nomadic Indian groups than the dry farming of small allotments. During the early years of the twentieth century, Indians on a number of plains reservations had been encouraged to go into the livestock business. In the Northern Plains this approach was successful so long as the allotments were held in trust and land was grazed communally, but by the end of World War I the tribal herds in that area had for the most part been broken up and sold off. Generally, the lands allotted continued to be used for grazing, but were leased now to white stockmen, and that situation persisted through the New Deal period on the Sioux reservations despite efforts by the bureau to promote Indian livestock operations. On a few other reservations, notably the Northern Cheyenne in Montana, successful tribal cattle herds were developed. The problem for most of these tribes was that there was not enough grazing land under tribal ownership to make cooperative ranching profitable, allottees were reluctant to exchange or sell their lands to the tribe, and white ranchers leasing Indian allotments resisted displacement from the grazing lands.[15]

Despite these obstacles the bureau did succeed in increasing Indian ownership of livestock through the promotion of cooperatives drawing on the revolving credit fund and relying on Indians to manage the herds, a break with bureau tradition, in which any tribally owned herds were handled by white stockmen. Land purchases authorized under the Wheeler-Howard Act and the transfer of leases from white to Indian use increased Indian grazing acreage by 15 percent between 1936 and 1940. Approximately

$900,000 was drawn from the revolving fund to purchase new breeding stock. By 1940 about 40 percent of the livestock on Indian lands was owned by Indians, largely through their 150 cooperative associations. The number of cattle, sheep, and horses grazed on the Indian range in 1941 was more than double what it had been only five years earlier, and the average value per head had increased by $6.50.[16]

While the rebuilding of tribal herds in the Northern Plains constituted a major accomplishment of the Indian New Deal, the bureau faced a strikingly different problem on the reservations of the Southwest. Here, and particularly on the Navajo Reservation, sheep and cattle herds had been encouraged—apparently in the expectation that the Indians were a disappearing race, since the land base had not increased after 1900. The result was severe overgrazing of the range, noticeable as early as 1910 and reaching a state of crisis two decades later.

The situation for the Navajos was the most critical. Various surveys by the bureau had indicated the extent of overgrazing during the 1920s, and in 1928 the Navajo council had passed a resolution charging grazing fees on herds of over 1,000 head in a futile effort to induce larger stockmen to reduce their herds. In 1930 a full-scale survey report was prepared by the bureau's Forestry Division which delineated the problem in detail: all of the agencies of the reservation had too many animals for the existing forage acreage; the worst were the Southern Navajo Agency, with over 73,000 surplus head, and the Northern Navajo, with over 32,000 surplus head. Most of the livestock held by the Navajos consisted of sheep and goats, both of which were extremely destructive of the range in their foraging habits. With the decline in prices for livestock in the 1920s, the Navajos had not sold their surplus animals as they might have done in normal conditions, and so the herds continued to breed and use up the eroded range. The report concluded that the range carried an excess of more than 500,000 head.[17]

The Navajos themselves did not see herd reduction as the obvious solution to their problem. While there were a few large herders among the forty thousand Indians on the reservation, the majority owned only a small number of sheep, goats, and horses and the loss of these, from their point of view, would mean their impoverishment, since their herds provided food and clothing as well as cash when necessary. The logical move for the government

so far as the Navajos were concerned was to expand their reservation, particularly in the eastern section, to replace land losses
resulting from allotment, and to irrigate more of the rangelands
during the dry seasons. This was the argument that Indian spokesmen brought before the Senate Committee on Indian Affairs when
it visited the Navajo country in 1931, and it continued to be their
refrain during the Collier years.[18]

During the winter of 1932 blizzards destroyed over 150,000
Navajo sheep, easing the situation somewhat, although goats were
considered a greater problem. Collier, apparently unaware of the
extent of overgrazing, instituted measures to replace the losses
early in 1933. Later in the year he reversed his position and proposed a full-scale stock reduction program for the Navajos. Herds
were to be reduced by 400,000 head of both sheep and goats, the
program to be implemented by the Soil Erosion Service of the
Department of the Interior. Losses in income resulting from the
reduction would be replaced by wage work until the range situation was stabilized.[19]

In October 1933, Collier presented this plan to the Navajo
council. He was eager to get the program started, since the Federal
Emergency Relief Agency had funds available to purchase the
stock, but the council balked, agreeing in the end to accept
reduction but leaving the mechanics of the operation to the local
jurisdictions. The plan was first tried in the western district, which
was scheduled to lose about 15,000 head. The large herders, however, refused to cooperate with any reduction program that would
require them to make greater sacrifices than their less fortunate
neighbors. As a compromise, the bureau arranged for an across-
the-board reduction of all the herds, regardless of size, rather than
reduction on a sliding scale as originally intended under Collier's
guidelines. The result, as had been predicted by Chee Dodge at the
October 1933 council, was that the larger herders culled their
herds of the less productive (nonbreeding) stock while smaller
herders experienced major losses of essential animals.[20]

The blatant inequality of the first stock reduction effort was
not its only fault. Most of the discussion between the bureau and
the Indians on the issue had taken place in the tribal council
meetings. The Navajos as a whole were not apprised of the necessity for the program; some outlying settlements were not even
aware that a tribal council existed or that it had any power over
them. Furthermore, the substitution of wages for livestock was

not a satisfactory alternative from the Indian point of view. "Livestock, not money, is their measure of wealth," one observer noted. These people were not part of a commercial economy to any great degree and regarded their herds as part of their social status. Most of the actual work of herding was traditionally done by Navajo women, and they were particularly resentful of the arbitrary diminution of their herds. The tribal council, which had no previous standing among the Navajos, became the target of their resentment and the focus of their complaints.[21]

At this unhappy juncture, the bureau introduced the tribal organization program. A tribal council meeting with Collier in March 1934 was set up to discuss the matter, but most of the discussion centered instead on stock reduction. Collier and his aides employed a combination of compliments and veiled threats to persuade the council to accept an additional reduction of 150,000 head (mostly goats) for the following year. Robert Marshall of the Forestry Division described the Navajo council (which Collier earlier that year had portrayed to Congress as a puppet government) as "truly representative . . . when it speaks, it is the voice of the tribe." In response to a question from a councilman, Collier asserted that the bureau had the authority to undertake stock reduction without consulting the Indians, but added, "We think . . . the Tribe itself should decide and act" on it. He also noted that the existing council could be dissolved at any time by the bureau, but that the Reorganization Act would ensure permanency to the tribal government.[22] Meanwhile, J. H. Stewart of the Land Division countered demands for a reservation boundary extension with the argument that the bureau could not support such demands unless stock reduction was continued. Under this kind of pressure the council agreed to continue stock reduction, but only after full discussion with their constituents and with a resolution that smaller herds would not be affected.[23]

The second effort was even more badly botched than the first had been. Less than a month after the March meeting, at which the council had been assured that the 150,000 head figure would be sufficient, Stewart reappeared to demand an additional 50,000 head reduction, mostly in sheep. The new program initiated in the fall of 1934 has been vividly described by David Aberle:

Agents in some areas put heavy pressure on . . . small owners to sell. It proved impossible to deliver all the goats to the railhead. So some were slaughtered and the meat given back to the Navajos; others were shot and left to rot; still others were shot and partly cremated with gasoline. . . . To the Navajos this waste was appalling and the attitude toward their valued resources was incomprehensible.[24]

After this debacle, stock reduction lost whatever degree of "voluntary" acceptance it might have previously aroused. In 1934 the Federal Emergency Relief Agency provided funds for further purchases, but the council took no action and only some 30,000 head were sold. In June of that year the referendum on the Wheeler-Howard Act was held and the Navajos rejected it, though by a close vote. The strongest opposition came from the northern and southern districts, which had been most affected by stock reduction, and the eastern district, which reacted against the delay of the boundary extension bill in Congress as well as stock reduction. In a singularly ill-conceived gesture, Collier sent a public letter to the Navajos through their superintendent, criticizing them for not ratifying the act and informing them that their action would have no effect on the stock reduction program. This proved to be indeed the case, and in 1936 the tribal council was completely overhauled to make it "representative." Subsequently, the reorganized council was taken over by a faction led by Jacob Morgan, a long-time critic of the Collier administration and the Wheeler-Howard Act.[25]

The stock reduction issue was not the only factor involved in the defeat of Indian reorganization among the Navajos, but it was symptomatic of the general deterioration of relations between the bureau and the Indians. Oliver La Farge observed, shortly after the referendum, that there was "complete confusion in the Indian mind due to treating soil erosion, stock reduction, the boundary bills and the reorganization bills and act all together. . . . Too many things have been happening on the reservation, and they are all linked in the Navajo mind. Like it or not, this was a vote of non-confidence in the present administration."[26]

Collier later admitted that errors had been made in handling the Navajo stock reduction problem but defended his reliance on the council in implementing the program rather than acting directly on his own authority. He also asserted that the experience proved a signal lesson both to him and to Hugh Bennett of the Soil Erosion Service of the need for extensive consultation with and participation by local people in any conservation program.[27] Certainly the stock reduction program was necessary, but the immediate result of the way in which it was carried out was the impoverishment of many Indians, their reduction to the status of wage earners, a fate distasteful to them, and the general disillusionment and demoralization of the Navajos. The participation of the tribal council did not in any way alleviate these developments, and the council could hardly be said to have been given a role in the process beyond that of carrier of the bad news to its constituents. With this as an example of democratic participation in administration, the Indians were understandably wary of further ventures with bureau-sponsored versions of self-government. When the Collier administration proceeded to reorganize the tribal council to make it conform more closely to the governments established under the Wheeler-Howard Act, the Navajos elected a new council which reflected all the grievances of the preceding five years.

Defenders of Collier, and Collier himself, have tended to treat the problems of the bureau and the Navajos as the result of a unique conjunction of unfortunate circumstances, but there were certain features of the situation that were not so unique: the emphasis on immediate action in the economic sphere, the use of the tribal council as a vehicle for approval of policies already determined by administrators, the failure to develop communications with the local communities—all these were characteristic of the economic programs under the Reorganization Act, as we have seen. Again, the administrators felt they had to act quickly to meet an emergency situation, and the council, which they believed to be representative "of the feudal Navajo sheep owners" rather than the tribe as a whole, did not appear prepared to produce any realistic or positive alternatives to the bureau's own initiatives.[28] But these considerations do not alter the fact that stock reduction was not the product of full and fair consultation between Indians and administrators. As one disgruntled Navajo put it: "We elected the council, but they couldn't do anything and we think they are just put in to try to get us to listen to Collier."[29]

The Collier administration did apply the lessons learned from the Navajo experience to stock reduction among other Indian groups, notably the western Pueblos. In 1935 the bureau initiated sheep reduction at Laguna and Acoma pueblos, meeting with village councils to devise equitable methods for culling the stock over a five-year period and implementing a program of soil conservation. Initially this program was to operate in conjunction with

a range purchase program drawing on funds from the Soil Conservation Service; when Congress failed to appropriate sufficient
funds for the purpose, Collier turned to the Resettlement Administration, which provided funds through its submarginal land
purchase program. Pueblo stock reduction was not without its
shortcomings; the Laguna council in 1941 complained that the
program was impoverishing them, having depleted half of their
herds, and that land purchases had been insufficient to increase
the range capacity. Nevertheless, on the whole the program
worked well and there was little friction.[30]

The haphazard experiments with range control in the Southwest
highlighted the need for a more systematic, planned approach to
Indian resource management which became the focus of bureau
economic policy in the period from 1936 to 1940, culminating
in the TC-BIA surveys and the Rio Grande watershed project. The
Meriam Report in 1928 had proposed the establishment of a planning division within the bureau, but that idea had been sidetracked
by the emergency conditions prevailing during the Rhoads administration and the initial period of Collier's tenure.

In January 1934, Ward Shepard, Collier's "special advisor on
land use matters," outlined a proposal for the establishment
of an Indian Land Planning Unit which would initiate surveys of
the resources of all Indian reservations and oversee the transfer
of national forest and other public lands to Indian use as well as
a submarginal land purchase program. Shepard anticipated that
this division would ultimately broaden its range of responsibilities
to embrace all facets of Indian affairs and would enlist the aid of
universities and foundations in research and planning activities.[31]
His proposal, which would have realized the goals of the Meriam
Report, did lead to the establishment of a Land Division, but the
ambitious aim for a wide-ranging planning organization was never
reached. Other divisions guarded their autonomy closely and
Collier sought to achieve coordinated economic programs through
joint ventures with other federal agencies.

We have already noted some of these cooperative ventures:
the Indian Emergency Conservation Work program, which was
officially part of the Civilian Conservation Corps but operated
relatively independently; the various land purchase programs that
drew upon funds supplied through the Federal Emergency Relief
Agency and, after 1936, the Resettlement Administration; and,
most important, the various programs carried out with the Soil

Conservation Service, of which Navajo stock reduction was an example.[32] The bureau also continued cooperative efforts, initiated under Rhoads, with the Public Health Service and the Bureau of Animal Industry, and included the Bureau of American Ethnology of the Smithsonian Institution in its experiment with an Applied Anthropology Unit.

One of the most beneficial of these joint ventures, from a financial point of view, was the submarginal purchase program carried out by the bureau with the Resettlement Administration (later the Farm Security Administration) between 1934 and 1940. During that period, more than 900,000 acres were purchased for Indian use at a cost of $2.4 million. The magnitude of this contribution to Indian land recovery can be recognized when it is compared with the land purchase program authorized by the Wheeler-Howard Act during the same period: 300,000 acres purchased at a cost of $3.5 million.[33] A congressional report criticized the practice of making submarginal land purchases (which included those made with Resettlement Administration funds and those authorized by specific congressional appropriations) as "not adapted to Indian use. It merely adds to the acreage they have." But Collier's rebuttal asserted that in none of the cases cited by the committee was the land in fact lying idle, and that much of it had been restored to use as pasture and grazing land.[34] He refrained in this instance from pointing out that one of the main reasons the bureau relied upon the submarginal land purchase program was that Congress had reduced appropriations for the Wheeler-Howard land purchase fund by more than 50 percent after 1937, and that by 1940 the total amount authorized represented little more than one-seventh the $2 million per year allowed under the act. The Resettlement Administration had its own appropriation battles to fight but its funds were not subject to the scrutiny of the Indian Affairs Committees of Congress.

Cooperative programs with the Soil Conservation Service (SCS) also operated with funds provided through the Department of Agriculture (to which the SCS had been transferred in 1935). To a greater extent than was the case with the Resettlement Administration, the bureau endeavored to integrate administratively with the SCS in their joint ventures.

Not surprisingly, cooperation did not always go smoothly and a considerable amount of energy was expended in resolving interagency disputes and working out lines of division between administrators. A portent of these difficulties emerged during the Navajo stock reduction program in 1935. The Indians were not alone in regarding herd reduction as unnecessary and badly managed. The first superintendent of the Central Agency, C. E. Faris, reached that conclusion by the end of 1934 and was reported to have "communicated his opinions down the line to the staff."[35] Meanwhile, the Indians, with the tacit approval of local officials, were agitating for the removal of all SCS agents from the reservation. The SCS, for its part, objected to the fact that it had no authority over land management, that being under the control of the superintendent, and unveiled a plan for the joint responsibility of the bureau and the SCS for a wide range of reservation affairs.[36] The problem was not resolved until Faris was replaced in 1935 by E. R. Fryer, who was amenable to stock reduction and the SCS.

The Navajo experience indicated to the heads of the bureau and the SCS the need for more forethought in devising economic programs for Indians and better procedures for interagency collaboration. Their contemplation of these matters eventuated in the establishment of the Technical Cooperation–Bureau of Indian Affairs (TC-BIA) project in December 1935. The purpose of TC-BIA, according to Woehlke, who was appointed coordinator for the project, was "the production of land utilization plans . . . on Indian reservations . . . to outline the best possible use of the reservation's resources, a use which will bring the human carrying capacity of the reservation to its maximum with complete conservation of the reservation's soil resources and with maintenance of an adequate standard of living."[37]

Basically, TC-BIA was to survey resources and draw up proposals whose recommendations would presumably be incorporated into joint SCS-BIA programs for Indian economic reconstruction. Woehlke also proposed to extend the Collier philosophy to the planning process, as he explained to Hugh Bennett of the SCS:

The most perfect technical land utilization and soil conservation plan will remain a dead letter unless the inhabitants of the area for which the plan is made can and will apply it. In almost every instance the technically perfect plan must be modified so as to make possible its application and execution by the inhabitants of the area. . . . In order to make such plans functionally effective they must be sold to the affected population, must be built into its consciousness until they become an integral part of its daily life.[38]

The surveys were initially undertaken in the Southwest on the

Papago, Hualapai, and Pima reservations in Arizona. The survey
was divided into three parts: a "reconnaissance survey" focusing
on technical matters, such as general land and water needs; a
"human dependency and economic survey," which would examine
the social and economic characteristics of the population; and a
"physical survey," which would carry out in-depth technical
surveys in the areas recommended by the reconnaissance unit. By
the end of 1938 thirty-four reservations in eight western states
had undergone intensive surveys, and an additional sixteen were
undergoing study when the United States entered the war in
1941.[39]

During the surveys certain questions were raised concerning
the extent of interagency cooperation and the control of the
program at the reservation level. While Collier and Bennett seem
to have been in agreement about the range of matters the surveys
should consider and the integration of the technical and human
resources aspects, other officials in the SCS questioned the pro-
priety of using their funds for anything more than land reclama-
tion work and would leave responsibility for all other surveys and
program implementation to the Indian Service. Woehlke sought to
counter these sentiments by asserting that the legislation authorizing the transfer of the SCS to the Department of Agriculture
endowed that agency with broad powers in the area of resource
management, and that "it is obvious that no feasible, practical
erosion-control and land-use plans can be made without taking
into consideration the dependency of the population on the land
and its yield."[40] Woehlke's arguments were legitimate and convincing, although he frankly admitted that the bureau sought to
use SCS money to circumvent the intent of Congress to keep
Collier's "social experiments" in check by withholding needed
appropriations.

A second administrative obstacle resulted from the bureau's
emphasis on decentralization. SCS survey operations in general
focused on physically integrated regional units such as water-
sheds. Few Indian reservations constituted such units, and on the
fragmented reservations of the Northern Plains, Indian- and white-
owned lands were extensively interspersed. SCS proposals tended
to emphasize large-scale plans embracing land use areas. In the
initial agreements on program coordination under TC-BIA, however, the Indian Service was assigned major administrative responsibility. Since the Collier administration was committed to

decentralization, in practice this meant that local superintendents were expected to exercise general coordination of programs recommended by the planning group. But those officials had neither the money nor the staff adequate to meet that demand, and they could not legally regulate the use of non-Indian lands on the reservations. Consequently, the burden of administration shifted back to the SCS, creating much friction between representatives of the two agencies.

Woehlke and Allan Harper, his successor in 1937 as director of TC-BIA, sought to overcome these difficulties in various ways. One method was to restrict actual programs to small land use units, such as the Red Shirt Table community at Pine Ridge, where the reservation agent could exercise real control. The weakness of this approach was that it would result in piecemeal action that would not resolve major problems of soil erosion and Indian land needs. A second method was to try to integrate TC-BIA projects into broader SCS programs for resource management where that agency had authority to develop measures for the regulation of non-Indian as well as Indian lands.[41]

A similar approach, independent of TC-BIA, was undertaken for the Rio Grande region in New Mexico by the bureau in cooperation with the SCS and the Resettlement Administration. In 1936, efforts by the bureau to develop lands and herds for the Indians of that area aroused opposition from Spanish American subsistence herders who resented the encroachments of federally subsidized Indian herds raised for commercial use on lands they had traditionally used. This was a complicated matter whose origins related to the dispute over Pueblo land claims which had stimulated the Indian reform movement of the 1920s. In that earlier period, Collier had emphasized the needs of the Indians, but now he argued that the interests of the Spanish-Americans must be taken into account, for "these two populations are going to rise and fall together . . . in the future there shall be important common utilities serving them both; and . . . their interests as social and economic groups stand over against the interests which would utilize the extremely limited natural resources for commercial purposes."[42] He proposed that an interagency program be designed for the sharing of range privileges on federal lands in the watershed and that a land purchase program be initiated to enable both groups to establish themselves on a subsistence herding basis.[43]

The interdepartmental board envisioned by Collier would embrace the entire Rio Grande valley from Texas to Colorado and would integrate all federal and state land use projects in the watershed for the basic purpose of "protecting the indigenous non-commercial rural population in the possession of its land, and in making available to it the feasible maximum use-rights to the renewable resources" controlled by federal and state agencies. In addition, land purchase projects "in key positions in the watershed" would "make possible the early introduction of conservation management in the entire region," as well as providing subsistence farming and grazing areas for landless people. The program as a whole would salvage lands exploited commercially and in imminent danger of soil exhaustion, improve and coordinate irrigation and water use generally, and provide a model, not unlike the Tennessee Valley Authority, "to many other regions of the country."[44] The board that was established under these guidelines in 1937 included representatives from the National Resources Planning Board and the Reconstruction Finance Corporation as well as the usual agencies from the Departments of Agriculture and the Interior. It was not, however, given any coordinating authority and acted mainly as a consultant with the various federal agencies operating in the area. By 1938, Woehlke was complaining that it was difficult to get agencies to provide funds for carrying out the recommendations of the board.[45] Ultimately, the Rio Grande Board was absorbed by the larger Land Use Planning program initiated by the Department of Agriculture in 1938. Despite its weaknesses, however, the board did widen bureau contacts with other government agencies, as Collier intended, and also, in the period from 1938 to 1942, provided a model for land use planning by other cooperating organizations in which the cultural framework of economic planning was emphasized.[46]

One drawback to those larger programs was that they tended to squeeze out of the picture the kind of small-scale projects in which Indians (and other local people) could participate directly. In 1938, Harper asserted that various proposals of TC-BIA were not being provided for in the reservations budgets, and Woehlke's argument that scarce funds should be reserved for major undertakings only reinforced Harper's point that the smaller projects were being sidetracked.[47] As in other phases of the Indian New Deal, priority was of necessity given to those measures that would produce maximum economic benefits, even though in the process they limited the bureau in its efforts to promote Indian participation.

Despite Woehlke's statements in 1938 that TC-BIA would encourage Indian involvement in economic programs, in fact his program was rather conventional, emphasizing technical matters and supplying services for Indians rather than providing a planning system in which Indian communities could find a role. Consequently, there was little Indian interest in or even awareness of the work of TC-BIA after it was initially introduced. Only when recommendations appeared to threaten some existing arrangement was there much Indian reaction.

An example of the latter situation developed at the Papago Reservation in Arizona. As in the case of the tribal cattle association, major opposition came from the larger cattle herders, who feared that the SCS would recommend a stock reduction program similar to that of the Navajos. Several of the villages held meetings in early 1937 calling for a halt to any further TC-BIA surveys there. To head off a confrontation, SCS representatives proposed that the socioeconomic survey team, which included several anthropologists, should go into the village before any technical men were brought in, to explain the broad aims of the survey and allay Indian suspicions. Indian spokesmen pointed out that in the past "surveys" had inevitably ended with the Papagos losing some of their land, but after discussion they agreed to allow the SCS into the area to complete its work.[48]

Indian fears appeared justified, since the recommended program included a 60 percent reduction in existing herds and the resettlement of many Papagos at the Colorado River and Pima reservations, where their main source of income would be jobs at local dam construction sites. This program would not radically have altered the immediate situation of most Papagos, since the cattle herds were concentrated in the hands of a few families and the majority of the Indians were currently employed on IECW projects, but it would have disrupted the cultural patterns of one of the most "self-reliant and independent" Indian communities in the country and required intensive "educational" work by the bureau. Federal officials were still trying to persuade the Papagos to accept this intrusion in their lives when the outbreak of World War II interrupted the program.[49]

This kind of dispute was rare, but the Papago erosion problem was uncommonly severe and the tribe unusually stubborn and cohesive in its resistance to unwanted changes. In most situations, the programs were too remote and the Indians too divided to take any position on them. The final legacy of TC-BIA and the other planning efforts of the Collier administration was a collection of valuable but generally unused survey reports on Indian conditions and needs. Administrators in Washington recognized the value of these planning tools and regarded them as an unprecedented achievement of the reformed Indian Service, which indeed they were. But few of their recommendations were put into full operation before the coming of war in 1941 interrupted their implementation, and to Indians and agents in the field they were not of major consequence. Like the elaborate surveys of the National Resources Planning Board and other departmental and interdepartmental planning groups of the New Deal era, TC-BIA, the Rio Grande Board, and similar forays by the bureau into planning for Indian resources left no lasting mark on the Indian communities or on the land.

8

THE WANING OF THE
INDIAN NEW DEAL

Despite its problems the Bureau of Indian Affairs proceeded with its program during the first six years of the Indian New Deal, with some indications of success in the form of tribal constitutions and organized governments and improvements in Indian economic conditions. After 1940, however, progress perceptibly slowed: planning projects ground to a halt, tribal reorganization declined, and the bureau's annual appropriations took a nosedive. When the United States entered World War II in December 1941, the Indian Service was itself moved from Washington, D.C., to Chicago to make way for assorted emergency bureaucracies deemed essential to the national war effort. Some bureau officials were sent to administer the Japanese relocation camps, where, perhaps unaware of the irony of the situation, they endeavored to inculcate a sense of community involvement among their reluctant wards. The war also drew off some of the best indigenous Indian leaders into military service, while many young men and women left the reservations to work in wartime industrial centers.

As the tribal organizations deteriorated, congressional critics mounted new and more effective assaults on Collier and his administration, ultimately forcing him to resign. Even that sacrifice was insufficient, however, and the new bureau leaders were pressured slowly to revive assimilation, under the guise of terminating federal responsibility for the Indians. Within a decade after his retirement, Collier's influence over the course of Indian affairs and his New Deal for them seemed only another transitory chapter in the melancholy history of Indian relations in the United States.

Yet even as the Indian New Deal faltered, a new pan-Indian movement began to take shape. In Denver, Colorado, in 1944 the National Congress of American Indians (NCAI) assembled. Its founders included an odd assortment of reform-minded and ambitious Indian politicians, Indians holding posts in the bureau and eager to further Collier's programs, unofficial delegates from some tribal councils, and Indians whose experiences in the Collier years had convinced them that future Indian policies should be initiated by Indians, not by white sympathizers, no matter how well intentioned. The early years of the NCAI were not particularly productive, but they did represent a by-product of the idea of Indian self-determination set in motion by the reforms of the 1930s.

Even supporters of the Wheeler-Howard Act in Congress, including Senator Wheeler himself, were always skeptical of Collier and his plans. The bill had been extensively revised in the House and Senate, and even then there were delays in bringing the new version to the floor. Furthermore, even in watered-down form the policies embodied in the act were sufficiently novel to raise congressional doubts about their practicality and desirability.

The initial struggle for appropriations for the Indian reorganization program in 1935 set the pattern for the future. Administered conservatively, the credit fund under the act drew only $5.6 million between 1935 and 1944, although Collier later noted that the total amount loaned Indians from various credit sources handled by the bureau came to more than $10 million.[1] The more controversial land purchase program was deliberately kept small as alarmed western congressmen discovered the extent of the contemplated land acquisition outlined by the National Resources Board. Collier's efforts to increase appropriations in this area were not helped by the revelation that he was able to tap outside agencies such as the Resettlement Administration for additional land purchase funds. Only $5.1 million was appropriated for land acquisition between 1935 and 1941, less than half the amount permitted under the act.[2]

The total Indian Service appropriation jumped from $28,146,105 in 1935 to $47,942,541 in 1938, but $19 million of the increase consisted of emergency relief funds, so there was no significant increase in the bureau's operating budget. Although the appropriation still came to $46 million in 1939, one-quarter of that amount was emergency funding which disappeared after 1941. By 1944 the appropriation for the bureau was down to $28 million.[3]

Up to the outbreak of World War II, Collier was able to make up losses in his authorized budget through funds from outside agencies, and he proved adept at this sort of maneuver. But the practice did not endear him to congressmen, and his critics sought other ways to harass his administration and discredit the Indian New Deal. Senator Wheeler, becoming increasingly hostile toward Collier and the program, used his position as chairman of the Senate Committee on Indian Affairs to criticize the bureau and investigate the administration of the reform program. Indian witnesses were brought in to testify about the incompetence or communistic tendencies of Collier and his colleagues. A favorite source of witnesses was the American Indian Federation, started in Oklahoma by Joseph Bruner. A subcommittee of Wheeler's Indian committee even held hearings on the American Indian Federation's proposal to distribute $3,500 to each Indian from trust funds, despite the protests of Ickes and Collier that the scheme was a "swindle." Ultimately, American Indian Federation leaders carried their tales of communism in the Indian Service to the Dies committee,[4] the predecessor of the House Committee on Un-American Activities.

It is unlikely that many congressmen took the Bruner group's charges very seriously, but they were useful for harassing Collier. The commissioner effectively counterattacked, exhibiting evidence linking the American Indian Federation with the Silver Shirts and other American Nazi sympathizers. By 1940 the organization had broken up into rival factions and lost its momentum.[5] More serious problems for the bureau came from delays or blockage of specific bills involving Indian matters, notably the Navajo eastern boundary extension bill, which was defeated largely through the efforts of Senator Dennis Chavez of New Mexico, a critic of Collier. The failure of the government to get the bill passed in 1935 contributed to the already bad relations with the Navajos.[6]

After 1937, Senate critics began launching direct assaults on the Indian Reorganization Act. Wheeler proposed to repeal the act bearing his name in 1937, and in the following session, the Senate

Committee on Indian Affairs reported out a bill embodying his proposal. The report was prepared by Chavez and relied heavily on testimony from the American Indian Federation as the basis for its charges. This bill was buried by the House Committee on Indian Affairs, but a similar one was resurrected by Senator Bushfield of South Dakota and a similar favorable report was presented by the Senate committee the following year. Once again Collier prevailed upon the House committee to kill the bill, and this time he felt the issue deserved an extensive, point-by-point refutation.[7] Although these bills were unlikely to succeed, they alarmed and exasperated Collier and Ickes.

Collier was generally able to count on support from the House Committee on Indian Affairs, but the House Appropriations Committee remained hostile, and ultimately brought his tenure as commissioner to an end. In March 1945 the subcommittee on the Interior Department appropriations threatened major cuts in the already skeletal bureau budget unless Collier resigned, and he bowed to the inevitable.[8]

The extent of opposition to the Indian New Deal in Congress is hard to ascertain, since Collier's critics were never obliged or never chose to carry their proposals to the floor. Unfortunately for Collier, men like Wheeler and Chavez occupied strategic positions on key committees relating to Indian affairs and could harass the bureau easily; and given the relatively low level of interest in and knowledge about Indian matters, their displacement by more sympathetic committee members was unlikely.

Collier tended to dismiss all such critics as spokesmen for "cattle interests, timber interests, oil interests, and other substantial corporation and regional interests . . . necessarily antagonized by those features of the Wheeler-Howard Act which . . . give to the tribe some measure of control over their own property."[9] There were, however, other motives. Wheeler, for example, seems to have developed a personal animosity toward Collier because of the latter's presumption that he alone understood the real needs of the Indians, and because of their fundamentally different approaches to Indian problems. His distaste was aggravated by Collier's use of *Indians at Work* to lobby for Roosevelt's court-packing plan in 1937.[10]

The main objection of Wheeler and other congressional critics, however, was that the reorganization program seemed directed less toward developing Indian self-sufficiency than toward setting

up tribal corporations as permanent controls over Indian resources. Since the corporations relied largely on bureau advisers,
the opportunity for eliminating the bureau in the near future
seemed remote. Moreover, a tribal corporation was more likely to
use Indian resources productively than to lease or sell them, which
meant that less would be available for local entrepreneurs when
and if federal supervision was terminated. General principles were
thus reinforced by the threat to the future interests of their
constituents in determining their position. Collier correctly identified the major source of opposition. Characteristically, he asserted that protection of Indian resources rather than perpetuation
of government controls was at the heart of the matter. His opponents were more likely to emphasize the latter aspect.

Collier and other historians of the Indian New Deal have assigned to Congress a major responsibility for the weaknesses of
that program, particularly in the area of economic reconstruction.
Certainly the revisions of the Wheeler-Howard Act making land
allotment exchanges voluntary, and the subsequent strangling of
the land purchase funds severely damaged the program. At the
same time, however, Collier was able to acquire land purchase
funds from other agencies and Ickes arranged for the transfer of
part of the public domain to Indian use. Moreover, the voluntary
exchange approach might have worked had the tribal governments
instilled any sense of confidence and loyalty in allottees. The
repercussions of the failure of the political features on the economic aspect of the Indian New Deal cannot be ignored.

Congress can also be charged with sabotaging tribal organization, albeit indirectly. Although the forays of the Senate committee were deflected with little difficulty, the presence of a body of
permanent critics capable of exploiting any fault reinforced a
sense of urgency within the Collier administration, the notion that
if the reforms were not achieved quickly, they would easily be
uprooted by a resurgent old guard. Oliver La Farge described their
predicament sympathetically:

It takes a good Commissioner of Indian Affairs about two years to learn his
job. A good man . . . needs four to get his program launched. Uncertainty of
appointment clouds that first term, creating a sense of haste. The virtual
certainty that eight years will be the limit is not as bad as the fear that the
next Commissioner will belong to an administration with a totally different
theory of government and will proceed to undo all that has been built up.[11]

In these circumstances the pressure to push tribal organization forward without delay was strong, despite Collier's own recognition that the process required patience and much preliminary exploratory work to ensure that the Indians would understand and respond to the opportunities presented. The program was hurriedly established and consequently viewed by Indians with their customary mistrust of government experiments and innovations. The congressional requirement of a referendum on the Wheeler-Howard Act and the subsequent efforts to repeal the act served to force the pace of tribal organization all the more.

Paradoxically, the Indian New Deal, which sought to reconstruct Indian societies on the basis of tribal loyalties, contributed more significantly to the development of pan-Indianism, a sense of shared problems and potentialities which transcended tribal and reservation boundaries. This was a new phenomenon in the history of American Indians. To be sure, they had not been completely immune to the forces of centralization that had reduced the isolation and parochialism of American communities in the late nineteenth century, and the operations of the Bureau of Indian Affairs in the years before Collier had provided them with a bond of shared experiences and grievances. But to an unusual degree the Indian remained outside the main current of American life, partly by choice, partly by circumstance.[12]

The Society of American Indians had functioned for a time as spokesman for all Indians, but it was composed largely of mixed-bloods educated at Carlisle or Hampton Institute. After its disappearance in the 1920s there was no truly indigenous Indian national organization except perhaps the American Indian Federation, whose numbers were small and aims dubious.

The Collier administration did not actively encourage inter-tribal contacts during the early stages of the Indian New Deal. Emphasis was placed on tribal organization. Yet the various conferences held in 1934 to explain the new program and arouse support for it brought together delegates from different tribes. They proved to be one-shot affairs, but they did present possibilities for future, and more permanent, assemblies on a regional basis. Forrest Stone, superintendent of the Blackfeet Agency, proposed to Collier that the bureau sponsor an "Indian Congress of the Northwest" composed of delegates from tribal councils on reservations in Montana and the Dakotas. This arrangement, Stone asserted, would provide for a greater degree of coordination of economic programs in the region and would enable top officials to have more regular contact with Indian leaders than was possible with a large number of tribal councils.[13] Nothing seems to have come of this suggestion, possibly because Stone seemed overly sanguine about the ability of the Indians to manage their own finances.

On the other hand, there were situations in which the bureau did seek to promote wider forms of organization. Collier was personally involved in efforts to promote an All-Pueblo Council and give it substantial powers over the villages. In other cases inadequate land resources dictated some degree of combination of scattered Indian groups: the Minnesota Chippewas are one example. A similar situation involved the Shoshones of Nevada, who lived in small bands. To encourage some degree of confederation the bureau established the Te Moak Band of Western Shoshones as the prospective nucleus for other bands and arranged for all credit and land purchases to be channeled through the council for this group. Despite these efforts, however, there were still separate councils operating elsewhere in Nevada in 1944.[14] The foregoing were exceptions to policy and did not prove very fruitful. On the whole, bureau leaders exhibited little interest in experimenting with regional intertribal arrangements.

Some Indians, however, were quick to see new opportunities in regional organization, notably the Sioux. The Great Sioux Reservation established in 1868 had been broken up in the intervening years and the bureau chose to organize separate tribal councils at the remnant agencies. Elected Sioux tribal leaders and dissidents alike sought bigger things. In April 1936, officers from the tribal councils at Pine Ridge, Cheyenne River, and Rosebud met at the Cheyenne River Agency to discuss common problems and, not surprisingly, decided that the tribal trust funds should be used to finance a permanent intertribal organization. After much discussion the bureau agreed to allow them to use the interest from trust funds for that purpose. Thereupon the Indians laid plans for a general council of the Sioux to be held in September 1937 and attended by congressmen from North and South Dakota. According to Antoine Roubideux, chairman at Rosebud, the assembly would discuss common problems of "old age, widowed mothers, extreme rehabilitation needs, care of orphans and children [from] broken homes . . . unemployment and education needs," all of which was highly desirable and met the approval of bureau officials.[15]

Matters took a turn for the worse when the Sioux proposed to focus on the perennial issue of claims under the 1868 treaty. Roubideux argued that much of the opposition to the Reorganization Act among the Sioux arose from the fact that the claims were unsettled and added, "If [the government] can appropriate millions to loan us [it] can just as easily pay our claims." Bureau officials did not object to discussing the claims problem per se, although there was little they could do to hasten the resolution of the question. They soon discovered, however, that the Indians were being urged by their claims attorney to discuss "the general state of reorganization," which would be certain to stir up a hornet's nest, and that the opponents of Collier were likely to use the assembly to air their grievances. William Zimmerman now recommended against the Sioux council, arguing, "It would be most unfortunate to have a gathering [of this] proportion and significance . . . defeat its own purpose through debates and discussions which have been settled and would only tend to widen any gap which may exist between . . . groups."[16] The meeting was held September 3–10, 1937, and established a Black Hills Sioux Council, but it received little fanfare from the bureau, which usually gave such examples of civic activity considerable publicity.

Following this assembly antireorganization Indians created a Treaty and Claims Council, which purported to represent all the Sioux in the Dakotas. There had in fact been a council of Sioux chiefs before the Indian New Deal which had been "genuinely conservative . . . rever[ing] the past," but it had never had legal status in the eyes of the bureau. By 1937 that organization had passed into the hands of more opportunistic Sioux politicians. In 1939 and 1940 leaders of the Treaty Council faction aired their grievances before various congressional committees. Presumably they reflected the feelings of many Sioux who were disillusioned with Collier and his program, but there is no evidence that this group ever had any substantial or permanent influence on an intertribal basis.[17]

Outside of the Sioux reservations the major area of intertribal activity among Indians was Oklahoma, and it was from here that the National Congress of American Indians began to take shape. A leading figure in Oklahoma Indian politics was Ben Dwight, who had been an aide to Oklahoma governor and U.S. senator Robert Kerr, a prominent member of the conservative wing of the Democratic party in the 1940s. Dwight, formal head of the Choctaw

Nation, had been a major supporter of the Thomas-Rogers Act, and had established an organization to work on behalf of the Indians of Oklahoma. He was able and energetic and was regarded by some Indians as a potential successor to Collier as commissioner of Indian affairs.[18]

Another major group contributing to the formation of the National Congress comprised Indian employees of the bureau, particularly D'Arcy McNickle, who began urging a national assembly before various Indian groups in early 1944. McNickle pointed out that an Indian national lobby could argue their case before Congress more effectively than the bureau because "Indians are listened to more attentively than are Government officials." He also noted that such an organization could probably get foundation support for projects that the bureau could not undertake because of lack of funds or legal restrictions.[19]

Among other Indian Service employees involved in planning the formation of the National Congress were Archie Phinney, Mark L. Burns, Peru Farver, Charles Heacock, and George LaMotte. Not surprisingly, the participation of these "bureau Indians" in the movement led critics of the Indian New Deal to grumble that it was another Collier scheme rather than a spontaneous Indian affair.

Bureau leaders were ambivalent toward the organization at the outset. Some field administrators were concerned that meetings of this type tended to produce a great deal of unrest among Indians over issues which the bureau could do nothing about. Even Zimmerman was skeptical, arguing that the first convention featured much political campaigning by ambitious Indian leaders like Robert Yellowtail rather than serious discussion of common problems.[20] Collier, on the other hand, seems to have been receptive to proposals for a new Indian organization, even though his old group, now the American Association on Indian Affairs, remained active. His later comments about the Indian convention in 1944 were largely approving.[21]

The issue of bureau involvement was discussed at the Denver meeting November 15–18, 1944, and a resolution was proposed to bar all Indians employed by the bureau from positions on any of the executive committees of the National Congress. The resolution was defeated, but the debate clearly indicated that the convention included Indians who had little liking for Collier or the Indian New Deal. One such critic asserted, "We have been as suspicious of the Indian Bureau as we are of the Japs and frankly we don't have any use for Collier." Ben Dwight had been elected chairman of the convention and did not participate in the debate, but Judge N. B. Johnson, also of Oklahoma, who was vice chairman (and subsequently was elected the first president of the NCAI) argued against the resolution on the ground that "the higher-ups formulate the policies of the Indian Department [and] I am sure that there are a lot of young people in the [bureau] who do not approve all of the policies of the Indian Service" and should have the opportunity to work for better policies through this organization.[22]

Another indication of the relative independence of the NCAI from the influence of Collier may be seen in two resolutions passed by the 1944 convention. One asserted that "various provisions of the tribal [powers under the Reorganization Act] have heretofore been ignored by the Secretary of the Interior and the Commissioner, thus causing unwarranted slighting of the programs of organized tribes," and urged that all tribal powers, explicit or implicit, be recognized. A second resolution called for greater attention to be paid to the problems of full-bloods, whose needs had been neglected by the bureau.[23]

A second problem for the Indians at the Denver assembly involved their status as representatives of all the Indians in the country. Although Judge Johnson noted that there were Indians "representing more than fifty Indian tribes, groups and associations," none of them had officially been chosen by their tribes as delegates. There were a number of tribal chairmen and former chairmen, but some shared the view of Antoine Roubideux that they had exceeded their authority by appearing to speak for their tribes. As McNickle later pointed out, the notion of an association extending beyond the tribe was far more novel to Indians than it might seem to the typical American "joiner." Further complicating matters was the tradition of decentralized leadership of the traditional Indian group; few Indians could presume to speak for their fellows without fear of contradiction.[24]

Despite these difficulties the NCAI was able to establish itself on a permanent basis and contributed more than marginally to the creation of the Indian Claims Commission, which it had set as its first priority. If it never emerged as a major force influencing Indian legislation in Washington, the NCAI could make an argument on behalf of the Indians with some effect on the bureau, particularly during the controversy over termination in the 1950s. The Indian New Deal did not create this organization, but it helped establish the conditions in which a national Indian pressure group could take shape and endure, even in the grim years following Collier's departure.

Between 1934 and 1945 the Bureau of Indian Affairs made an unprecedented effort to provide the Indian tribes of the United States with some degree of political autonomy, financial assistance for economic rehabilitation, and the legal tools for managing their own affairs in the future. Whatever the shortcomings of that effort, it was motivated by a genuine desire to reverse the policies of the past.

From its beginnings the Indian New Deal faced formidable obstacles. White communities in the West and their congressional spokesmen sought to limit the more far-reaching goals of the program envisioned by Collier and his staff and continued to snipe at it through a series of investigations. Each year the battle for adequate appropriations had to be renewed by Collier, with diminishing success as hostility or indifference toward the Indian program increased. Local bureau officials often misconstrued the objectives of the new policy and in some cases sought deliberately to undermine it. The Indians themselves remained ignorant of the full measure of opportunities provided them, or fell to squabbling over matters that the administrators felt to be irrelevant to their most urgent needs.

Yet there were enduring achievements. The tribal constitutions and governments remained, still relatively powerless, but providing a semblance of self-rule, more than had existed before the Collier era. Even as the tribal reorganization program was collapsing, a new phenomenon appeared, the first genuinely Indian pressure group since the eclipse of the Society of American Indians, and one far more representative of diverse Indian communities than the earlier group had been. More than perhaps they intended, the designers of the Indian New Deal had helped establish the conditions for a pan-Indian movement in the United States. While the influence of the NCAI on Indian policy fluctuated considerably in the next three decades, it acted in turn as a stimulus for more outspoken and militant Indian groups.

Another lasting achievement of the Collier era was the establishment in 1946 of the Indian Claims Commission, patterned after the Pueblo Lands Board, and envisioned in the original draft of the Indian Reorganization Act in 1934. The Claims Commission did not resolve all the demands of the Indians to their satisfaction, but it was a functioning part of the administration of Indian affairs for thirty-two years.

In retrospect, the Indian New Deal left a mixed legacy. Its economic programs had substantial effect only in specific situations and did not permanently improve Indian living standards. For these failings Collier's defenders could with some justification place the responsibility on a niggardly and hostile Congress. Its political programs produced institutions and arrangements that survive, but the goal of genuine Indian self-determination remains a dream; and for this failure Collier and his colleagues bear greater responsibility. At the same time, the Indian New Deal in peculiar and unexpected ways did help produce among Indians, if not a "spiritual reawakening," at least a reinvigorated sense of pride in their cultural heritage. Washington policy makers could revert to assimilation, but few Indian leaders could openly urge fellow Indians to accept it again. A new generation of leaders emerged, more aware of the intricacies of white politics and legal procedures.

The long-range results of the Indian New Deal were a natural outgrowth of the administrative process. Regardless of their initial commitment to genuine Indian autonomy, administrators felt constrained by budgetary limitations and the growing intensity of congressional criticism to channel their main efforts into economic rehabilitation of the reservations, even where it brought them into conflict with the Indian leaders they had helped to establish. For their part, Indian leaders accepted the promises of the Indian Reorganization Act and challenged what seemed to them to be administrative attempts to curtail their freedom and exercise of new powers. Regardless of whether the situation on individual reservations was harmonious or acrimonious, those Indians who acquired political office became more aware of their potential power and their mutuality of interests with Indian leaders on other reservations. But the structure of the new self-governing institutions restricted this growing political self-consciousness and activism to a small educated and ambitious elite. Only when that elite was challenged from below could the promise of the Indian New Deal extend to the Indian people as a whole.

APPENDIX 1
DATA ON ASSIMILATION

This table constitutes a rather crude but useful summary of the distribution of Indian groups on reservations in terms of assimilation, insofar as it can be measured by statistical information available from census data and social and economic indices compiled by the Civil Works Administration in 1933–34, and the Land Planning Unit of the National Resources Board in 1934–35.

The three major factors considered are (1) intermarriage between Indians and non-Indians, as indicated by degrees of blood recorded by the Bureau of Indian Affairs up to 1936; (2) the extent of allotted land which had been patented in fee and/or alienated by 1934, according to the National Resources Board report; (3) the extent of literacy in any form, as determined by the U.S. Census Bureau. Each of these measures is based on sources which are not entirely satisfactory; hence there is no claim that the statistics are totally reliable, and no effort has been made to arrange the groups in an exact series.

The definition of mixed-blood varied from tribe to tribe and according to who was doing the census. Figures were taken by the U.S. Census Bureau for the 1930 census, and by the Civil Works Administration (CWA) in 1933–34. The CWA figures are probably more accurate, as well as more detailed since they broke down groups into five categories of mixed blood, but are complete for only thirty-three tribes, mostly in the plains region. The literacy figures are taken from the Census Bureau but are sometimes hard to accept, particularly when matched against CWA figures for education on the thirty-three reservations it surveyed. For example, the Census Bureau figures indicate that over 80 percent of the Chippewas over ten years old were literate, while the CWA figures show that only 17 percent of the Chippewas had any formal education at all in 1932. Presuming, however, that some rudimentary form of literacy may be acquired without formal education, I have used the census figures, including the CWA figures in parentheses in the table where there is a serious discrepancy between the two figures.

The information on land patenting is probably the most reliable, based on intensive surveys of existing land as well as historical information. The one point to be noted is that fee patenting was only one form of Indian land acquisition by local whites. Many allottees whose land was still in trust leased it. The patent measure does, however, indicate the extent to which a tribe was considered acculturated by the Bureau of Indian Affairs, since patents were, in theory, issued only to Indians deemed competent to manage their own resources, although that determination of competency was often farcical and sometimes criminal.

Despite these drawbacks, the table does give a broad view of the range of tribal groups, and indicates which were more likely to retain tribal cohesion. I have subdivided them into five major groups, which actually fall on a continuum ranging from high to low assimilation (see table on page 42 in the text), complicated by the fact that some tribes which were relatively highly assimilated culturally had escaped patenting, and so retained a tribal economic base. There were only two converse situations in which patenting had occurred extensively but cultural and biological assimilation was relatively slight: among the Cheyenne-Arapahoes and the Pawnees, both in Oklahoma. All but two of the forty-four groups examined in this sample fit readily into these two dimensions.

The sample itself was not drawn randomly, but was determined by the availability of information, especially in the CWA and National Resources Board surveys. It does not seem to be skewed, however, since it constitutes a selection of the major reservations in each region (except the East). The total population of the forty-four reservations equalled 76 percent of the total Indian population enumerated in 1935.

Tribe or Reservation	Percent Mixed-Blood	Percent Patented	Percent Literate
Turtle Mountain (Chippewa)	97	39	78
Chippewa	87	85	82 (17)
Flathead	81	80	52
Menominee	77	—	83
Blackfeet	75	14	78
Osage	73	70	97
Five Civilized Tribes	71	67	90 (26)
Spokane	68	23	30
Potawatomi	68	64	81
Yankton (Sioux)	66	84	78
Iroquois	63	—	86
Fort Belknap (Cheyenne)	62	—	79
Colville	60	25	—*
Umatilla	59	41	—*
Ottawa	58	—	79
Cheyenne River (Sioux)	56	67	78
Klamath	55	—	—*
Sacramento	55	—	—*
Rosebud (Sioux)	53	46	78
Crow	51	—	78
Pine Ridge (Sioux)	48	28	78
Fort Peck (Assiniboin)	47	21	—*
Fort Berthold (Mandan, Hidatsa, Arikara)	42	6	78
Crow Creek (Sioux)	40	44	—*
Mission	38	—	—*
Fort Hall (Shoshone, Bannock)	32	55	—*
Standing Rock (Sioux)	32	37	78
Fort Totten (Sioux)	30	61	—*
Northern Cheyenne	28	—	—*
Kiowa	28	29	74
Uintah-Ouray	28	26	—*
Winnebago	28	55	84
Pawnee	27	68	—*
Shoshone	24	7	61
Cheyenne-Arapaho	18	67	—*
Warm Springs (Apache)	17	9	—*
Ute	16	—	53
Walker River (Paiute)	12	—	—*
Yuma	6	—	74
Fort Apache	4	—	71

Tribe or Reservation	Percent Mixed-Blood	Percent Patented	Percent Literate
Sells (Papago)	2	—	46
Pima	1	—	73
Navajo	1	—	16
Hopi	—	—	69

*Information not available.

APPENDIX 2

Indian Ethnic and Economic Characteristics Correlated with
Vote on Indian Reorganization

Agency	Percent Full-Blood*	Percent Vote No on IRA	Percent Vote No on Constitution
Walker River	88	14	—**
Warm Springs	83	19	—**
Tongue River	72	33	—**
Uintah-Ouray	71	8	—**
Couer d'Alene	70	38	—**
Standing Rock	61	33	—**
Mission	60	40	—**
Wind River	58	45	—**
Fort Berthold	56	21	33
Crow	55	70	—**
Pine Ridge	52	27	26
Cheyenne River	51	32	25
Umatilla	47	44	—**
Crow Creek	46	52	—**
Rosebud	46	14	20
Fort Belknap	45	8	4
Colville	43	34	—**
Fort Peck	39	56	—**
Klamath	38	61	—**
Yankton	34	17	—**
Blackfeet	25	10	9
Menominee	21	1	—**
Fort Totten	20	45	—**
Chippewa	20	7	20
Flathead	20	14	—***
Turtle Mountain	3	46	—**

*Percentage based on ratio of full-bloods to total adult population over age twenty-one.
**No referendum held on a constitution at this agency.
***No information available on referendum for this agency.

Indian Economic Status Correlated with Vote
on Indian Reorganization Act

Agency	Percent Landless	Percent Vote Yes on Act*
Yankton	80	25
Turtle Mountain	83	22
Mission	78	8
Fort Hall	58	34
Uintah Ouray	57	54
Fort Belknap	56	61
Rosebud	54	27
Flathead	50	41
Sacramento	41	40
Umatilla	38	23
Crow Creek	33	22
Chippewa	32	30
Winnebago	31	30
Warm Springs	29	66
Pine Ridge	23	29
Colville	22	25
Fort Totten	21	28
Crow	19	11
Fort Peck	17	27
Walker River	13	12
Cheyenne River	13	46
Menominee	0	58

*Percentage of total voting population (adults over age twenty-one).

Sources: Records of Civil Works Administration social and economic survey of Indian reservations, 1933–34, in Records of the Bureau of Indian Affairs, Record Group 75, National Archives; Theodore H. Haas, *Ten Years of Tribal Government under IRA* (Washington, D.C.: Government Printing Office, 1947), pp. 14–20; George E. Fay, comp., *Charters, Constitutions and By-Laws of the Indian Tribes of North America,* 14 pts. (Greeley, Colo.: Museum of Anthropology, Colorado State College, 1967).

Indian Participation in Indian Reorganization Act Referenda, 1934–35

Agency	Voting Population	Percent Vote on Act	Percent Vote on Constitution
PLAINS AND NORTHWEST			
Blackfeet	1,785	56	58
Cheyenne River	1,420	78	66
Chippewa	6,351	35	34
Colville	1,420	59	—*
Crow	982	82	—*
Fort Belknap	604	70	56
Fort Berthold	661	93	74
Fort Hall	971	42	46
Fort Peck	1,027	83	—*
Fort Totten	521	72	—*
Klamath	666	70	—*
Nez Percé	608	77	—*
Pine Ridge	4,075	56	59
Red Lake	828	50	—*
Rocky Boy's	344	54	44
Rosebud	3,126	41	52
Standing Rock	1,559	75	—*
Taholah	1,345	50	—*
Tongue River	757	68	78
Tulalip	1,280	64	—*
Umatilla	681	67	—*
Warm Springs	394	85	—*
Yakima	1,392	81	—*
SOUTHWEST (excluding Oklahoma)			
Carson	1,609	59	—*
Colorado River	402	56	61
Fort Apache	1,340	56	—*
Fort McDowell	111	65	56
Fort Hall	109	57	—*
Gila River	2,308	56	—*
Hoopa Valley	703	76	—*
Hopi	1,320	62	57
Mescalero	367	74	80
Mission	2,725	37	—*
Navajo	15,900	98	—*
Papago	3,028	47	63

Agency	Voting Population	Percent Vote on Act	Percent Vote on Constitution
Pueblo	6,333	60	—*
Sacramento	1,815	58	—*
Salt River	592	44	53
San Carlos	1,473	35	—*
Southern Ute	129	73	53
Uintah-Ouray	780	58	46
Ute Mountain	225	45	46
Western Shoshone	489	49	—*
PLAINS Average		66	57
SOUTHWEST Average		58	57
Combined Average		62	57
		(43 agencies)	(18 agencies)
National Average		58	57
		(96 agencies)	(25 agencies)

*No referendum held on constitution at this agency.

NOTES

Preface

1. "American Indian Policy Review Report," excerpt from *Final Report of the American Indian Policy Review Commission* in *Indian Law Reporter* 4 (1977): M19-M22.

2. John Collier, *Indians of the Americas*, pp. 21-22, 267-82. See also William Zimmerman, "The Role of the B.I.A. since 1933," *Annals of the Academy of Political and Social Sciences* 311 (1957): 31-36; Harold E. Fey and D'Arcy McNickle, *Indians and Other Americans: Two Ways of Life Meet*, pp. 91-124; Oliver La Farge, *As Long as the Grass Shall Grow*; Randolph C. Downs, "A Crusade for American Indian Reform, 1922-1934," pp. 331-54.

3. Lawrence C. Kelly, *The Navajo Indians and Federal Indian Policy, 1900-1940*, pp. 158-70, 190-94; Donald H. Parman, *The Navajos and the New Deal*, pp. 25-80, 193-216, 290-96.

4. Kenneth R. Philp, *John Collier's Crusade for Indian Reform, 1920-1954*, pp. 1-3, 187-95, 210-12. Other recent reexaminations of John Collier and the Indian New Deal include Gary Stein, "Tribal Self Government and the I.R.A. of 1934," *Michigan Law Review* 70 (April 1972): 955-86; Stephen J. Kunitz, "The Social Philosophy of John Collier," pp. 213-29; Lawrence C. Kelly, "The Indian Reorganization Act: The Dream and the Reality," pp. 291-312; Graham Taylor, "The Tribal Alternative to Bureaucracy: The Indian's New Deal, 1933-1945," pp. 128-42.

Chapter 1

1. Felix Cohen, *Handbook of Federal Indian Law* (Washington, D.C.: Government Printing Office, 1941), p. 122.

2. Wilcomb Washburn, *Red Man's Land / White Man's Law*, pp. 66–68.

3. See Harold E. Driver, *Indians of North America*, pp. 325–52, for a summary of patterns of Indian political organization.

4. Karl N. Llewelyn and E. Adamson Hoebel, *The Cheyenne Way*, pp. 67–69, 96–98. See also R. G. Fisher, "An Outline of Pueblo Government," in *So Live the Works of Man*, ed. D. D. Brand and F. O. Harvey (Albuquerque: University of New Mexico Press, 1939), pp. 147–57; Edward H. Spicer, *Cycles of Conquest: The Impact of Spain, Mexico, and the United States on the Indians of the Southwest, 1533–1960*, pp. 380–83; M. E. Opler, "The Creek 'Town' and the Problem of Creek Indian Political Reorganization," in *Human Problems in Technological Change*, ed. Edward H. Spicer (Boston: John Wiley, 1962), pp. 165–70.

5. A. L. Kroeber, "The Nature of the Land-holding Group," p. 304. See also Alden Vaughan, *The New England Frontier* (Boston: Little Brown, 1965), for a discussion of divergent concepts of landholding between Indians and American colonists.

6. Bernard W. Sheehan, *Seeds of Extinction: Jeffersonian Philanthropy and the American Indian,* p. 167. See also Roy Harvey Pearce, *Savagism and Civilization: A Study of the Indian and the American Mind* (Baltimore: Johns Hopkins University Press, 1967), pp. 69–73.

7. Quoted in Fey and McNickle, *Indians and Other Americans*, pp. 74–75.

8. See H. Craig Miner, *The Corporation and the Indian: Tribal Sovereignty and Industrial Civilization in Indian Territory, 1865–1907,* pp. 11–19, 210–12, on corruption among the Five Civilized Tribes. In order to prevent the misuse of moneys, Congress began a policy in the 1870s of releasing tribal funds from the U.S. Treasury only by special act of Congress. This restriction was to hamper the operations of the new tribal governments in the New Deal. See Commissioner of Indian Affairs, *Annual Report, 1935–36* (Washington, D.C.: Government Printing Office, 1936), p. 199.

9. Delos S. Otis, *The Dawes Act and the Allotment of Indian Lands*, ed. Francis Paul Prucha, pp. 19–20. This study, which John Collier commissioned Otis to prepare, was originally published in the hearings of the House Committee on Indian Affairs on the Wheeler-Howard bill in 1934. Although highly critical of the Dawes Act, the study was carefully researched. Prucha regards it as probably the best study of the subject. For a more sympathetic treatment, see Loring B. Priest, *Uncle Sam's Stepchildren: The Reformation of United States Indian Policy, 1865–1887.* The text of the Dawes Act can be found in Wilcomb Washburn, ed., *The American Indian and the United States*, 3:2188–94.

10. Quoted in Francis Paul Prucha, ed., *Americanizing the American Indians*, p. 225; quoted in Washburn, *The American Indian*, 1:425.

11. Otis, *The Dawes Act*, pp. 58, 73–75, 86ff.

12. "Report of Walter W. Liggett on Blackfeet Indian Reservation," U.S. Congress, Senate Committee on Indian Affairs, *Survey of Conditions of Indians of the United States*, 71st Cong., 2d sess. (Washington, D.C.: Government Printing Office, 1930), p. 12747.

13. Lewis Meriam et al., *The Problem of Indian Administration* (Washington, D.C.: Brookings Institution, 1928), p. 471. See also reports of the commissioner of Indian affairs for 1918 and 1919, in Washburn, *The United States and the American Indian*, 2:881, 889–92.

14. These percentages were calculated from material in National Resources Board, Land Planning Committee, *Report on Land Planning, Part 10: Indian Land Tenure, Economic Status, and Population Trends* (Washington, D.C.: Government Printing Office, 1935), pp. 28–35.

15. Arthur L. Bach, "The Administration of Indian Resources in the United States, 1933–1941," p. 71.

16. Meriam, *Indian Administration,* p. 461.

17. Percentages were calculated from the records of the National Resources Board Land Unit's economic surveys in 1934 and 1935, in the National Archives, Washington, D.C., Record Group 75, Records of the Bureau of Indian Affairs (hereafter cited as NA, RG 75).

18. Figures are from Meriam, *Indian Administration*, pp. 446–51, and from the records of the Civil Works Administration, Social and Economic Survey of Indian Reservations, 1933–1934, in NA, RG 75.

19. Meriam, *Indian Administration*, pp. 115–17.

20. Ibid., pp. 140–42, 155.

21. U.S. Congress, House Committee on Indian Affairs, *Hearings on H.R. 7902*, 73d Cong., 2d sess. (Washington, D.C.: Government Printing Office, 1934), p. 36.

22. Quoted in Prucha, *Americanizing the American Indians*, p. 137.

23. Hazel W. Herzberg, *The Search for an American Indian Identity: Modern Pan-Indian Movements*, pp. 59–70.

24. U.S. Congress, House Committee on Indian Affairs, *Report on H.R. 25242*, 62d Cong., 2d sess. (Washington, D.C.: Government Printing Office, 1912), pp. 4–6.

25. Franklin K. Lane to Senator Henry Ashurst, April 18, 1916, in U.S. Congress, Senate Committee on Indian Affairs, *Hearings on S. 5335*, 64th Cong., 1st sess. (Washington, D.C.: Government Printing Office, 1916), pp. 3ff.

26. Kenneth R. Philp, "Albert Fall and the Protest from the Pueblos," pp. 237–54; idem, *John Collier's Crusade for Indian Reform*, pp. 26–49.

27. John Collier, *From Every Zenith: A Memoir*, pp. 81–84, 93–96, 230–34; idem, *The Indians of the Americas*, pp. 9–11; idem, "Community

Councils: Democracy Every Day," *Survey* 40 (1918): 604–14, 689–91. See also Kunitz, "The Social Philosophy of John Collier," pp. 219–21.

28. Meriam, *Indian Administration*, pp. 21–22, 38–40, 140–48, 468–74, 495–97.

29. Downs, "A Crusade for Indian Reform," pp. 344–45.

30. Commissioner of Indian Affairs, *Annual Report, 1931* (Washington, D.C.: Government Printing Office, 1931), pp. 3–5; C. J. Rhoads and H. Scattergood, "U.S. Indian Service, March 3, 1933," mimeographed, Manuscript Division, Philadelphia Public Library, pp. 10–12. See also Kenneth R. Philp, "Herbert Hoover's New Era: A False Dawn for the American Indian, 1929–1932," pp. 53–60.

31. C. J. Rhoads to Senator Lynn Frazier, December 18, 1929, in *Congressional Record*, vol. 71, 71st Cong., 2d sess. (Washington, D.C.: Government Printing Office, 1929), pp. 1052–54. See also Philp, *John Collier's Crusade for Indian Reform*, p. 94.

32. U.S. Congress, Senate Committee on Indian Affairs, *Hearings on S. 3588*, 72d Cong., 1st sess. (Washington, D.C.: Government Printing Office, 1932), pp. 3–4.

Chapter 2

1. Lawrence C. Kelly, "Choosing a New Deal Indian Commissioner: Ickes versus Collier," pp. 282–87.

2. Indian Rights Association, *51st Annual Report of the Board of Governors*, Philadelphia, December 1933, p. 5.

3. Commissioner of Indian Affairs, *Annual Report, 1933–1934* (Washington, D.C.: Government Printing Office, 1934), pp. 69–71. See also Donald H. Parman, "The Indian and the Civilian Conservation Corps," pp. 39–56.

4. The bills include S. 529, introduced by Senator Lynn Frazier of the Senate Committee on Indian Affairs, March 20, 1933; H.R. 4603; introduced by Representative James Sinclair (R., N.Dak.), April 4, 1933; and H.R. 4803 and H.R. 4813, introduced by Representative Edgar Howard (D., Nebr.), and Representative Roy Ayers, respectively, April 10, 1933. *Congressional Record*, vol. 77 (Washington, D.C.: Government Printing Office, 1933), pp. 618, 1240, 1453.

5. Oliver La Farge, memorandum of conversation with Allan G. Harper, November 16, 1933, Papers of the American Association on Indian Affairs, Princeton University Library, Princeton, N.J. (hereafter cited as AAIA Papers).

6. La Farge to Harper, November 22, 1933; La Farge to Jonathan Steere, president, Indian Rights Association, November 22, 1933. AAIA Papers. The text of the Cosmos Club resolutions is in House Committee on Indian Affairs, *Hearings on S. 2103*, 76th Cong., 3d sess. (Washington, D.C.: Government Printing Office, 1940), pp. 409–12.

7. U.S. Congress, House Committee on Indian Affairs, *Hearings on H.R. 7902*, 73d Cong., 2d sess. (Washington, D.C.: Government Printing Office, 1934), pp. 1–12. See also Michael T. Smith, "The Wheeler-Howard Act of 1934: The Indian New Deal," pp. 524–26.

8. *Hearings on H.R. 7902*, pp. 20–22.

9. See Philip Selznick, *T.V.A. and the Grass Roots* (Berkeley: University of California Press, 1949), pp. 219–26, for a discussion of the basic differences among federal land use programs of the New Deal.

10. *Hearings on H.R. 7902*, p. 64. Werner was considered a major obstacle to the bill in the committee by the Indian Defense Association, which issued a news release in April 1934, charging him with "the use of every technical rule to prevent consideration of the Wheeler-Howard bill" (AAIA Papers).

11. *Hearings on H.R. 7902*, pp. 23, 59.

12. Ibid., pp. 60–61. See also John L. Freeman, "The New Deal for the Indians: A Study of Bureau-Committee Relationships in American Government" (Ph.D. diss. Princeton University, 1952), pp. 82–83, for an analysis of Collier's views on assimilation.

13. *Hearings on H.R. 7902*, pp. 66–68.

14. Flora Seymour, "Trying It on the Indians," *New Outlook*, May 1934, pp. 22–25; Oliver La Farge, "The American Indian's Revenge," *Current History* 11 (May 1934): 163–68.

15. *Hearings on H.R. 7902*, pp. 118–20, 134. Collier was at this time seeking a new Pueblo relief bill that would increase the authority of the Pueblo Lands Board in settling questions of compensation.

16. Franz Boas to John Collier, May 9, 1934; Ralph Linton to Collier, April 16, 1934, Records relating to the Wheeler-Howard Act, NA, RG 75 (hereafter cited as Wheeler-Howard Records, NA, RG 75).

17. *Congressional Record*, vol. 78 (Washington, D.C.: Government Printing Office, 1934), pp. 9265–66. Assemblies were held at Rapid City, South Dakota; Salem, Oregon; Santo Domingo, New Mexico; Fort Defiance and Phoenix, Arizona; Riverside, California; and Anadarko, Oklahoma. See also Freeman, "The New Deal for the Indians," p. 143.

18. Allan G. Harper to Oliver La Farge, May 6, 1934, AAIA Papers.

19. Freeman, "The New Deal for the Indians," pp. 252–53.

20. U.S. Congress, *House Report 1804*, 73d Cong., 2d sess. (Washington, D.C.: Government Printing Office, 1934), p. 5. See also *Senate Report 1080*, 73d Cong., 2d sess. (Washington, D.C.: Government Printing Office, 1934).

21. *Congressional Record*, 78: 11126–39.

22. Ibid., 78: 11744.

23. U.S. Congress, *Laws Relating to Indian Affairs*, 73d Cong., 2d sess. (Washington, D.C.: Government Printing Office, 1934), pp. 381–82.

24. Collier, *The Indians of the Americas*, p. 265.

Chapter 3

1. Cohen, *Handbook of Federal Indian Law*, p. 132.

2. Collier, *From Every Zenith*, p. 236.

3. Clyde Kluckhohn and Robert Hackenberg, "Social Science Principles and the Indian Reorganization Act," in *Indian Affairs and the Indian Reorganization Act: The Twenty-Year Record*, ed. W. H. Kelly, p. 29.

4. In the first annual report of the commissioner of Indian Affairs after the passage of the Wheeler-Howard Act, Collier complained that the land purchase and revolving credit funds provided for in the act were inadequate, and that the provisions for transfer of heirship lands were at best "a first, hesitant step toward a solution of this problem" (Commissioner of Indian Affairs, *Annual Report, 1934-35*, pp. 79-82).

5. Collier, *From Every Zenith*, p. 224.

6. Jay B. Nash, Oliver La Farge, and W. Carson Ryan, eds., *The New Day for the Indians* (Washington, D.C.: Government Printing Office, 1938), p. 27.

7. In April 1934, while the Indian Reorganization bill was still in committee, Interior Secretary Ickes sent out a directive requiring bureau employees not to criticize the bill in public, and threatened those who defied the order with dismissal. This order aroused ire in Congress as a "gag rule" which unfairly silenced opponents of the bill, since Collier and his staff were touring the country promoting their version throughout this period. See *Congressional Record*, 78: 11738.

8. John Collier to M. L. Burns, June 21, 1934, Wheeler-Howard Records, NA, RG 75.

9. Commissioner of Indian Affairs, *Annual Report, 1935-36*, p. 115.

10. The voting results for the referenda on the Indian Reorganization Act are tabulated in Theodore H. Haas, *Ten Years of Tribal Government under the I.R.A.*, pp. 14-20. According to Haas's figures, 194 Indian groups voted to come under the act and 74 rejected it, while 12 more were brought under the act either because they did not vote or because the number of voters constituted less than 30 percent of those eligible. In one case, the Indians refused to vote (Santa Rosa at Sacramento Agency, California), and in another the act was rejected but only 27 percent of the eligible voters participated (Walker River at Carson Agency, Nevada).

11. Commissioner of Indian Affairs, *Annual Report, 1935-36*, p. 116.

12. Freeman, "The New Deal for the Indians," p. 226; Oliver La Farge to Allan G. Harper, July 1, 1935, AAIA Files; M. K. Sniffen, executive secretary, Indian Rights Association, to J. M. Steere, president, Indian Rights Association, August 19, 1935, Indian Rights Association Papers, Pennsylvania Historical Society, Philadelphia.

13. John Collier to Harold Ickes, February 15, 1935; Collier to Ickes, March 6, 1935, Collier Papers, Yale University. See also Smith, "The Wheeler-Howard Act of 1934," p. 532.

14. Commissioner of Indian Affairs, *Annual Report, 1935-36*, p. 115. Actually, the overall appropriations for the Indian Service were to increase from $19 million in 1935 to $35 million in 1940, although a large part of these additions came from "emergency funds" for IECW and other relief projects. See Freeman, "The New Deal for the Indians," pp. 436-38.

15. The text is in Haas, *Ten Years*, p. 41.

16. William N. Paul, attorney, Alaska Native Brotherhood, to A. J. Dimond, Alaska delegate to Congress, June 2, 1935, Tribal Organization Records, Alaska File, NA, RG 75.

17. Haas, *Ten Years*, p. 42. O. H. Lipps of the bureau concluded in 1937 that the villages were too small to function successfully as independent corporations, and suggested that several villages be encouraged to combine resources to make the corporations economically feasible (O. H. Lipps et al., "Report on Organization in Alaska," February 5, 1937, Tribal Organization Records, Alaska File, NA, RG 75).

18. On the Oklahoma Indians, see B. T. Quinten, "Oklahoma Tribes, the Great Depression, and the Indian Bureau," pp. 29-43; and Angie Debo, *And Still the Waters Run: The Betrayal of the Civilized Tribes*, pp. 351-79.

19. Freeman, "The New Deal for the Indians," pp. 279-89. See also Peter Wright, "John Collier and the Oklahoma Indian Welfare Act of 1936," pp. 347-71.

20. Freeman, "The New Deal for the Indians," pp. 290-96.

21. The text of the bill is in Haas, *Ten Years*, pp. 13 15.

22. Haas, *Ten Years*, p. 28; Debo, *And Still the Waters Run*, pp. 372-73.

23. Commissioner of Indian Affairs, *Annual Report, 1936-37* (Washington, D.C.: Government Printing Office, 1937), pp. 200-201; Haas, *Ten Years*, pp. 22-27. The figures given do not include tribal constitutions and charters in Oklahoma and Alaska. As noted earlier, eighteen groups organized under the Oklahoma Indian Welfare Act, and all but five of these ratified corporate charters as of 1944. In Alaska, forty-six native communities were organized and all were issued charters of incorporation as of 1945.

24. The criticism of standardization was made by Charlotte T. Westwood, assistant solicitor of the Interior Department, in a letter to Collier, November 16, 1935, Tribal Organization Records, Chippewa Files, NA, RG 75. The criticism of linguistic obfuscation was made by Alida C. Bowler, superintendent, Carson Agency, Nevada, in a letter to Collier, December 28, 1938, Tribal Organization Records, Carson File, NA, RG 75. The Westwood letter was discovered by a hostile senatorial investigating committee, which printed it in order to discredit the Wheeler-Howard Act and justify its repeal. See *Senate Report 1031*, 78th Cong., 2d sess. (Washington, D.C.: Government Printing Office, 1944), pp. 5-6. Collier's response to this particular item is in House Committee on Indian Affairs, *Hearings on H.R. 166*, 78th Cong., 1st sess. (Washington, D.C.: Government Printing Office, 1944), pt. 4, p. 20.

25. Collier to Ickes, June 1, 1934, Collier Papers.

26. Commissioner of Indian Affairs, *Annual Report, 1936–37*, p. 200. On the role of anthropologists in the Indian Service, see David L. Marden, "Anthropologists and Federal Indian Policy prior to 1940," pp. 19–26; Graham D. Taylor, "Anthropologists, Reformers, and the Indian New Deal," pp. 151–62; and Lawrence C. Kelly, "Anthropology in the Indian New Deal: The Personality and Government Project," paper presented at meeting of the Organization of American Historians, Atlanta, Georgia, April 8, 1977.

27. Circular on Indian Reorganization, 1936, Wheeler-Howard Records, NA, RG 75. Daiker was succeeded as head of the division by D'Arcy Mc-Nickle, a Flathead Indian, who later became assistant commissioner. Without exception the Indians from the bureau who attended the first session of the National Congress of American Indians at Denver in 1944 were, or had been, in the Indian Organization Division.

Chapter 4

1. In this respect, it is interesting to note that studies of the process of acculturation were not undertaken on a large scale by American anthropologists before the 1930s; emphasis was placed in research on the identification of "traditional" customs and institutions. See Ralph Linton, "Acculturation and the Processes of Cultural Change," in *Acculturation in Seven Indian Tribes,* ed. Ralph Linton (New York: Appleton-Century, 1940), pp. 463–64.

2. Commissioner of Indian Affairs, *Annual Report, 1934–35*, p. 114.

3. Collier, *From Every Zenith*, pp. 440–41.

4. Ibid., p. 240.

5. House Committee on Indian Affairs, *Hearings on H.R. 7902*, p. 21.

6. The data on admixture of blood among Indian tribes are based on a survey of social and economic conditions on thirty-three Indian reservations carried out by the Civil Works Administration in 1933–34, and on information in U.S. Census Bureau, *The Indian Population of the United States,* comp. L. Truesdell (Washington, D.C.: Government Printing Office, 1937), pp. 76–79, which was based largely on statistics in the Fifteenth Census (1930). Information on literacy rates is also based on *The Indian Population of the United States*, pp. 146–47. The statistics for tribal land alienation (which were computed as percentages of total allotted land rather than total reservation land) were compiled by the National Resources Board, Land Planning Unit, which carried out land surveys of all the major Indian reservations in 1934 and 1935; the summary of this research is in *Indian Land Tenure, Economic Status, and Population Trends*, passim. The records of the Civil Works Administration and National Resources Board surveys which I used in preparing these tables are in NA, RG 75. See Appendix 1 for a discussion of the sources and the tables on which this table is based.

7. See Robert F. Berkhofer, Jr., "The Political Context of a New Indian History," pp. 363–71, for a discussion of the importance of factionalism

within Indian tribes even before the reservation era and the implications of factionalism among Indians for the concept of the tribe.

8. Morris E. Opler, "Report on Observations at Mescalero Reservation," 1936; J. C. Cavill, superintendent, Mescalero Reservation, to Collier, May 7, 1935, Tribal Organization Records, Mescalero File, NA, RG 75.

9. Morris E. Opler to Collier, February 22, 1937; Opler to Allan G. Harper, April 19, 1937; A. G. Stover, superintendent, Jicarilla Agency, Dulce, N. Mex., to Collier, August 14, 1937, Tribal Organization Records, Jicarilla File, NA, RG 75. The constitution was ratified in July 1937, with only two dissenting votes.

10. Oliver La Farge to Collier, September 21, 1934, Collier Papers.

11. A. C. Plake to A. H. Kneale, superintendent, Pima-Maricopa Agency, Scottsdale, Arizona, July 25, 1934, Tribal Organization Records, Pima File, NA, RG 75. There were other "Montezumist" groups among the agencies in the Southwest, including Sells (Papago) Reservation in Arizona and Isleta pueblo in New Mexico. See Spicer, *Cycles of Conquest*, p. 530.

12. Oliver La Farge to M. K. Sniffen, February 17, 1937, Indian Rights Association Papers; Collier to Ickes, February 9, 1937, Collier Papers; Elizabeth Sergeant, "Memorandum of Santa Clara Objections to the Washington Draft of the Constitution and By-Laws," November 19, 1935, Tribal Organization Records, Pueblo File, NA, RG 75.

13. Collier to Ickes, June 1, 1936; Collier to All-Pueblo Council, June 13, 1936; Collier to Jay B. Nash, June 19, 1938, Collier Papers. Peyote had long been used by Indians in the Southwest and Mexico, but in the early years of the twentieth century a peyote cult emerged, and thrived on the plains reservations, integrating various elements of traditional Indian religions and Christianity with the use of the drug. During the 1930s the peyote church experienced a revival on the southwestern reservations, where it had hitherto been relatively weak, particularly among the Navajos. See James Slotkin, *The Peyote Religion* (Glencoe, Ill.: Free Press, 1956); David H. Aberle, *The Peyote Religion among the Navaho*.

14. C. E. Faris, superintendent, Northern Pueblos, Santa Fe, N. Mex., to Collier, August 17, 1934, Tribal Organization Records, Pueblo File, NA, RG 75; D'Arcy McNickle, interview, April 1973.

15. Theodore B. Hall, superintendent, Sells Agency, Arizona, to Collier, October 17, 1935, Tribal Organization Records, Sells File, NA, RG 75.

16. Ruth Underhill, *The Navajos*, p. 231.

17. Theodore B. Hall to Collier, October 17, 1935; John H. Holst and Kenneth A. Marmon, "Memorandum . . . Papago Cattle Association," October 29, 1935, Tribal Organization Records, Sells File, NA, RG 75; John Pearmain, TC-BIA field coordinator, to Allan G. Harper, August 4, 1938, Records of the Technical Cooperation-Bureau of Indian Affairs Project, Soil Conservation Service Records, NA, RG 114 (hereafter cited as TC-BIA Records, NA, RG 114).

18. Parman, *The Navajos and the New Deal*, pp. 17–20. See also Lawrence C. Kelly, *The Navajo Indians and Federal Indian Policy*, pp. 158–63.

19. Ivan Drift to Collier, December 29, 1933, Tribal Organization Records, Pine Ridge File, NA, RG 75.

20. Collier, testimony on March 30, 1940, in Senate Committee on Indian Affairs, *Hearings on S. 2103*, 76th Cong., 3d sess. (Washington, D.C.: Government Printing Office, 1940), p. 59. In his study of the Pine Ridge Sioux for the Personality and Government Project, carried out jointly by the Indian Service and the University of Chicago, Gordon Macgregor argued that the Sioux males, deprived of opportunities to participate in traditional ceremonies like the sun dance, turned their combative instincts inward, generating petty conflicts in their homes and in the community. See Gordon Macgregor, *Warriors without Weapons: A Study of the Society and Personality Development of the Pine Ridge Sioux*, pp. 207–9.

21. William O. Roberts, superintendent, Rosebud Agency, S. Dak., to Collier, August 14, 1934, Tribal Organization Records, Rosebud File, NA, RG 75.

22. These Indians were particularly bewildered by the 1934–35 referendum on the Wheeler-Howard Act, which was a binding, never-to-be-repeated vote. Several groups that had voted against the act later asked to be allowed to hold another referendum since they had changed their minds. In at least one case (the Colville Reservation in Washington), the bureau sought special legislation to enable them to do so. Helen Tandon to Collier, May 27, 1939; William Zimmerman, assistant commissioner, to Louis Balsam, superintendent, Colville Agency, Washington, August 15, 1939, Tribal Organization Records, Colville File, NA, RG 75. In other cases, especially on the Sioux reservations, Indians who had voted to come under the act later changed their minds and refused to proceed further with preparing constitutions or charters, and sought to have Congress repeal the act as it applied to their reservations. See House Committee on Indian Affairs, *Hearings on H.R. 5878, to Amend the Wheeler-Howard Act*, 76th Cong., 3d sess. (Washington, D.C.: Government Printing Office, 1940).

23. *The Indian Population of the United States*, pp. 89, 147.

24. Opler, "Report on Observations at Mescalero Reservation."

25. This favoritism toward mixed-bloods on the part of Indian Service agents was a rather recent phenomenon. Clark Wissler, an anthropologist who visited numerous plains reservations in the 1900–1910 period, encountered a good deal of contempt among bureau employees toward "half-breeds," who were regarded as mentally and morally inferior to "real Indians." See Clark Wissler, *Red Man Reservations*, pp. 183–84.

26. Ruth Underhill to W. Duncan Strong, Applied Anthropology Staff, October 29, 1935, Tribal Organization Records, Sells File, NA, RG 75.

27. John H. Holst to Collier, June 4, 1938, Tribal Organization Records, Sac and Fox File, NA, RG 75.

28. Amos Red Owl to Collier, May 11, 1938, Tribal Organization Records, Pine Ridge File, NA, RG 75.

29. D'Arcy McNickle, Memorandum on Tribal Organization, September 13, 1941, Wheeler-Howard Records, NA, RG 75; Hiram N. Clarke, "Observations on Flathead Tribal Council," 1935, Tribal Organization Records, Flathead File, NA, RG 75.

30. Collier to Allan G. Harper, November 1936, Collier Papers.

31. M. K. Sniffen to Collier, August 28, 1933, Tribal Organization Records, Colville File, NA, RG 75.

32. William Zimmerman, assistant commissioner, to W. J. Bulow, April 21, 1940, Tribal Organization Records, Rosebud File, NA, RG 75, Zimmerman was writing in reference to a particular problem at the Yankton Subagency, but it is representative of a situation on many reservations in the plains.

33. Dick Red Bear to Harold Ickes, April 9, 1940, Tribal Organization Records, Pine Ridge File, NA, RG 75.

34. John H. Holst, "Considerations Affecting the Method of Organizing the Minnesota Chippewa Indians," 1935, Tribal Organization Records, Consolidated Chippewa File, NA, RG 75.

35. R. H. Bitney, superintendent, Red Lake Agency, Minnesota, to Collier, December 13, 1935; Bitney to Collier, July 31, 1941, Tribal Organization Records, Consolidated Chippewa File, NA, RG 75.

36. Bitney to Collier, March 17, 1936; Minutes of Meeting, Red Lake Tribal General Council, March 14, 1936, ibid. The affair was even more complicated than indicated here. Morrison had been head of the trading post at Red Lake and had created a Red Lake Business Association in 1934 to undermine the control of Peter Graves, a full-blood and head of the Red Lake General Council, who had been his personal rival since 1917, when Morrison was president of the Chippewa General Council and Graves had led the Red Lake secession movement. The Red Lake Chippewas also suspected that the new general council would use up Red Lake assets to finance the cooperative, and they distrusted the managerial ability of the other Indians. The bureau attempted to get the Indians to distinguish between the two ventures, but the Red Lake group believed tribal organization and the cooperative to be integrally related and made a very plausible argument linking them.

37. "Report of Walter W. Liggett on Blackfeet Indian Reservation," in Senate Committee on Indian Affairs, *Survey of Conditions of Indians in the United States*, 23: 12746–47.

38. Allan G. Harper to Walter V. Woehlke, September 1, 1935, Collier Papers; "Reconaissance Survey of the Blackfeet Indian Reservation," April 1939, TC-BIA Records, NA, RG 114. Woehlke had written a highly laudatory account of the five-year plan when it was initiated. See W. V. Woehlke, "Hope for the Blackfeet," *Sunset Magazine*, December 1923, pp. 9–11, 97–100.

39. William Zimmerman to James White Calf, January 11, 1936, Tribal Organization Records, Blackfeet File, NA, RG 75.

40. H. Scudder Mekeel to C. E. Faris, Report on Blackfeet Reservation, November 23, 1937; Stuart Hazlett, chairman, Blackfeet Tribal Council, to Collier, June 7, 1938, ibid.

41. Testimony of Joseph Brown, Blackfeet Tribal Council, in House Committee on Indian Affairs, *Hearings on H.R. 166,* pt. 3, August 4, 1944, pp. 402-8.

42. Testimony of William Zimmerman, Brian Connolly, and Leo Kennerly in *Hearings on H.R. 166,* pt. 3, pp. 294, 409-11, 425-30; Leo Kennerly, Blackfeet Tribal Council, to Ickes, April 11, 1941, Tribal Organization Records, Blackfeet File, NA, RG 75.

43. Charles Heacock to D'Arcy McNickle, December 19, 1945, Tribal Organization Records, Blackfeet File, NA, RG 75.

44. Vine Deloria, Sr., interview, April 1970.

45. C. M. Dollar and R. J. Jensen, *Historian's Guide to Statistics* (New York: Holt, Rinehart and Winston, 1971), pp. 97-103.

46. Robert Burnette and John Koster, *The Road to Wounded Knee* (New York: Bantam, 1974), pp. 116-17.

47. Sometimes the situation took a reverse twist. At the Colville Agency in Washington, supporters of the Reorganization Act complained, after the referendum had resulted in rejection by the Indians there, that they had been misled by the superintendent into thinking that withheld votes would be counted as votes in favor of the act. Peter Gunn, president, Colville Indian Association, to Collier, July 26, 1935, Tribal Organization Records, Colville File, NA, RG 75.

48. Ivan Drift to Collier, December 29, 1933, Tribal Organization Records, Pine Ridge File, NA, RG 75; Floyd Pollock, "Navajo-Federal Relations as a Social-Cultural Problem," pp. 316-17.

49. W. R. Centerwall, superintendent, Tongue River Agency, Lame Deer, Montana, to Collier, August 17, 1934; George LaVatta to Fred H. Daiker, Tribal Organization Division, November 6, 1935, Tribal Organization Records, Tongue River File, NA, RG 75.

50. Robert Yellowtail, superintendent, Crow Agency, Montana, to Collier, May 2, 1935, Tribal Organization Records, Crow File, NA, RG 75. Yellowtail was a Crow who had been elected superintendent by his fellow tribesmen in 1933 and was very popular there, but was suspected of opposing the Reorganization Act. W. R. Centerwall to Collier, February 16, 1935, Tribal Organization Records, Tongue River File, NA, RG 75. Yellowtail was also friendly with Senator Wheeler and later developed political ambitions of his own.

51. *Hearings on H.R. 7902,* pp. 136-38.

52. Fred H. Daiker to Dick Red Bear, April 29, 1940, Tribal Organization Records, Pine Ridge File, NA, RG 75.

53. Opler, "Report on Observations at Mescalero Reservation."

Chapter 5

1. Kroeber, "The Nature of the Land-holding Group," p. 303.

2. This view of tribalism among Indians has been contested. D'Arcy McNickle, *Native American Indian Tribalism: Indian Survivals and Renewals*, pp. 7-10, argues on the basis of studies by A. I. Hallowell of Indian tribal psychological characteristics, that tribalism has been a persistent feature of Indian cultural groups. Anthropologist Robert Hackenberg, "The Parameters of an Ethnic Group: A Method for Studying the Total Tribe," *American Anthropologist* 69 (October 1967): 478-79, suggests that anthropologists' generalizations about tribal societies may have been limited because they have tended to focus on smaller units of Indian life rather than on larger cultural entities.

3. Marshall D. Sahlines, *Tribesmen* (Englewood Cliffs, N.J.: Prentice-Hall, 1968), pp. 5-6, 49.

4. E. Adamson Hoebel, *The Law of Primitive Man* (Cambridge, Mass.: Harvard University Press, 1964), pp. 22-28.

5. Archie Phinney, "Memorandum on Ward Shepard Plan of Reorganization of the Bureau of Indian Affairs," August 30, 1942, Tribal Organization Records, General Files, NA, RG 75.

6. Morris E. Opler, "Memorandum in Regard to Creek Towns," May 1937: A. C. Monahan, Oklahoma regional coordinator, to Collier, June 18, 1937, Tribal Organization Records, Five Tribes File, NA, RG 75. It appears that the Creeks themselves were not much interested in any form of tribal organization, being mainly concerned with acquiring credit; only three towns were eventually organized under the Oklahoma act. Monahan to Collier, March 10, 1938, ibid.

7. McNickle, *Native American Tribalism*, pp. 153-55.

8. F. L. Kirgis to Collier, July 15, 1937, Tribal Organization Records, Five Tribes File, NA, RG 75.

9. Of the thirty-one community organizations under the Indian Reorganization Act, nine were in California and five in Nevada, where the Indians historically had never developed tribal organizations and the reservations consisted mainly of scattered small plots of land, or rancherias. Seven others were in Michigan and Minnesota, where most of the Indian lands had been released in fee patent. The other ten community groups were scattered, but fit one or the other of these categories.

10. John Backus, superintendent, Yankton Subagency, Rosebud, South Dakota, to Collier, November 17, 1936; Kenneth Meicklejohn to Allan G. Harper, December 3, 1936, Tribal Organization Records, Rosebud File, NA, RG 75.

11. C. B. Suszen Timentoe to Collier, March 6, 1935; H. K. Meyer, superintendent, Colville Agency, Washington, to Collier, May 20, 1935; William Zimmerman to Willie Red Star, Colville, Washington, March 29, 1935, Tribal Organization Records, Colville File, NA, RG 75. In fact, the bureau could have permitted the arrangement demanded by the Indians on the grounds

of historical differences: most of the full-bloods in the south half of the
Colville Reservation were of the Nez Percé, not the Colville, tribe. That it
was not done indicates that economic criteria were considered the most
important.

12. Kenneth A. Marmon, Regional Office, Duchesne, Utah, to Fred H.
Daiker, Tribal Organization Division, June 17, 1942, Tribal Organization
Records, Uintah-Ouray File, NA, RG 75.

13. C. E. Faris, superintendent, Northern Pueblos, Santa Fe, New Mexico,
to Collier, August 17, 1934, Tribal Organization Records, Pueblo File, NA,
RG 75. See also Ralph Beals, "An Outline of Pueblo Government," in Brand
and Harvey, *So Live the Works of Man*, pp. 147-57.

14. Fred C. Eggan, *Social Organization of the Western Pueblos*, pp. 106-9.
Spicer, *Cycles of Conquest*, pp. 380-81, points out that in the period before
significant white contact the western Pueblos were more united than the Rio
Grande Pueblos, who often fought one another. By the twentieth century,
however, this situation seems to have changed.

15. Ruth Underhill to W. Duncan Strong, October 30, 1935, Tribal Organization Records, Sells File, NA, GR 75; see also Ruth Underhill, *Red
Man's America*, pp. 190-93.

16. Underhill, *Red Man's America*, pp. 254-55.

17. C. E. Faris to Collier, June 17, 1936, Tribal Organization Records,
Jicarilla File, NA, RG 75.

18. Margaret Welpley, "Preliminary Report on the Political Situation at
San Carlos," December 11, 1934, Tribal Organization Records, San Carlos
File, NA, RG 75.

19. Kelly, *The Navajo Indians and Federal Indian Policy*, pp. 49-54,
192-93.

20. House Committee on Indian Affairs, *Hearings on H.R. 7902*, p. 38. In
a 1924 article in *Sunset Magazine* entitled "The Fate of the Navajos," Collier
had a good deal of praise for Navajo superintendent H. J. Hagerman, the man
whom he charged in 1930 and in 1934 with having destroyed "traditional"
Navajo government in order to rob the Indians of their oil leases.

21. Kelly, *The Navajo Indians and Federal Indian Policy*, pp. 190, 193.

22. Oliver La Farge to Collier, December 5, 1933, Wheeler-Howard
Records, NA, RG 75.

23. Clyde Kluckhohn and Dorothea Leighton, *The Navaho*, pp. 100-101.

24. La Farge to Collier, December 5, 1933, Wheeler-Howard Records,
NA, RG 75.

25. Aberle, *The Peyote Religion among the Navaho*, pp. 42-43.

26. Quoted in Pollock, "Navajo-Federal Relations," p. 280. This comment, like most of the rest of Dodge's discourse on events after 1933 was self-
serving, but it represented the view of one of the most influential traditional
Navajo spokesmen. See Parman, *The Navajos and the New Deal*, pp. 17-21.

27. Ruth Underhill, "The Native Culture System of the Pueblo through
Which the Present Indian Administration Operates," *Indians at Work*, April

1940, pp. 22–25; Minutes of meeting of Commissioner of Indian Affairs with Laguna Council, September 2, 1941; Sophie Aberle, superintendent, United Pueblos Agency, Albuquerque, New Mexico, to Joe Jennings, Tribal Organization Division, January 31, 1941, Tribal Organization Records, Pueblo File, NA, RG 75.

28. Collier to La Farge, May 28, 1935; Collier to Henry A. Wallace, Secretary of Agriculture, December 22, 1939, Collier Papers. The Rio Grande Board is discussed further in Chapter 7. See also John H. Provinse, "Cultural Factors in Land Use Planning," in *The Changing Indian,* ed. Oliver La Farge, pp. 55–71.

29. Laura Thompson and Alice Joseph, *The Hopi Way,* pp. 28–29; Spicer, *Cycles of Conquest,* pp. 196–98.

30. Oliver La Farge to Collier, September 21, 1934, Collier Papers.

31. Ibid.

32. Constitution and By-Laws of the Hopi Tribe of Arizona, December 19, 1935, reprinted in G. E. Fay, comp., *Charters, Constitutions and By-Laws of the Indian Tribes of North America* (Greeley, Colorado: Museum of Anthropology, Colorado State College, 1967), pt. 16, p. 75. See also D'Arcy McNickle, *Indian Man: A Life of Oliver La Farge,* pp. 107–12.

33. Fay, *Charters,* pp. 76–80.

34. See, for example, McNickle, *Indian Man,* p. 112. Spicer in *Cycles of Conquest,* p. 206, however, argues that the tribal constitution only exacerbated intervillage conflict, and that "a majority of Hopis" regarded it "as a rubber stamp organization for the Indian Bureau superintendent."

35. Collier, *From Every Zenith,* p. 218.

36. Laura Thompson, *Personality and Government: Findings and Recommendations of the Indian Administration Research Project* (Mexico: Instituto del America Indiginesta, 1951), pp. 152–56, 161–62.

37. Ruth Underhill, "Social Organization of the Papago Indians," *Columbia University Contributions in Anthropology* 30 (1939): 63–65; see also Alice Joseph, Rosamund Spicer, and Alice Chesky, *The Desert People: A Study of the Papago Indians of Arizona.*

38. Annual Report of Superintendent, Sells Agency, Arizona, 1935–36; Theodore B. Hall, superintendent, Sells Agency, to Collier, October 17, 1935; Hall to Fred H. Daiker, assistant to the commissioner, July 3, 1936, Tribal Organization Records, Sells File, NA, RG 75.

39. Ruth Underhill to W. Duncan Strong, October 30, 1935, ibid.

40. John H. Holst, "Organization of the Papago under I.R.A.," May 5, 1936, ibid.; Allan G. Harper to Collier, December 19, 1936; Collier to Harper, December 21, 1936, Collier Papers.

41. Constitution and By-Laws of the Papago Tribe of Arizona, in Fay, *Charters,* pt. 4, pp. 45–48.

42. John D. Pearmain, soil conservationist, Sells Agency, Arizona, to Lucy W. Adams, TC-BIA, February 24, 1937; Permain to D. E. Harrison, TC-BIA,

March 8, 1937; Lucy W. Adams, "Notes on Papago Situation," March 3, 1937, TC-BIA Records, NA, RG 114.

43. D. E. Harrison to Allan G. Harper, March 8, 1938, ibid.

44. Pearmain to Harper, August 4, 1938; L. B. Holloway, extension agent, to Theodore B. Hall, superintendent, Sells Agency, February 24, 1939, ibid.

45. Thompson, *Personality and Government*, pp. 101–2.

46. Kenneth A. Marmon, Tribal Organization Division, to Hall, April 8, 1938; Hall to Jose Ignacio, chairman, Papago Tribal Council, April 11, 1938; Tribal Organization Records, Sells File, NA, RG 75.

47. Marmon, "Report on Papago Tribe," February 29, 1940, ibid.

48. Ibid.

49. Beulah Head, superintendent, Sells Agency, to Collier, June 11, 1943, Tribal Organization Records, Sells File, NA, RG 75.

50. Spicer, *Cycles of Conquest*, pp. 143–44.

51. Robert Lowie, *Indians of the Plains* (New York: McGraw-Hill, 1954), pp. 6–11.

52. Llewelyn and Hoebel, *The Cheyenne Way*, pp. 67–130; see also George Bird Grinnell, *The Cheyenne Indians: Their History and Ways of Life*, 2 vols. (New Haven: Yale University Press, 1923), 2: 56–79; and Robert H. Lowie, *The Origin of the State* (New York: Russell and Russell, 1927), pp. 103–4, on the significance of military societies as state-building institutions.

53. Stephen Feraca, "The Political Status of the Early Bands and Modern Communities of the Oglala Dakota," *University of South Dakota Museum News* 27 (January 1966): 1–3; Lowie, *Indians of the Plains*, pp. 91–95.

54. Ernest Wallace and E. Adamson Hoebel, *The Comanches: Lords of the Southern Plains*, p. 209.

55. L. W. Shotwell, superintendent, Flathead Agency, Dixon, Montana, to Collier, January 3, 1936; John H. Holst, "Observations on the Former Flathead Reservation," April 3, 1943, Tribal Organization Records, Flathead File, NA, RG 75.

56. A. R. Serven to Fred F. Daiker, June 17, 1936, Tribal Organization Records, Fort Belknap File, NA, RG 75.

57. A. C. Monahan, Oklahoma regional coordinator, to Collier, July 8, 1937, Tribal Organization Records, Kiowa File, NA, RG 75; Mildred Mayhall, *The Kiowas* (Norman: University of Oklahoma Press, 1962), pp. 207–10, 273–74.

58. John H. Holst, "Organization on Fort Berthold Reservation," November 16, 1935, Tribal Organization Records, Fort Berthold File, NA, RG 75.

59. C. E. Schaffer, Report on Council Election at Flathead Reservation, December 21, 1935, Tribal Organization Records, Flathead File, NA, RG 75.

60. "Observations on Flathead Tribal Council," n.d. (ca. 1936), ibid.

61. L. W. Shotwell to Collier, January 11, 1936, and December 8, 1937, ibid.

62. Martin Charlo to Ickes, April 29, 1940; Baptiste Mathias to Walter V. Woehlke, March 17, 1943, ibid. During 1939 and 1940 several Indians from the Flathead reservation appeared before the Senate Committee on Indian Affairs and produced petitions urging repeal of the Reorganization Act. Local bureau officials linked these complainants to Joseph Bruner's American Indian Federation, which had been seeking a foothold at Flathead for several years. H. O. Decker, acting superintendent, Flathead Agency, to Daiker, July 19, 1939, ibid.

63. John H. Holst, "Observations on the Former Flathead Reservation."

64. Spicer, *Cycles of Conquest*, p. 413.

65. Burnette and Koster, *The Road to Wounded Knee*, pp. 116–17, argue that the tribal councils established under the Wheeler-Howard Act represented only a minority of self-interested Indian politicians. If the reports cited here by Holst and others are accurate, this charge, however exaggerated, may not be far off the mark in explaining the roots of internal tribal friction in the post-Collier era.

66. According to the report of the Division of Extension and Industry on the IRA loan program as of June 30, 1939, Tongue River had arranged for a loan of $2,090,931, and had been advanced $287,724 since 1937, which was the largest single advance granted to any tribe under the program. This amount increased to $751,531 (16 percent of the total loans under the IRA) as of 1943, and $464,551 of the advance had been repaid in full. See House Committee on Indian Affairs, *Hearings on H.R. 166*, pt. 4, p. 22.

67. F. A. Asbury and C. H. Jennings, "The Tongue River Steer Enterprise," *Indians at Work*, August 1939, pp. 15–16.

68. Minutes of Northern Cheyenne Tribal Council, January 21, 1937; C. E. Faris to C. H. Jennings, superintendent, Tongue River Agency, Harlem, Montana, October 23, 1937, Tribal Organization Records, Tongue River File, NA, RG 75.

69. Kenneth Meicklejohn to Fred H. Daiker, November 3, 1937, ibid.

70. Archie Phinney to Joe Jennings, regional coordinator, Minneapolis, Minnesota, March 16, 1938; Mark L. Burns to Collier, August 3, 1938, Tribal Organization Records, Consolidated Chippewa File, NA, RG 75.

71. Phinney to Collier, November 1, 1938; transcript of meeting of tribal delegates and local council officers of White Earth Reservation, September 17, 1938, ibid.

72. D'Arcy McNickle to Kenneth Meicklejohn, November 5, 1938; Meicklejohn to McNickle, November 21, 1938, ibid.

73. Feraca, "Early Bands and Modern Communities," pp. 2–4; H. Scudder Mekeel, "A Short History of the Teton Dakota," *North Dakota Historical Quarterly* 10 (October 1943): 137–205.

74. H. Scudder Mekeel to Collier, April 7, 1934, Wheeler-Howard Records, NA, RG 75.

75. William O. Roberts, "Administration at the Rosebud Jurisdiction

through Indian Organization," August 22, 1935, Tribal Organization Records, Rosebud File, NA, RG 75.

76. W. F. Dickens, superintendent, Cheyenne River Agency, South Dakota, to Collier, August 30, 1935, Tribal Organization Records, Cheyenne River File, NA, RG 75.

77. Ben Reifel to Fred H. Daiker, October 27, 1935; Mekeel to Daiker, October 31, 1935, Tribal Organization Records, Pine Ridge File, NA, RG 75.

78. Charles Brooks, memorandum on Pine Ridge constitution, n.d. (ca. 1938), ibid.

79. William O. Roberts, "Dakota Indians: Successful Agriculture within the Reservation Framework," *Applied Anthropology* 2 (June 1943): 37–44; Thompson, *Personality and Government*, pp. 87–90.

80. Ben Reifel to Daiker, August 25, 1935; William Zimmerman to C. R. Whitlock, superintendent, Rosebud Agency, South Dakota, April 21, 1937; J. J. Backus, superintendent, Yankton Subagency, to Whitlock, May 18, 1938, Tribal Organization Records, Rosebud File, NA, RG 75.

81. Whitlock to Joe Jennings, Indian Organization Division, February 5, 1938, ibid.; House Committee on Indian Affairs, *Hearings on H.R. 5878*, pp. 110–12.

Chapter 6

1. The *Handbook of Federal Indian Law* was published in 1942 by the Department of the Interior and was not reissued in its original form until 1968, when it was reprinted by the University of New Mexico Press. The *Handbook* did not have the force of law, but it remains the only complete study of an extremely complex subject. See R. L. Bennet and F. M. Hart, Foreword, *Felix Cohen's Handbook of Federal Indian Law* (Albuquerque: University of New Mexico Press, 1968), pp. v–vi.

2. See Freeman, "The New Deal for the Indians," pp. 377–87, for an analysis of the complaints of Indian witnesses before various congressional investigating committees in the period 1937–44.

3. Critical analyses of the tribal organization program include Kelly, "The Indian Reorganization Act," pp. 310–11; and Philp, *John Collier's Crusade for Indian Reform*, pp. 163–66. At a panel at the convention of the Organization of American Historians in Chicago in April 1973, where Philp and Kelly presented papers arguing their position, D'Arcy McNickle, in his commentary, maintained that they had missed the point, since the main purpose of the Indian New Deal had been to restore the economic bases of Indian life to form the underpinnings for future tribal self-determination; hence, carping over the failures on the political side in the early years was irrelevant. My response to this criticism is developed in this chapter and in Chapter 7.

4. Murray Wax, *Indian Americans: Unity and Diversity* (Englewood Cliffs, N.J.: Prentice-Hall, 1971), p. 74.

5. Freeman, "The New Deal for the Indians," p. 272.

6. Margold's opinion is in U.S. Department of the Interior, *Decisions of the Department of the Interior*, vol. 55 (Washington, D.C.: Government Printing Office, 1938), pp. 14–67. The opinion appears to have been based on a study by Felix Cohen, "The Power of an Indian Tribe," which appeared in modified form in *Handbook of Federal Indian Law*, pp. 122–82. See also E. R. McGimpsey, "Indian Tribal Sovereignty," in "Studies in American Indian Law," ed. Ralph W. Johnson, 2 vols., mimeographed (University of Washington Law School, Seattle, Washington), 2:1–75.

7. *Senate Report 1031*, 78th Cong., 2d sess. (Washington, D.C.: Government Printing Office, 1944), p. 5.

8. Statement by John Collier, *Hearings on H.R. 166*, p. 20.

9. Constitution and By-Laws of the Ute Mountain Tribe, June 6, 1940, in Fay, *Charters*, pt. 5, p. 99.

10. Under the Indian Reorganization Act some fifty tribes established tribal courts, which operate under simplified legal codes and whose jurisdiction has been compared to justice of the peace courts. They have jurisdiction over most civil matters and criminal acts involving Indians within the territorial limits of the tribe (the reservation), as well as whites residing on the reservation. The tribal courts established under the 1934 act replaced courts that had hitherto existed at the sufferance of the reservation agent under an Interior Department directive of 1884. See Cohen, *Handbook of Federal Indian Law*, pp. 145–49. See also Marilyn Sloan, "The Indian Bill of Rights," in Johnson, "Studies in American Indian Law," 1:36–42, for a critical appraisal of the tribal court system. On the pre-1935 reservation court system, see William T. Hagan, *Indian Police and Judges* (New Haven: Yale University Press, 1966).

11. These conclusions are based on an examination of twenty constitutions established under the Indian Reorganization Act between 1935 and 1945, and on a similar survey of twenty-two constitutions in M. C. Sykes, "A History of Attempts of the U.S. Government to Reestablish Self-Government among the Indian Tribes, 1934–1949" (master's thesis, Bowling Green State University, 1950). Under the article "Powers of the Council," the items enumerated by Margold and the Wheeler-Howard Act were included in the model constitutions. The same provisions, generally using the same words, in nine of the twenty-six powers enumerated, were found in 86 percent of all the constitutions examined, and another four in over 70 percent of the constitutions, so that it could generally be concluded, on the basis of this sample, that in over two-thirds of all the constitutions, more than half of the provisions relating to tribal council powers were taken directly from the model constitution.

12. Welpley, "Preliminary Report on the Political Situation at San Carlos."

13. Collier to Henry Chinn, January 6, 1934; Welpley, "Preliminary Report on the Political Situation at San Carlos," Tribal Organization Records, San Carlos File, NA, RG 75.

14. James Kitch, superintendent, San Carlos Agency, Arizona, to Collier, April 24, 1936; O. J. Berry to Louis Glavis, Division of Investigations, Bureau of Indian Affairs, May 30, 1936, ibid. A somewhat different version of events at San Carlos is offered by Spicer, *Cycles of Conquest*, p. 250. According to his account, thre was a tribal council of sorts in existence throughout the 1920s, and that council prepared the constitution which was ultimately ratified by the San Carlos Apaches in 1935. This version differs markedly from my own reconstruction of events, but it is impossible to determine the sources of his account, since he does not use direct references. I can only say that my account is derived from documents in the Tribal Organization Records as cited above. This conflict in accounts may stand as an example of the general murkiness of recent Indian history.

15. William O. Roberts, superintendent, Rosebud Agency, to Fred H. Daiker, November 27, 1935, Tribal Organization Records, Rosebud File, NA, RG 75.

16. Bonnin was the husband of Gertrude Bonnin, who had figured prominently in the Indian reform movement of the 1920s and later established the National Council for American Indians, a group of indeterminate size and influence among Indians. See Herzberg, *The Search for an American Indian Identity*, pp. 207–8.

17. J. A. Barkley, chief clerk, Rosebud Agency, South Dakota, to Collier, August 28, 1936, Tribal Organization Records, Rosebud File, NA, RG 75.

18. William Zimmerman to C. R. Whitlock, superintendent, Rosebud Agency, August 28, 1936, ibid.

19. Roberts to Daiker, November 27, 1935; Joe Jennings, field representative, Indian Organization Division, to Daiker, September 17, 1939, ibid.

20. Allan G. Harper, "Yankton Organizational Problem," January 14, 1937, ibid. Harper felt that this resolution was "not representative of the tribe as a whole."

21. Kenneth Meicklejohn to D'Arcy McNickle, May 4, 1937, ibid.

22. Not all constitutions included all these provisions. Several simply gave the tribe a veto over the sale or lease of land but did not mention whether it could initiate such action; some did not include any reference to the chartering of subordinate organizations. About 10 percent of the constitutions had clauses reserving to the tribes powers not enumerated, but for the most part it seems that that was not considered necessary because of the "inherent powers" position of the Interior Department outlined by Margold in 1934.

23. Cohen, *Handbook of Federal Indian Law*, pp. 130–31. The instances of the latter phenomenon included an attempt by the Oglala Sioux Council at Pine Ridge to delegate powers of taxation to the local bureau agent, a Rocky Boy's Council's proposal for a departmental review of ordinances relating to financial contracts with the federal government for an indefinite period, and a measure passed by the Fort Belknap Council delegating leasing powers to the local superintendent.

24. Cohen, *Handbook of Federal Indian Law*, pp. 105–7, 114, 332–33, 341–44, 348–51.

25. Ibid., p. 135.

26. C. H. Jennings, superintendent, Tongue River Agency, Lame Deer, Montana, to Collier, May 28, 1937, Tribal Organization Records, Tongue River File, NA, RG 75.

27. J. M. Stewart, September 2, 1937, ibid. Some constitutions had provisions eliminating from the roll tribal members who had moved away from the reservation, and all had a residency requirement of some sort, ranging from thirty days to two years, to qualify to vote in tribal elections.

28. Meicklejohn to Daiker, September 27, 1937, ibid.

29. Cohen, *Handbook of Federal Indian Law*, p. 136.

30. Ibid., pp. 349–51, 142–43.

31. Meicklejohn to Daiker, February 23, 1937; McNickle to Meicklejohn, February 24, 1937, Wheeler-Howard Records, NA, RG 75.

32. O. H. Lipps to Collier, June 30, 1937, Tribal Organization Records, Flathead File, NA, RG 75. Lipps's views are intriguing, since he was one of the bureau's old guard, and was regarded as not being fully in sympathy with the measures introduced by the Collier administration.

33. Cohen, *Handbook of Federal Indian Law*, pp. 105–7, 345. Cohen noted that there were "statutes authorizing the expenditures of tribal funds without express reference to the wishes of the tribe," but that "the omission of express reference . . . does not necessarily imply the absence of such consent," and that in practice some form of consent was usually sought. These rulings, of course, referred only to tribal funds held in trust by the U.S. Treasury.

34. Freeman, "The New Deal for the Indians," p. 438.

35. Cohen, *Handbook of Federal Indian Law*, pp. 105–6, 346.

36. Freeman, "The New Deal for the Indians," pp. 387–88; Harold Ickes, *The Secret Diary of Harold Ickes*, vol. 2 (New York: Simon and Schuster, 1953), pp. 506–7; Hiram N. Clark, Report on Montana Reservations, May 2, 1939, Tribal Organization Records, Blackfeet File, NA, RG 75.

37. See statement by William Zimmerman in *Hearings on H.R. 166*, pt. 4, pp. 294–95.

38. Joe Jennings to D'Arcy McNickle, November 8, 1939, Wheeler-Howard Records, McNickle File, NA, RG 75.

39. Collier to Ickes, March 6, 1935, Collier Papers; Collier to M. C. Burns, June 21, 1935, Wheeler-Howard Records, Burns File, NA, RG 75.

40. L. W. Shotwell, superintendent, Flathead Agency, to Collier, October 29, 1937, Tribal Organization Records, Flathead File, NA, RG 75.

41. Quoted in Cohen, *Handbook of Federal Indian Law*, p. 246.

42. *Senate Report 1031*, pp. 11–13.

43. *Hearings on H.R. 166*, pt. 4, p. 23.

44. As of June 30, 1944, Congress had appropriated only $4,273,400 for the credit fund, but there were loan commitments in the amount of

$7,147,166 (of which $5,533,082 had been advanced), made possible by re-payments of $2,532,798 on earlier advances, leaving a balance of $1,273,116 in the fund. *Hearings on H.R. 166*, pt. 4, pp. 144–45.

45. Figures are compiled from the annual reports of the Division of Extension and Industry, Bureau of Indian Affairs, 1943, NA, RG 75. The totals do not include figures for Oklahoma, which operated under a separate fund established by the Oklahoma Indian Welfare Act of 1936. Under that act, forty-three credit associations had been advanced loans totaling $686,500, an average of $16,000 per association. Virtually all of those loans went to individual Indians.

46. Bach, "Administration of Indian Resources in the United States," pp. 144–48; *Hearings on H.R. 166*, pt. 4, pp. 144–45.

47. See Sidney Baldwin, *Poverty and Politics: The Rise and Fall of the Farm Security Administration* (Chapel Hill: University of North Carolina Press, 1968), pp. 198–99.

48. Lipps to Collier, June 30, 1937, Tribal Organization Records, Flathead File, NA, RG 75.

49. *Hearings on H.R. 166*, pt. 4, pp. 416–18, 451–60; it also came out in testimony by Zimmerman, pp. 429–30, that the bureau had taken over administration of the Blackfoot oil revenues because "the tribe has not always been wise in the expenditure of the large sums it receives as income."

50. Mekeel, "An Appraisal of the Indian Reorganization Act," pp. 211–12.

51. Kluckhohn and Hackenberg, "Social Science Principles and the Indian Reorganization Act," p. 31.

52. "Collier Replies to Mekeel," *American Anthropologist* 46 (July–September 1944): 425.

53. G. B. Lindquist to M. K. Sniffen, June 33, 1937; O. H. Lipps to Sniffen, September 9, 1937; John H. Holst to Sniffen, n.d., Indian Rights Association Papers.

54. Collier appointed as editor of *Indians at Work* Mary Heaton Vorse, later accused by Elizabeth Bentley of being a member of the Communist party. This was about the closest the Collier administration came to being influenced by "communism," a favorite charge by hostile congressmen.

55. W. F. Dickens, superintendent, Cheyenne River Agency, South Dakota, to Collier, November 9, 1934, Tribal Organization Records, Cheyenne River File, NA, RG 75.

56. These comments by superintendent Upchurch of Port Madison Agency, Washington, were quoted by Kenneth Meicklejohn in a letter to Allan G. Harper, December 14, 1936, Wheeler-Howard Records, Meicklejohn File, NA, RG 75.

57. Ben Reifel to Daiker, August 25, 1935; Mekeel to W. Duncan Strong, August 14, 1935, Tribal Organization Records, Rosebud File, NA, RG 75.

58. William O. Roberts to Frank Wilson, chairman, Pine Ridge Tribal

Council, July 29, 1936; Wilson to Collier, September 1, 1936; Collier to Wilson, September 21, 1936; Wilson to Roberts, March 27, 1937, Tribal Organization Records, Pine Ridge File, NA, RG 75.

59. Roberts to Zimmerman, May 11, 1945; Roberts to J. C. McCaskill, assistant commissioner, July 16, 1945, Tribal Organization Records, Pine Ridge File, NA, RG 75. Harry Conroy to Ben Dwight, acting secretary, National Congress of American Indians, Pine Ridge, South Dakota, October 16, 1945, NCAI Files.

60. D'Arcy McNickle to William Brophy, commissioner of Indian affairs, November 18, 1945, Tribal Organization Records, Pine Ridge File, NA, RG 75.

61. Reifel to Collier, August 2, 1938, Wheeler-Howard Records, NA, RG 75.

62. Hiram N. Clark, Report to Indian Organization Division, May 2, 1939, Tribal Organization Records, Flathead File, NA, RG 75.

63. Allan G. Harper to Walter V. Woehlke, April 25, 1938; Harper, "Planning for the Economic Independence of Indians," paper delivered before the National Conference for Social Work, Buffalo, New York, June 22, 1939, Collier Papers.

64. House Committee on Indian Affairs, *Hearings on H.R. 7902*, pp. 3–4, 41.

65. Cohen, *Handbook of Federal Indian Law*, pp. 149–50.

66. By 1945, Yellowtail was actively campaigning among Northern Plains tribes for support in his effort to become commissioner of Indian affairs after Collier. Yellowtail was not the only Indian leader with this ambition; Ben Dwight, executive secretary of the National Congress of American Indians, also lobbied for the post. In the end, their ambitions were frustrated and Indians had to wait another twenty years to get an Indian as commissioner. William Zimmerman to William Brophy, September 27, 1945, Tribal Organization Records, Pine Ridge File, NA, RG 75; Hiram N. Clark to Ben Dwight, February 19, 1946, NCAI Files.

67. "Memorandum covering the conference held in the Commissioner's office on April 23 to discuss certain questions," April 24, 1936, AAIA Files.

68. Ibid.

Chapter 7

1. See Paul Conkin, *Tomorrow a New World: The New Deal's Community Program* (Ithaca, New York: Cornell University Press, 1966), on the subsistence homesteads program.

2. On the Land Use Planning program, see Richard S. Kirkendall, *Social Scientists and Farm Politics in the Age of Roosevelt* (Columbia: University of Missouri Press, 1966), pp. 150–64; Ellen S. Parks, "Experiment in the

Democratic Planning of Public Agricultural Activity" (Ph.D. diss., University of Wisconsin, 1947). The parallels with the Indian Service program were clearly drawn by Allan G. Harper in "Planning for the Economic Independence of Indians," p. 8.

3. Harper, "Planning for the Economic Independence of Indians," p. 7.

4. Bach, "Administration of Indian Resources in the United States," p. 105.

5. Collier, *From Every Zenith*, pp. 219–20; David Aberle, *The Peyote Religion among the Navaho*, pp. 75–77.

6. Commissioner of Indian Affairs, *Annual Report, 1934–35*, p. 82.

7. During the decade after Collier's departure, Congress initiated measures to terminate federal control over tribal properties, giving the Indians the option of having tribal resources sold and the proceeds distributed on a per capita basis. While the National Congress of American Indians and tribal council spokesmen vigorously opposed the policy, there are indications that a substantial number of Indians in tribes affected were indifferent or favored the proposal. In some cases more than 70 percent of the tribesmen were reported to favor termination. See Fey and McNickle, *Indians and Other Americans*, pp. 155–65; N. H. Holland, "The Last Days—An Inquiry into the Proposed Colville Termination," in Johnson, "Studies in American Indian Law," 2:333–39.

8. *Hearings on H.R. 7902*, pp. 25–27.

9. Ibid., p. 36. On the Taylor Grazing Act, see E. Louise Peffer, *The Closing of the Public Domain* (Stanford, Calif.: Stanford University Press, 1951); and Philip O. Foss, *Politics and Grass* (Seattle: University of Washington Press, 1960).

10. Allan G. Harper, acting director, Lands Division, to William Zimmerman, April 20, 1943, Tribal Organization Records, Jicarilla File, NA, RG 75.

11. Figures are in Bach, "Administration of Indian Resources," pp. 51–56.

12. Harper, "Planning for the Economic Independence of Indians," p. 7; see also Bach, "Administration of Indian Resources," pp. 49–50.

13. Commissioner of Indian Affairs, *Annual Report, 1936–37*, p. 247; Bach, "Administration of Indian Resources," pp. 68–71.

14. National Resources Board, *Indian Land Tenure, Economic Status and Population Trends*, p. 30; Bach, "Administration of Indian Resources," pp. 70–72.

15. "Statement by Commissioner Collier concerning Conditions on the Sioux Reservations," March 30, 1940, in *Hearings on H.R. 5878*, pp. 57–58; Bach, "Administration of Indian Resources," pp. 106–8; Asbury and Jennings, "The Tongue River Steer Enterprise," pp. 15–16.

16. Annual Report, Division of Agriculture and Industry, Bureau of Indian Affairs, 1939, NA, RG 75; Bach, "Administration of Indian Resources," pp. 105–8.

17. Aberle, *The Peyote Religion among the Navaho*, pp. 52–54; Kelly, *The Navajo Indians and Federal Indian Policy*, pp. 112–14. Kelly notes that one reason the 1928 resolution failed to have any effect was that no Navajos owned more than 1,000 head of livestock of any sort, a point made by the Navajos at the time.

18. Aberle, *The Peyote Religion among the Navaho*, p. 53; Pollock, "Navajo-Federal Relations as a Social-Cultural Problem," pp. 100–4. In 1934, Senator Bronson Cutting of New Mexico introduced a Navajo boundary extension bill in Congress, but it was blocked after Cutting's death and his replacement by Dennis Chavez in 1935.

19. Kelly, *The Navajo Indians and Federal Indian Policy*, pp. 158–59.

20. Minutes, Navajo Tribal Council, Tuba City, Arizona, October 30–November 1, 1933, Tribal Organization Records, Navajo File, NA, RG 75.

21. Kelly, *The Navajo Indians and Federal Indian Policy*, p. 115.

22. Minutes, Navajo Tribal Council, Fort Defiance, Arizona, March 12–13, 1934, Tribal Organization Records, Navajo File, NA, RG 75.

23. Aberle, *The Peyote Religion among the Navaho*, p. 57.

24. Ibid. Aberle's description was based on interviews with Navajos, whose portrayal of the situation has been questioned as exaggerated by recent historians. See Parman, *The Navajos and the New Deal*, pp. 64–65.

25. Minutes, Navajo Tribal Council, Fort Defiance, Arizona, June 11, 1935; Collier to E. R. Fryer, superintendent, Central Navajo Agency, June 21, 1935, Tribal Organization Records, Navajo File, NA, RG 75.

26. Oliver La Farge to Allan G. Harper, July 1, 1935, AAIA Papers. Kelly in *The Navajo Indians and Federal Indian Policy* offers a different explanation: The Navajos rejected tribal organization because they were satisfied with their council, were not in danger of allotment, and could not make use of the land purchase funds so long as the boundary bill was pending. Thus Reorganization had no appeal for them for the moment. This argument is plausible, but the stock reduction program and related issues led to a heavy turnout at the referendum, and the tribal council could hardly have been very popular from its association with stock reduction. See Parman, *The Navajos and the New Deal*, pp. 51–80.

27. Collier, *The Indians of the Americas*, pp. 277–79.

28. Walter Woehlke to Collier, January 15, 1935, Collier Papers.

29. Quoted in Pollock, "Navajo-Federal Relations," p. 278.

30. Underhill, "The Native Culture System of the Pueblo," pp. 22–25; minutes, Laguna Pueblo Council, September 2, 1941, Tribal Organization Records, Pueblo File, NA, RG 75.

31. Ward Shepard, "Memorandum of Program of Reestablished Indian Land Planning Unit and Permanent Planning Agency," January 31, 1934, Collier Papers.

32. Commissioner of Indian Affairs, *Annual Report, 1935-36*, p. 119; *Annual Report, 1938-39*, pp. 62–63.

33. Bach, "Administration of Indian Resources," pp. 60–66.

34. *Senate Report 1031*, pp. 8–9; *Hearings on H.R. 166*, pt. 4, pp. 24–25.

35. Woehlke to Collier, January 15, 1935, Collier Papers.

36. La Farge to Collier, July 18, 1935, Collier Papers.

37. Walter Woehlke, Memorandum on TC-BIA, January 7, 1936, TC-BIA Records, NA, RG 114.

38. Woehlke to Hugh H. Bennett, Soil Conservation Service, March 16, 1936, ibid.

39. Collier, Circular on TC-BIA, July 30, 1937; Harper, "Planning for the Economic Independence of Indians," pp. 4–5; Ickes to R. G. Tugwell, Resettlement Administration, June 22, 1935, Collier Papers.

40. Collier to Bennett, December 30, 1935; Woehlke, "Draft of Confidential Memo on Indian Service–Soil Conservation Service Relations," n.d. (ca. 1936), ibid.

41. Woehlke to Harper, Denver, Colorado, May 10, 1938; Harper, Report to Regional Conservators, August 22, 1938, ibid.

42. Collier to Lewis C. Gray, Resettlement Administration, October 16, 1936, ibid.

43. Collier to Ickes, December 30, 1936; Collier to Wallace, December 30, 1936; Collier to E. P. Herring, March 23, 1937, ibid.

44. Woehlke, "Recommendations concerning Rio Grande Board," June 14, 1937, ibid.; Commissioner of Indian Affairs, *Annual Report, 1938–39*, pp. 64–65.

45. Woehlke to Collier, February 2, 1938, Collier Papers.

46. John H. Provinse, "Cultural Factors in Land Use Planning," in La Farge, *The Changing Indian*, pp. 55–71. See also M. L. Wilson, "The Democratic Processes and the Formulation of Agricultural Policy," *Social Forces* 19 (October 1940): 1–11.

47. Harper to Woehlke, April 25, 1938; Woehlke to Harper, May 2, 1938; Collier to Harper, August 22, 1938, Collier Papers.

48. John Pearmain, TC-BIA field coordinator, to Lucy W. Adams, Sells Agency, Arizona, February 24, 1937; Lucy Adams, "Notes on the Papago Situation," March 3, 1937, TC-BIA Records, NA, RG 114.

49. Pearmain to Harper, August 4, 1938; D. E. Harbison to Harper, March 8, 1938; Harper to Collier, January 24, 1939, ibid. After the war, the establishment of new mines in the neighborhood provided employment for the Papagos, so their wholesale removal was avoided, although the Indian Service was still seeking to encourage the resettlement of some families at Colorado River (where the local Indians did not want them) in 1949. See Thompson, *Personality and Government*, pp. 125–29; Spicer, *Cycles of Conquest*, pp. 555–56.

Chapter 8

1. House Committee on Indian Affairs, *Hearings on H.R. 166*, pt. 4, pp. 22–23.

2. Kelly, "The Indian Reorganization Act," pp. 306–8, points out that the Bureau of the Budget was also responsible for substantially reducing Collier's land purchase fund requests, particularly after 1938. In 1940 it actually cut off all funds for that purpose while Congress kept the program going for another year so that current land purchases could be completed.

3. Figures are in Freeman, "The New Deal for the Indians," p. 441.

4. Freeman, "The New Deal for the Indians," pp. 353–54, 387–88; Ickes, *Secret Diary*, 2:506–7.

5. House Committee on Indian Affairs, *Hearings on H.R. 5878*, p. 60; see also Philp, *John Collier's Crusade for Indian Reform*, pp. 200–202.

6. Pollock, "Navajo-Federal Relations," pp. 100–107.

7. *Congressional Record*, 75th Cong., 1st sess. (Washington, D.C.: Government Printing Office, 1937), p. 1665; *Senate Report 1947*, 76th Cong., 1st sess. (Washington, D.C.: Government Printing Office, 1939); *Senate Report 1031; House Report 2091 on House Res. 166*, 78th Cong., 2d sess. (Washington, D.C.: Government Printing Office, 1944).

8. Parman, *The Navajos and the New Deal*, p. 289.

9. Collier to Ickes, February 15, 1935, Collier Papers.

10. Burton K. Wheeler and P. F. Healy, *A Yankee From the West: The Autobiography of Burton K. Wheeler* (Garden City, N.Y.: Doubleday, 1962), p. 315.; Philp, *John Collier's Crusade for Indian Reform*, pp. 198–99.

11. La Farge, *As Long as the Grass Shall Grow*, p. 58.

12. See Evon Z. Vogt, "The Acculturation of American Indians," *Annals of the American Academy of Political and Social Sciences* 311 (May 1957): 137–46, for a discussion of the factors underlying Indian resistance to assimilation and the origins of pan Indianism.

13. Forrest R. Stone to Collier, January 23, 1934, Wheeler-Howard Records, NA, RG 75.

14. Alida C. Bowler, superintendent, Carson Agency, Stewart, Nevada, to Allan G. Harper, December 16, 1936; D'Arcy McNickle to J. H. Stewart, Land Division, Bureau of Indian Affairs, June 30, 1940, Tribal Organization Records, Carson File, NA, RG 75.

15. Luke Gilbert, chairman, Cheyenne River Council; Antoine Roubideux, chairman, Rosebud Council; Frank Wilson, chairman, Pine Ridge Council, to Collier, April 24, 1936; minutes of meeting at Bureau of Indian Affairs, April 24, 1936; Roubideux to C. R. Whitlock, superintendent, Rosebud Agency, South Dakota, July 9, 1937, Tribal Organization Records, Rosebud File, NA, RG 75.

16. Ralph Case, Sioux attorney, Washington, D.C., to Roubideux, July 19, 1937; William Zimmerman to Whitlock, September 2, 1937, ibid.

17. William O. Roberts, superintendent, Pine Ridge, South Dakota, to Collier, March 7, 1938. Tribal Organization Records, Pine Ridge File, NA, RG 75. See also *Hearings on H.R. 5878*.

18. Hiram N. Clark, to Ben Dwight, February 14, 1946, NCAI Files; Angie Debo, *And Still the Waters Run*, p. 369.

19. Remarks by D'Arcy McNickle to an Indian group in Chicago, January 1944, Wheeler-Howard Records, NA, RG 75; D'Arcy McNickle, interview, April 1973.

20. Roberts to J. C. McCaskill, July 30, 1945; William Zimmerman to William Brophy, September 27, 1945, Tribal Organization Records, Pine Ridge File, NA, RG 75.

21. Freeman, "New Deal for the Indians," pp. 415–16; Collier, *The Indians of the Americas*, p. 265.

22. Minutes of the National Congress of American Indians convention, November 15–18, 1944, Denver, Colorado, pp. 30–34, NCAI Files. Of the fifty-one positions available on the eight executive committees of the NCAI, ten were given to Indians who had been or continued to be officials with the Bureau of Indian Affairs.

23. Ibid., p. 56.

24. Fey and McNickle, *Indians and Other Americans*, pp. 238–39.

BIBLIOGRAPHICAL ESSAY

Historical analysis of Indian affairs in the Collier era is still being developed. There have been significant recent studies of the subject by Lawrence C. Kelly, Donald H. Parman, and Margaret Szasz, and Kenneth R. Philp's biography of Collier provides the first major historical account of his career and the course of reform. My primary interest has been in the Indian Reorganization Act and its program, but any definitive study of the period must also draw upon the papers of the Indian reform groups, notably the Association on American Indian Affairs (AAIA), recently acquired by the Princeton University Library. The AAIA was the result of a merger in the 1930s between the Eastern Association of Indian Affairs and Collier's organization, the American Indian Defense Association, both of which had been formed initially in the early 1920s to combat the Bursum bill. Princeton's holdings include the office files and pamphlets of both groups, but the collection is much more complete for the period after the merger. The other major Indian reform group, the Indian Rights Association, has deposited its papers for this period with the library of the Pennsylvania Historical Society in Philadelphia. The holdings include some interesting critical surveys of the New Deal programs by association observers.

One other Indian group whose papers I examined was the

National Congress of American Indians, established in 1944. I was allowed to go through their office files, some of which have since been microfilmed, in Washington, D.C. Their records for this early period consist primarily of material such as official convention minutes, press releases, and pamphlets, but include scattered pieces of correspondence between Indian leaders after 1945.

Probably the most important sources for Collier and the reform movement are in the John Collier Papers at the Sterling Memorial Library of Yale University. In addition to Collier's personal correspondence throughout this period and beyond, the collection includes a substantial number of official government memoranda, particularly between Collier and Interior Secretary Harold Ickes and between Collier and his key aides, Walter Woehlke and Allan G. Harper. Both the Collier Papers and the AAIA records were being reorganized when I used them, and future researchers should benefit from those efforts.

By far the most important materials relating to the operation of the Indian Reorganization Act in the 1934–45 period are in the National Archives, Record Group 75, in Washington, D.C. The general records relating to Indian tribal organization have been separated from the Bureau of Indian Affairs Central Classified Files, and are broadly divided into two groups: those relating to the preparation of the Wheeler-Howard bill in 1933 and 1934, which I have cited as the Wheeler-Howard Records, and those relating to the administration of the Indian Reorganization Act from 1934 to 1945, broken down alphabetically by tribes or reservations. The latter I have cited as the Indian Reorganization Records and have given the file title rather than file number because the records are separate and the title gives a clearer indication of the source. Also in the National Archives are records relating to the administration of the Technical Cooperation–Bureau of Indian Affairs (TC-BIA) project between 1936 and 1942, located in Record Group 114, the records of the U.S. Soil Conservation Service.

There was a proliferation of congressional investigations of Indian affairs during the New Deal, although the unreliability of the testimony is more indicative of the position of critics of the Collier administration than of the general response of Indians to the New Deal programs. The most massive of these investigations was the *Survey of Conditions of Indians of the United States,* initiated by Senate Resolution 308 in the 70th Congress, 2d session, in 1928, and continuing until 1939. The hearings of the Senate Committee of Indian Affairs were published in thirty-seven parts between 1929 and 1939; thirty-two of the volumes of testimony were gathered before October 1933, and only volume 37 dealt with the Wheeler-Howard Act, but the survey contributed to demands for reform legislation throughout the Hoover period. The hearings of the House Committee of Indian Affairs on House Resolution 7902, the Indian Reorganization bill, 73d Congress, 2d session (1934) include the original draft of the bill by the Bureau of Indian Affairs and revealing testimony by Collier and other witnesses on the aims of the program. The House committee version of the bill is in *House Report 1804*, 73d Congress, 2d session (1934). I also consulted the Senate Committee on Indian Affairs, *Hearings on S. 2755*, 73d Congress, 2d session (1934).

On the Oklahoma Indian Welfare (Thomas-Rogers) Act, see House Committee on Indian Affairs, *Hearings on H.R. 6234*, 74th Congress, 2d session (1935), and Senate Committee on Indian Affairs, *Hearings on S. 2047*, 74th Congress, 2d session (1935). The major congressional hearings on the administration of the Indian Reorganization Act by the House Committee on Indian Affairs include *Hearings on H.R. 5878*, 76th Congress, 1st–3d sessions (1939–40); *Hearings on S. 2103*, 76th Congress, 3d session (1940); and, most useful, *Hearings on H.R. 166*, 78th Congress, 1st session (1944), in four parts. In the report on this last investigation, *House Report 2091*, 78th Congress, 2d session (1944), an extensive response by the bureau to charges of mismanagement made by the Senate Committee on Indian Affairs in *Senate Report 1047*, 76th Congress, 1st session (1939), and *Senate Report 1031*, 78th Congress, 2d session (1944), can be found. An insightful study of the struggles between Collier and Congress is John L. Freeman, "The New Deal for the Indians: A Study in Bureau-Committee Relations in American Government," (Ph.D. diss., Princeton University, 1952).

In addition to the congressional surveys, there were other governmental and quasi-governmental investigations of Indian conditions that proved useful in reconstructing the problems faced by the Collier administration. The most significant was the Brookings Institution report, *The Problem of Indian Administration*, compiled by Lewis Meriam and his associates, and published in 1928. Almost equally valuable, however, was the report of the Land Planning Committee of the National Resources Board,

Indian Land Tenure, Economic Status and Population Trends
(Washington, D.C.: Government Printing Office, 1935). The
records upon which this report was based are now held in Record
Group 75 at the National Archives, as are records of a social and
economic survey of thirty-three Indian reservations carried out by
the Civil Works Administration in 1933–34. Both of these collections of survey data were extremely useful in determining the
social and economic characteristics of Indian groups. Also worthwhile was the final report of the Indian Administration Research
Project, an anthropological study financed by the University of
Chicago and the Bureau of Indian Affairs. The report, by Laura
Thompson, *Personality and Government: Findings and Recommendations of the Indian Administration Research* (Mexico,
1951), emphasized the social and psychological impact of the
New Deal on the Indians.

No study of Indian legal and political institutions could be
adequately done without Felix Cohen's *Handbook of Federal
Indian Law* (Washington, D.C.: Government Printing Office,
1941), which pieced together a clear description of the subject
from a hitherto chaotic collection of laws, regulations, and treaty
provisions relating to Indian tribes. The texts of the tribal constitutions established under the Indian Reorganization Act are in
George Fay, comp., *Charters, Constitutions and By-Laws of Indian
Tribes of North America* (Greeley, Colo.: Museum of Anthropology, Colorado State College, 1967), in fourteen parts.

The bureau's version of the development of Indian reorganization may be followed in the annual reports of the Commissioner
of Indian Affairs in the *Annual Reports of the Secretary of the
Interior* (Washington, D.C.: Government Printing Office, 1934–
44), and in *Indians at Work*, an in-house journal produced by
Collier from 1937 to 1944.

Most of the major figures involved in the Indian New Deal are
deceased, but I was fortunate in being able to interview D'Arcy
McNickle, who had been in the Indian Organization Division, in
April 1973; and Vine Deloria, Sr., who had been at Pine Ridge
during the 1930s, in April 1970; and to discuss the general aims
of the Indian New Deal with former interior secretary Oscar
Chapman, who was assistant secretary of the interior throughout
the New Deal, at various times in 1970 and 1971.

Below are listed the major secondary works consulted in the
preparation of this study of the Indian New Deal:

Published

Aberle, David H. *The Peyote Religion among the Navaho.* Chicago: Aldine Publishing Co., 1966.

Berkhofer, Robert F., Jr. "The Political Context of a New Indian History." *Pacific Historical Review* 40 (August 1971): 363–82.

Boyce, George A. *When the Navajos Had Too Many Sheep: The 1940's.* San Francisco: Indian Historian Press, 1974.

Collier, John. "United States Indian Administration as a Laboratory of Ethnic Relations." *Social Research* 12 (September 1945): 265–303.

_____. *The Indians of the Americas.* New York: W. W. Norton, 1947.

_____. "The Indian Bureau and Self-Government: A Reply to John F. Embree." *Human Organization* 8 (Summer 1949): 22–26.

_____. *From Every Zenith: A Memoir.* Denver: Sage Books, 1962.

Debo, Angie. *And Still the Waters Run: The Betrayal of the Civilized Tribes.* Princeton: Princeton University Press, 1940.

Downs, Randolph D. "A Crusade for Indian Reform, 1922–1934." *Mississippi Valley Historical Review* 32 (December 1945): 331–54.

Driver, Harold E. *Indians of North America.* Chicago: University of Chicago Press, 1961.

Eggan, Fred C. *Social Organization of the Western Pueblos.* Chicago: University of Chicago Press, 1950.

Embree, John F. "The Indian Bureau and Self-Government." *Human Organization* 8 (Spring 1949): 11–14.

Fey, Harold E., and McNickle, D'Arcy. *Indians and Other Americans: Two Ways of Life Meet.* New York: Harper Brothers, 1959.

Haas, Theodore H. *Ten Years of Tribal Government under I.R.A.* Washington, D.C.: U.S. Department of the Interior, 1947.

Hagan, William T. *American Indians.* Chicago: University of Chicago Press, 1971.

Herzberg, Hazel W. *The Search for an American Indian Identity: Modern Pan-Indian Movements.* Syracuse, N.Y.: Syracuse University Press, 1971.

Hyde, George. *A Sioux Chronicle.* Norman: University of Oklahoma Press, 1956.

Joseph, Alice; Spicer, Rosamund; and Chesky, Alice. *The Desert People: A Study of the Papago Indians of Arizona.* Chicago: University of Chicago Press, 1949.

Kelly, Lawrence C. *The Navaho Indians and Federal Indian Policy, 1900–1945.* Tucson: University of Arizona Press, 1968.

_____. "Choosing the New Deal Indian Commissioner: Ickes versus Collier." *New Mexico Historical Review* 49 (October 1974): 269–88.

_____. "The Indian Reorganization Act: The Dream and the Reality." *Pacific Historical Review* 46 (January 1975): 291–312.

Kelly, William H., ed. *Indian Affairs and the Indian Reorganization Act: The Twenty Year Record.* Tucson: University of Arizona Press, 1954.

Kinney, Jay P. *A Continent Lost; A Civilization Won: Indian Land Tenure in America*. Baltimore: Johns Hopkins University Press, 1937.

Kluckhohn, Clyde, and Leighton, Dorothea. *The Navaho*. Cambridge, Mass.: Harvard University Press, 1946.

Kroeber, A. L. "The Nature of the Land-holding Group." *Ethnohistory* 2 (Fall 1955): 303–13.

Kunitz, Stephen J. "The Social Philosophy of John Collier." *Ethnohistory* 18 (Summer 1971): 213–29.

La Farge, Oliver. *As Long as the Grass Shall Grow*. New York: Longmans, Green and Co., 1940.

_____, ed. *The Changing Indian*. Norman: University of Oklahoma Press, 1942.

Llewelyn, Karl N., and Hoebel, E. Adamson. *The Cheyenne Way*. Norman: University of Oklahoma Press, 1941.

Macgregor, Gordon. *Warriors without Weapons: A Study of the Society and Personality Development of the Pine Ridge Sioux*. Chicago: University of Chicago Press, 1946.

McNickle, D'Arcy. *The Indian Tribes of the United States*. New York: Oxford University Press, 1962.

_____. *Indian Man: A Life of Oliver La Farge*. Bloomington: Indiana University Press, 1971.

_____. *Native American Tribalism: Indian Survivals and Renewals*. New York: Oxford University Press, 1973.

Marden, David L. "Anthropologists and Federal Indian Policy Prior to 1940." *Indian Historian* (Winter 1972): 19–26.

Mekeel, H. Scudder. "An Appraisal of the Indian Reorganization Act." *American Anthropologist* 46 (April–June 1944): 209–18.

Miner, H. Craig. *The Corporation and the Indian: Tribal Sovereignty and Industrial Civilization in Indian Territory, 1865–1907*. Columbia: University of Missouri Press, 1976.

Otis, Delos S. *The Dawes Act and the Allotment of Indian Lands*. Edited by Francis Paul Prucha. Norman: University of Oklahoma Press, 1973.

Parman, Donald H. "The Indian and the Civilization Conservation Corps." *Pacific Historical Review* 40 (February 1971): 39–56.

_____. *The Navajos and the New Deal*. New Haven: Yale University Press, 1976.

Philp, Kenneth R. "Albert Fall and the Protest from the Pueblos." *Arizona and the West* 12 (Autumn 1970): 237–54.

_____. "Herbert Hoover's New Era: A False Dawn for the American Indian, 1929–1932." *Rocky Mountain Social Science Journal* 9 (April 1972): 53–60.

_____. "John Collier and the Crusade to Protect Indian Religious Freedom." *Journal of Ethnic Studies* 1 (Spring 1973): 22–38.

_____. *John Collier's Crusade for Indian Reform, 1920–1954*. Tucson: University of Arizona Press, 1977.

Priest, Loring B. *Uncle Sam's Stepchildren: The Reformation of United States Indian Policy, 1865-1887*. New Brunswick, N.J.: Rutgers University Press, 1942. Reprinted Lincoln: University of Nebraska Press, 1975.

Prucha, Francis Paul, ed. *Americanizing the American Indians: Writings by the "Friends of the Indians," 1880-1900*. Cambridge, Mass.: Harvard University Press, 1973. Reprinted Lincoln: University of Nebraska Press, 1978.

Quinten, B. T. "Oklahoma Tribes, the Great Depression, and the Indian Bureau." *Mid-America* 49 (January 1967): 29–43.

Sheehan, Bernard W. *Seeds of Extinction: Jeffersonian Philanthropy and the American Indian*. Chapel Hill: University of North Carolina Press, 1973.

Smith, Jane F., and Kvasnicka, Robert M., eds. *Indian-White Relations: A Persistent Paradox*. Washington, D.C.: Howard University Press, 1976.

Smith, Michael T. "The Wheeler-Howard Act of 1934: The Indian New Deal." *Journal of the West* 10 (July 1971): 524–34.

Spicer, Edward H. *Cycles of Conquest: The Impact of Spain, New Mexico, and the United States on the Indians of the Southwest, 1533-1960*. Tucson: University of Arizona Press, 1962.

Szaz, Margaret. *Education and the American Indian: The Road to Self-Determination, 1928-1973*. Albuquerque: University of New Mexico Press, 1974.

Taylor, Graham D. "The Tribal Alternative to Bureaucracy: The Indian's New Deal, 1933-1945." *Journal of the West* 13 (January 1974): 128–42.

———. "Anthropologists, Reformers, and the Indian New Deal." *Prologue* 7 (Fall 1975): 151–62.

Thompson, Laura, and Joseph, Alice. *The Hopi Way*. Chicago: University of Chicago Press, 1944.

Tyler, S. Lyman. *A History of Indian Policy*. Washington, D.C.: U.S. Department of the Interior, 1973.

Underhill, Ruth. *Red Man's America*. Chicago: University of Chicago Press, 1953.

———. *The Navajos*. Norman: University of Oklahoma Press, 1956.

Wallace, Ernest, and Hoebel, E. Adamson. *The Comanches, Lords of the Southern Plains*. Norman: University of Oklahoma Press, 1952.

Washburn, Wilcomb E. *Red Man's Land / White Man's Law*. New York: Scribners Sons, 1971.

———, ed. *The American Indian and the United States: A Documentary History*. 4 vols. New York: Random House, 1973.

Wissler, Clark. *Indians of the United States*. Garden City, N.Y.: Doubleday, 1940.

———. *Red Man Reservations*. 2d ed. New York: Macmillan, 1971.

Wright, Peter. "John Collier and the Oklahoma Indian Welfare Act of 1936." *Chronicles of Oklahoma* 50 (Autumn 1972): 347–71.

Unpublished

Bach, Arthur L. "The Administration of Indian Resources in the United States, 1933–1941." Ph.D. dissertation, State University of Iowa, 1942.

Johnson, Ralph W., ed. "Studies in American Indian Law." 2 vols. Mimeographed. University of Washington Law School, Seattle, 1971–72.

Philp, Kenneth R. "John Collier and the American Indian, 1920–1945." Ph.D. dissertation, Michigan State University, 1968.

Pollock, Floyd. "Navajo-Federal Relations as a Social-Cultural Problem." Ph.D. dissertation, University of Southern California, 1942.

ACKNOWLEDGMENTS

This study of tribal organization in the Indian New Deal evolved from a broader study of community organization in government programs of the New Deal era undertaken with the late John Shover at the University of Pennsylvania. Most of the financial assistance for the research and writing was provided by the Dalhousie University Research and Development Fund from 1973 to 1975. I am particularly grateful for the help provided in my research by Robert Kvasnicka and his staff at the National Archives and Records Service in Washington, D.C., and to the manuscript division staffs at the Sterling Memorial Library of Yale University and at the Princeton University Library. I benefited considerably from discussions of my work with D'Arcy McNickle, Larry Kelly, Ken Philp, Jack Crowley, Hazel Herzberg, and Michael Glazier, who first encouraged me to undertake this book. Judy Campbell typed the manuscript, and my wife, Deb, conscientiously edited and reedited drafts of the work. Of course, I am solely responsible for any errors or omissions of fact or interpretation.

195

INDEX

Aberle, David, 72, 128, 183 n. 24

Aberle, Sophie, 74

Alaska Reorganization Act, 34–35, 67

Allotment: and assimilation, 7; and Dawes Act, 4–6; obstacle to Indian New Deal, 122–23, 125; stopped by Ickes, 18

All Pueblo Council, 47, 69, 74, 145. See also Pueblos

American Indian Defense Association, 12, 13, 18, 19, 147

American Indian Federation, 36, 107, 141–42, 144, 175 n. 62. See also Bruner, Joseph

American Indian Policy Review Commission, ix

Apaches, 2, 63, 82; Chiricahua Apaches, 46, 50; Jicarilla Apaches, 46, 70, 123; Mescalero Apaches, 45–46, 50, 62, 110; San Carlos Apaches, 70, 71, 98–99. See also Reservations: Mescalero Apache, San Carlos Apache

Applied Anthropology Staff, 37, 77, 113, 132

Appropriations: and Indian Reorganization Act, 33–34, 165 n. 14; and Rhoads administration, 14, 16; reduced by Bureau of the Budget, 185 n. 2; reduced by Congress, 132, 140–41

Arapahoes, 35, 44, 152

Arikaras, 81

Ashurst, Henry, 27

Assimilation: and allotment, 7; extent of, among tribes, 41–44; in nineteenth century, 3; revival after Indian New Deal, 139–40, 182 n. 7; statistics on, 151–54, 166 n. 6

Assiniboins, 82

Atwood, Stella, 12

Ayers, Roy, 18

Bennett, Hugh, 130, 134

Blackfeet: assimilation among, 44; factionalism among, 55–57, 104; traditional organization, 2; tribal

197

loan fund, 111, 123
Boas, Franz, 24–25, 39
Bonnin, R. T., 100–101, 178 n. 16
Bruner, Joseph, 36, 84, 107, 141.
    See also American Indian Feder-
    ation
Bureau of American Ethnology, 37,
    132
Burge, Moris, 99
Burke, Charles, 14
Burke Act, 5, 11
Burnette, Robert, 59
Burns, Mark L., 87, 147
Bursum, Holm, 11, 12
Bursum bill, 11, 13
Buster v. *Wright*, 105

Charlo, Martin, 84
Chavez, Dennis, 141, 142
Cherokees, 1, 2, 92
Cheyenne-Arapahoes. *See* Arapa-
    hoes
Cheyennes: cooperative land plan-
    ning initiated, 121, 125; dispute
    over tribal membership, 104;
    traditional organization, 2, 81;
    tribal loan to, 110, 175 n. 66;
    tribal organization in New Deal,
    86–87. *See also* Reservations:
    Tongue River
Chickasaws, 2, 92
Chinn, Henry, 71, 98–99
Chippewas: communal organiza-
    tion, 66, 87–88, 145; faction-
    alism among, 53–55, literacy
    among, 152; results of allot-
    ment, 6, 45; suffer in Depres-
    sion, 119; tribal constitution,
    97. *See also* Reservations: Red
    Lake, White Earth
Choctaws, 2, 3, 92
Civil Works Administration, 7, 41,
    151
Cohen, Felix, 33, 37, 108, 112;
    compiles Indian laws, 92; and

Indian Reorganization Act, 20,
    30; on Indian self-government,
    1, 103; and San Carlos Apache
    tribal constitution, 99
Collier, John: and Alaska Reor-
    ganization Act, 34–35; attacks
    American Indian Federation,
    141–42; appointed Indian com-
    missioner, 17–18; background,
    12; defends Bureau of Indian
    Affairs, 113; and criticism of In-
    dian tribal constitutions, 97, 98;
    criticized in Congress, 141–42;
    on factionalism among Indians,
    61–62; forced to resign, 139,
    142; and Hugh Bennett, 130,
    134; on Indian New Deal, x–
    xi, 30, 31, 121, 143; as Indian
    reformer, 12–13, 15; and Indian
    Reorganization Act, 19–20, 23–
    25, 28, 150; on Indian tradi-
    tional societies, 13, 40; on
    mixed-blood Indians, 52; and
    Navajos, 71, 127–30; and Okla-
    homa Indian Welfare Act, 34,
    35–36; attitude toward pan-
    Indian groups, 145, 147; and
    Pueblos in New Deal, 46–47,
    131; proposes Rio Grande Board,
    135; and Salish-Kootenais, 108;
    and San Carlos Apaches, 99;
    defends submarginal land pur-
    chases, 132; defends tribal loans,
    109; on tribal power to remove
    bureau employees, 117, 118;
    and tribal referenda, 32
Comanches, 2, 35, 63, 81, 82
Community organization: among
    Indians before New Deal, 72;
    among Chippewas, 87–88; Col-
    lier and, 12; established under
    Indian Reorganization Act, 68,
    171 n. 9; at Pine Ridge, 89–
    90; at Yankton, 90–91
Competency commission, 5, 44

Constitutions, tribal: characteristics
of, 96–98, 177 n. 11; arrangements for land exchanges in,
123; limitations on, 101–3;
powers of appointment and removal in, 117–18
Cooley, A. C., 118
Cosmos Club Conference, 19
Councils, tribal. *See* Government,
tribal
Courts, Tribal, 21, 25, 28, 177 n.
10
Credit Unit, 109–11
Creeks (Muskogees), 2, 45, 67–68
Crows, 33, 44, 60, 61, 81

Daiker, Fred H., 37, 99
Dance Order, 69
Dawes Allotment Act, 4, 5, 20, 41
Dickens, W. F., 89
Dodge, Chee, 48, 72–73, 127
Dodge, Tom, 48
Dwight, Ben, 146–47, 148, 181 n.
66

Eastern Association on Indian Af-
fairs, 13, 19
Eastman, Charles A., 9
Education, Indian, 14 15, 119

Factionalism: traditional, within
tribes, 45, 49; and tribal organi-
zation in New Deal, 45–62
Fall, Albert B., 11, 12, 13
Faris, C. E., 56, 133
Farver, Peru, 147
Federal Emergency Relief Adminis-
tration, 127, 129, 131
Five Civilized Tribes, 2, 5, 35, 36,
44. *See also* Cherokees; Chicka-
saws; Choctaws; Creeks
Frazier, Lynn, 15
Fryer, E. R., 133
Funds, tribal, 106–7

Government, tribal: and community organizations, 87–91; failure to represent communities,
65–66, 85–86; formal powers of,
defined, 95–96; and Indian Reorganization Act, 28, 65; limits
placed on authority of, 93–94;
pre–New Deal business committees, 49–50, 70–72, 83; and
Stephens bill, 9; traditional, 2
Greenaway, Isabel, 23
Gros Ventres, 82

Hackenberg, Robert, 31, 113
Hall, Theodore, 77, 79
Harper, Allan G., 112; coordinator
of TC-BIA program, 117, 121,
135, 136; and Indian Reorganization Act, 19, 21; on land exchanges, 123, 124; and Navajos,
121
Hastings, William, 22–23, 35
Heacock, Charles, 147
Heirship lands, 6, 124
Holst, John H., 51, 77, 82–83,
85, 114
Hopis: traditional organization, 74,
173 n. 34; tribal constitution,
97; tribal organization in New
Deal, 75–76, 80, 88
House Committee on Indian Affairs:
and appropriations, 33–34, 142;
and Indian Reorganization Act,
20–22, 28–29, 33, 142
Howard, Edgar, 20
Hualapais, 134

Ickes, Harold, 19, 103; appointed
secretary of the interior, 18;
denounces American Indian Federation, 107, 141–42; imposes
"gag rule" on critics, 113,
164 n. 7; increases Indian
lands, 143; stops allotment, 18

Indian Claims Commission, 15, 149–50
Indian Emergency Conservation Works, 18, 77, 79, 80, 119, 131
Indian Organization Division, 37–38, 92, 105, 108, 118
Indian Reorganization Act, x, 20–21, 26–29, 102, 104, 120, 150
Indian Rights Association, 2, 13, 15, 18, 33, 113
Indian Truth, 113–14
Indians at Work, 114, 142
Iroquois, 2, 33, 63

Jennings, Joe, 108
Johnson, Edwin, 10
Johnson, N. B., 148

Kelly, Lawrence C.: on Indian New Deal, xi, 176 n. 3; on Navajos, 71, 183 n. 26
Kiowas, 35, 44
Kirgis, F. L., 67
Kitch, James, 71, 98–99
Klamaths, 15, 33, 85
Kluckhohn, Clyde, 31, 72, 113
Kroeber, A. L., 63, 64

La Farge, Oliver, 33, 46, 47, 69; and Hopi tribal organization, 74–76; and Indian Reorganization Act, 19, 21, 143; on Navajos, 72, 129; on San Carlos Apaches, 99
Lamotte, George, 147
Land use planning program, 120, 136
Lane, Franklin K., 10, 11
Leighton, Dorothea, 72
Linton, Ralph, 24–25
Lipps, Oscar H., 106, 114, 165 n. 17
Livestock cooperatives: and Cheyennes, 86–87; and Papagos, 77, 80; at Pine Ridge, 90; promoted in New Deal, 125–26
Loans, tribal: administration of, 109–11, 140; and Cheyennes, 86–87; and Chippewas, 88; and Indian Reorganization Act, 27, 121; and Oklahoma Indian Welfare Act, 36; and Salish-Kootenais, 108
Lowie, Robert, 33
Luhan, Mabel Dodge, 12, 47

McCarran, Pat, 27
Macgregor, Gordon, 168 n. 20
McNickle, D'Arcy: on Indian New Deal, x, 176 n. 3; heads Indian Organization Division, 166 n. 27; on Indian tribalism, 171 n. 2; supports licensing fees at Cheyenne River, 105; investigates Pine Ridge situation, 116
Mandans, 81
Margold, Nathan: and Indian Reorganization Act, 20, 37; on tribal constitutional powers, 92, 95, 97; on tribal loans, 109
Marmon, Kenneth, 77, 79, 80
Marshall, Robert, 128
Meicklejohn, Kenneth, 68, 87, 101, 104, 105
Mekeel, H. Scudder, 37, 56, 89, 113, 115
Menominees, 44, 85, 119
Meriam, Lewis, 13, 19
Meriam Report, 6, 13–14, 131
Merritt, Edgar, 18
Mirabel, Antonio, 47, 74
Montezuma, Carlos, 46, 167 n. 11
Morgan, Jacob, 129
Morgan, Thomas J., 4

Nash, Jay B., 18
National Congress of American Indians, 115, 140, 146–49

National Resources Board, 136, 140; report on Indian lands, 5, 6, 7, 41, 124, 151–52

Navajos: economic divisions among, 48, 49; and Hopis, 74; land overgrazed, 120, 126; livestock reduction in New Deal, 126–30, 132–33; reject Indian Reorganization Act, 33, 38, 128–29; traditional organization, 2; tribal council before New Deal, 71–73

Nez Percés, 52

Oklahoma Indian Welfare Act, 34–36, 67, 147, 180 n. 45

Oneidas, 6

Opler, Morris, 46, 62, 67

Osages, 44

Otis, Delos S., 4

Paiutes, 2, 123

Papagos: economic divisions among, 48; linguistic problems, 51; and TC-BIA surveys, 134, 137, 184 n. 49; traditional organization, 70, 76; tribal organization in New Deal, 77–80. *See also* Reservations; Sells

Parker, Arthur C., 9

Parman, Donald H., xi–xii

Pawnees, 152

Personality and Government Project, 168 n. 20

Peyote church, 47, 74, 167 n. 13

Philp, Kenneth R., xii, 176 n. 3

Phinney, Archie, 66, 69, 87, 88, 147

Pimas, 46, 79, 134

Planning: declining interest in after 1940, 139; and Indian Reorganization Act, 22, 120; proposals of Ward Shepard, 131; and TC-BIA, 120, 121

Potawatomis, 6

Pueblo Lands Board, 13, 24, 149

Pueblos: and Bursum bill, 11, 13; and Collier, 12, 13, 73–74; factionalism among, 46–47; land overgrazed, 120; and livestock reduction in New Deal, 73, 130–31; and Rio Grande Board, 135; traditional organization, 2, 69–70, 172 n. 14; tribal organization in New Deal, 88

Pugh, George, 115

Red Shirt Table, 90, 115, 135

Referenda, tribal, 32–33, 144, 155–58, 164 n. 10

Reifel, Ben W., 89, 90, 100, 115, 116, 118

Reservations: Cheyenne River, 105, 114, 118, 123, 145; Colorado River, 79, 137; Colville, 52, 68, 86, 168 n. 22, 170 n. 47, 171 n. 11; Flathead, 52, 82, 83–85, 106, 111, 175 n. 62; Fort Belknap, 44, 82; Fort Berthold, 82 83; Fort Peck, 33; Kiowa, 82; Lower Brulé, 6; Mescalero Apache, 45–46, 110; Pine Ridge, 49, 52, 61, 89–91, 100, 115–16, 135, 145, 168 n. 20; Red Lake, 53–55, 119, 169 n. 36; Rocky Boy's, 83; Rosebud, 6, 44, 49, 61, 100, 115, 145; San Carlos Apache, 70–71, 98–99, 178 n. 14; Sells, 77, 78; Standing Rock, 61; Tongue River, 86, 104, 110; Turtle Mountain, 33, 44; Uintah-Ouray, 68; White Earth, 87; Yankton, 44, 61, 68, 86, 100–101, 103

Resettlement Administration (Farm Security Administration): close relations with BIA under Collier, 120, 132, 140; contributions to Indian lands, 124, 131, 132; and Chippewa land program, 87–88; lending program, 110; and Rio Grande Board, 74, 135

Rhoads, Charles, 14, 15, 16, 107, 119, 132

Rio Grande Board, 74, 120, 131, 135–36, 138. *See also* Resettlement Administration; Soil Conservation Service

Roberts, William O., 89–91, 114–16

Rogers, Will, 35

Roosevelt, Franklin D., 18, 25, 27, 142

Roubideux, Antoine, 145, 146, 148

Ryan, W. Carson, 14

Sac and Fox, 51

Sahlins, Marshall D., 64

Salish-Kootenais: dispute over tribal funds, 108; dispute over tribal loans, 111; and establishment of Flathead Reservation, 82; tribal organization in New Deal, 83–85. *See also* Reservations: Flathead

Senate Committee on Indian Affairs: hostility toward Collier administration, 107, 141–42; and Indian Reorganization Act, 20, 22; investigation of Bureau of Indian Affairs, 14, 127; opinion of Indian constitutions, 97

Sergeant, Elizabeth S., 47

Seymour, Flora, 24

Shepard, Ward, 18, 33, 131

Shoshones, 2, 145

Sioux, 63; community organization in New Deal, 89–91; constitutional controversies involving, 100–101, 103, 104; factionalism among, 49–50, 62, 168 n. 20; attitude toward Indian Reorganization Act, 59–60; intertribal organization among, 145–46;

results of allotment, 6; traditional organization, 2, 81, 82, 89. *See also* Reservations: Cheyenne River, Pine Ridge, Rosebud, Yankton

Smith, Clement, 100–101

Sniffen, Matthew K., 15

Society of American Indians, 9, 10, 144, 149

Soil Conservation Service: disputes with Bureau of Indian Affairs, 132–33; and Navajo livestock reduction, 127–28, 129, 133; and Papago survey, 137; and Pueblo livestock reduction, 130–31; and Red Shirt Table development project, 90; and Rio Grande Board, 74, 120; and TC-BIA, 78–79, 117, 120, 133–35. *See also* Bennett, Hugh; Technical Cooperation–Bureau of Indian Affairs

Stephens bill, 9, 10, 117

Stewart, J. M., 104, 128

Stone, Forrest W., 144

Strong, W. Duncan, 37

Technical Cooperation–Bureau of Indian Affairs (TC-BIA), 78, 117, 120, 131, 133–38. *See also* Soil Conservation Service

Teller, Henry, 9

Thomas, Edgar, 35

Tribe: concept of, 2, 63–64; focus of Indian Reorganization Act, 66

Underhill, Ruth, 51, 77, 78

Utes, 68–69, 97

Werner, Theodore, 22, 163 n. 10

Wheeler, Burton K.: critical of Collier, 140, 141, 142; and Indian Reorganization Act, 20, 25, 26, 141

Whitlock, C. R., 90

Wilson, Frank, 115
Winnebagos, 6
Wissler, Clark, 39, 168 n. 25
Woehlke, Walter V.: confidant of
  Collier, 18; coordinator of TC-
  BIA, 133–37; and San Carlos
  Apaches, 99
Worcester v. *Georgia*, 95
Work, Hubert, 13

Yellowtail, Robert, 33, 61, 118,
  147, 170 n. 50, 183 n. 66

Zimmerman, William, 112; and
  Blackfeet, 56, 57; on Indian New
  Deal, x; and Indian Reorganization Act, 20, 25; attitude toward
  pan-Indian groups, 146, 147;
  and Yankton constitution, 101